W9-DHT-485

Israel and the Developing Countries: *New Approaches to Cooperation*

Israel and the Developing Countries: *New Approaches to Cooperation*

by LEOPOLD LAUFER

THE TWENTIETH CENTURY
FUND / NEW YORK / 1967

THE TWENTIETH CENTURY FUND

founded in 1919 and endowed by Edward A. Filene, is a nonprofit foundation which, through research and publication, seeks to throw light upon emerging issues of our times. Major fields of interest of the Fund are economics, social problems and international affairs. The study of which this volume is a report has been defined and supported by the Fund's Board of Trustees. The Fund attempts to ensure the scholarly quality of works appearing under its imprint; the Trustees and the staff, however, accord the author or authors complete freedom in the statement of opinions and the interpretation of facts.

Printed in the United States of America
By Quinn & Boden Company, Inc., Rahway, N. J.
Library of Congress Catalog Card Number: 67-29176

Foreword

The economic gap between the technologically advanced, highly industrialized countries and the less developed countries appears to be widening. This is so despite massive aid programs, a variety of experiments in development and unremitting study of new ways to foster development.

Since World War II the United States, the Soviet Union, Japan and countries of Western Europe, among others, have engaged in aid programs, but the problems continue and deepen. In recent years a new element has been introduced: the contribution of the emerging nations themselves.

It appeared to be useful for the Twentieth Century Fund to look into the possibilities of this approach. Have the emerging nations a potential for helping each other? Can these nations, new or old, contribute knowledge, experience and cooperative effort to stimulate growth and advancement among themselves? Indeed, might they have special insights that are lacking in the efforts of larger and wealthier countries?

Israel seemed a good central point from which to conduct such a study. Here was a nation that came into existence in 1948 and was immediately faced with the problem of making a place for itself in the family of nations. Israel knew at first hand what it meant to be new, small and developing. Moreover, Israel has, during the last decade, made a conscious effort to share its knowledge and technical skills with other developing countries in Asia, Africa, Latin America and elsewhere.

The present work examines in depth Israel's experiences in international technical cooperation and also reviews briefly similar programs undertaken by other countries. As recorded here, there were, of course, some failures and partial successes, along with the outright successes. The study was undertaken to see what value these activities might have that could prove enlightening or helpful to other developing nations. As a whole, the record seems impressive. The Twentieth Century Fund hopes that it has served a useful purpose in assembling this record and making it generally available. Perhaps the approaches analyzed here indeed may also indicate some directions toward attaining peaceful advancement in the Middle East.

The Fund wishes to thank officials and directors of programs and departments and institutions in the many cooperating countries who made it possible to complete this study. It is a pleasure to express the Fund's gratitude for the dedication and professional competence with which Leopold Laufer carried out the study.

JOHN E. BOOTH, *Acting Director*
The Twentieth Century Fund

41 East 70 Street, New York City
July 1967

Preface

As this book goes to press, the lands of the Middle East are again torn by a major convulsion. The present study is not directly related to the problem of Arab-Israeli relations and was completed before the hostilities of June 1967. It is my hope, however, that its theme and some of its conclusions may contribute insights that will help in the long search for peace that lies ahead.

Each successive major Arab-Israeli confrontation has resulted in far-reaching transformations. Israel emerged from the first confrontation in 1948 as an independent, struggling state, requiring the support of the so-called "developed world." This it received, and, eventually, also its respect.

The second eruption of the Arab-Israeli conflict, at Suez in 1956, had only slightly less dramatic consequences on Israel's position and role in the world. One of the important effects of that confrontation, as the present study shows, was a new dimension in Israel's foreign policy, based on cooperation and friendship with the peoples of developing countries. Except for countries in the Arab bloc, most developing countries accepted Israel and became its partners in cooperation.

The Middle East is for the third time at a historic crossroads. The perils in the situation are all too clear, but not, perhaps, the opportunities for constructive action. These must be seen in the context of earlier events. The period between the 1956 and the 1967 crises, covered by the present study, is marked by an expanding volume of increasingly sophisticated cooperative activity between Israel and the developing world.

Where could the insights and experiences acquired from this activity over the past decade be more fittingly utilized than within the region of which Isreal is a part? Israel's program of technical cooperation has proved strongest in precisely those areas in which needs are most acute among Israel's Arab neighbors—arid zone agriculture, development and utilization of water resources, integrated regional development, youth training for nation-building.

Two important elements in the art of international cooperation which the present study illustrates are particularly relevant to the potential future course of relations in the Middle East: first, large nonmaterial benefits can accrue to partners in international cooperation from small inputs of capital and manpower; second, the initiation of fruitful cooperative relations between countries need not await the resolution of all their major political conflicts. Recommendations made in Chapter 15 provide for an international mechanism that would be well suited to initiate the first modest steps in Middle East cooperation.

The present study was undertaken to probe the potentials of cooperation between developing countries in general. In order to evaluate the Israeli program and assess the readiness and potential of the various countries for mutual aid and the sharing of technical resources, extensive observations were made at project sites and discussions were held in Israel and in Turkey, Ethiopia, Ghana, Ivory Coast, Kenya, Nigeria, Senegal, Tanzania, Upper Volta, Argentina, Chile, Costa Rica, Ecuador, Mexico, Peru and Venezuela. The field research was supplemented by conferences at the headquarters of the United Nations and its specialized agencies in New York, Paris, Geneva, Rome, Addis Ababa and Santiago de Chile; the Organization of American States in Washington; the Organization of African Unity in Addis Ababa; the Organisation for Economic Cooperation and Development in Paris; the Central Treaty Organization in Ankara; and the Washington headquarters and overseas missions of the U. S. Agency for International Development. Special thanks are due the staff of the Department for International Cooperation of Israel's Ministry for Foreign Affairs and the staffs of various Israeli training institutions and to Israeli experts and diplomats in many countries for their patience and readiness to respond to innumerable questions and requests for information. The interest and candid approach to complex, often delicate problems by government officials in all the countries visited and by officials of international organizations were vital.

It is impossible to name individually the hundreds of people on five continents who aided in this study in various ways. Their contributions are woven into the book, though specific attribution was not always feasible. This is particularly true of unpublished material made available by various government officials and of the wealth of facts, insights and observations gathered in personal interviews. Factual statements made in the text without clear attribution of source can be documented from project files.

The U. S. Agency for International Development proved to be a most understanding employer, granting me a two-year leave to carry out the study. I am especially grateful for the steadfast encouragement and support of Richard E. Lippincott, former Deputy Director, Office of Caribbean Affairs; to Dr. Alvin Mayne, former economic consultant to the Coordinator of the Alliance for Progress; and to David Mayer, former Director of Analysis in the Office of Research and Analysis.

I also owe much to other friends and colleagues who read the manuscript in whole or in part and made constructive suggestions for its improvement: Dr. Robert E. Asher of the Brookings Institution, Professor Joseph W. Eaton of Pittsburgh University, Mrs. Caryl Holiber of the Economic Development Administration of the U. S. Department of Commerce, Andrew E. Rice of the Society for International Development, Dr. Walter Sedwitz of the Organization of American States, Dr. Judith Shuval of the Israel Institute for Applied Social Research and the Hebrew University, Dr. Saadia Touval of the University of Tel Aviv, and Dr. Raanan Weitz of the National and University Institute of Agriculture at Rehovoth, Israel. Mrs. Holiber, moreover, made important contributions to the design and conceptualization of the study.

Professor Elihu Katz of the University of Chicago and the Hebrew University in Jerusalem made valuable suggestions for the implementation of a special survey of Israeli technical assistance experts and instructors, conducted for the present study by the Israel Institute for Applied Social Research. The study was directed by Professors Uriel Foa and Yitshak Schlesinger. Uzi Peled, Assistant Director of the Institute, extended the hospitality of the Institute to me, which helped make my year's stay in Jerusalem both pleasant and intellectually stimulating. I am particularly grateful for the unfailing cooperation of Aharon Remez and David Golan, former Directors of the Department for International Cooperation of Israel's Ministry for Foreign Affairs, their assistant, Hagai Eylon, and former Acting Director Tsvi Brosh; Gershon Fradkin, Director of the Foreign Training Department of

Israel's Agricultural Extension Service; Akiva Eger, Director of the Afro-Asian Institute for Labour Studies and Cooperation; Naftali Glaser, Director of the Center for Cooperative and Labour Studies; and Mrs. Mina Ben Tsvi, Director of the Mount Carmel International Training Center for Community Services. David Atar of Kibbutz Givat Chaim contributed from his rich experience as youth leader and educator to my understanding of Israel's philosophy of youth training and leadership. At different stages of the study I had the able assistance of Yaacov Shiboleth and Glenn Pierce, who performed valuable research assignments. To them and all the others who had a part in this undertaking I express my heartfelt thanks. On the other hand the conclusions expressed and responsibility for any errors of judgment or fact are mine alone.

No author or researcher could ask for a sponsor more understanding, generous and committed to the cause of free, unfettered research than the Twentieth Century Fund. The personal interest taken by August Heckscher, former Director of the Fund, John E. Booth, Acting Director, and Elizabeth Blackert, Chief Editor, enabled me to weather many a crisis. Most important for the eventual fruition of the study was the assistance and critical advice of two other staff members: Isador Lubin, Economic Consultant, whose incisive mind and wealth of professional experience enabled me to crystallize my ideas and greatly improve the design and final shape of the study; and Frances Klafter, Associate Editor, who combines superior professional qualities with patience, sympathy and an unsparing dedication to the task at hand. No brief acknowledgment could do full justice to the extent of her contribution. Credit must also go to Herbert Kaufman, who performed the exacting task of preparing the index, and to Virginia May and Mary Mish, who conscientiously saw the manuscript through its various stages of typing, checking and proofreading.

Finally, a word must be said about the part which my wife has had in this study. Although burdened by the problems arising from the temporary relocation of a large family and my frequent absences from home, she not only accepted these hardships, but became an important and active partner in my work. As my sharpest and perhaps least inhibited critic, she performed an invaluable service to which I pay grateful tribute.

LEOPOLD LAUFER

Contents

Tables

Appendix Tables

Charts

Israel and the Developing Countries: *New Approaches to Cooperation*

Chapter 1

Introduction

REVOLUTIONARY changes are shaping new conditions of life and bringing expectations for a better, more affluent future to the three fifths of humanity who live in the shadow of hunger, ignorance and disease in what we call, for want of a better word, the "developing" countries. Yet the sharp contrast between their world and that of their more prosperous neighbors in the economically advanced countries creates an ominous gap—not only in material wealth but also in status, in the fulfillment of aspirations for self-respect and dignity.

The status gap, perhaps a heritage of colonialism and other forms of domination, is as perilous and potentially destructive as the material gap. External infusions of capital and skills alone cannot close it. The gap will disappear only as the emerging world acquires strength and confidence in its ability to carry forward the nation-building effort. Cooperation between the developing countries, particularly in promoting the growth of human and institutional resources, can help build this strength and confidence.

Assistance in development is usually thought of in terms of transfers of capital and skills from economically advanced countries to developing countries and the mobilization of internal resources by individual developing countries. The potentialities of mutual assistance between the emerging countries, a form of assistance still in its infancy, have often been overlooked or underestimated. The present study is a modest attempt to look at this aspect of the manifold efforts being made to bridge the gap between the developed and the developing worlds.

It examines the results and problems of this approach in actual practice and its possibilities for the future. The study falls into three broad parts: first, the experience in mutual assistance of Israel, a country that has itself only recently achieved a relatively high stage of economic and social development; second, a brief review of multilateral and bilateral cooperation between some of the developing countries of Africa, the Middle East (excluding Israel) and Latin America, including the role of international agencies and the economically advanced countries in encouraging and supporting such cooperative relationships; and third, conclusions and recommendations based on the findings of the study.

In order to comprehend what is essentially a new force in the development process—mutual aid between developing countries—it is helpful to examine briefly its rationale and evolution.

A Chain Reaction in Technical Assistance

As countries go through successive stages of growth, they acquire knowledge and techniques valuable to other countries experiencing similar stages of development. This accumulated knowledge, passed from one developing country to another, can form a chain reaction, quickening the tempo of development. John Kenneth Galbraith, former U. S. Ambassador to India, recognized this when he suggested that we think of the countries of the world ". . . as spaced along a line representing various stages of development . . . each country has something to gain from those that are in front . . . something to offer those that follow. The provision of aid is seen as it should be seen, as a cooperative endeavor in which all countries may participate. And while there will be differences in what is given and what is received . . . I am not sure that the contribution of the less developed countries is necessarily less. . . . Development is a task in which many need help and as many have something to offer." [1]

[1] *Economic Development,* Harvard University Press, Cambridge, 1964, pp. 51–52.

The value of a chain reaction, sometimes also called a "multiplier effect," in technical assistance has long been known. Simply stated, it means that at least some of those who learn become teachers of others, who in turn transmit their knowledge to a third group, and so forth, so that the original input of knowledge or investment in teaching is multiplied many times over. What has not been sufficiently realized is that a chain reaction between developing countries can be at least as effective as a chain reaction between an economically advanced and a developing country, or perhaps even more so. Skill or knowledge useful in a developed country must ordinarily undergo considerable modification and adaptation before it can be put to use in a developing country. Another developing country, next along the chain, can be spared much of the often lengthy and costly process of adaptation if it uses techniques or insights already modified for conditions similar to its own.

Israel's program of cooperation with other developing countries offers striking evidence of the chain reaction effect in technical assistance. A survey undertaken in connection with the present study shows, for example, that at least one out of five Israelis who came to the United States as trainees under the Point Four program for technical assistance in the 1950's later participated in Israel's own program of cooperation.[2] Most of these felt that their U. S. training had been helpful to them in training others from developing countries.

U. S. technical assistance has also had a significant chain reaction effect in Israel's approach to agricultural extension work. The Israelis, having modified and adapted U. S. agricultural methods to their own needs, now claim techniques of agricultural development among their most successful "exports" to other developing countries.

In Venezuela Israel helped found an agricultural training and planning center, which has been so successful that Chile recently requested the Venezuelan center to assist it in establishing a similar institution. The Organization of American States (OAS) has also

[2] All 370 ex-trainees trained in the United States between 1951 and 1960 were included in the mail survey, and 55 per cent responded. Sixty-three respondents, or 17 per cent of all the trainees, indicated that they had participated in Israel's program of cooperation. Allowing for the probability that some who did not respond also participated in the program, the estimate of at least 20 per cent seems justified.

requested the center to open its doors to trainees from other Latin American countries. If, as seems entirely possible, the Venezuelan center is requested to share its planning experience with an Israeli sister institution, the chain reaction will have run full circle.

In another type of activity, Uganda in 1965 contemplated establishing a new cooperative marketing organization and sent its people to Tanzania, where the Israelis had for some time been helping to establish just such an enterprise.

An interesting chain reaction that started in Israel was recently described by a U. S. Agency for International Development (AID) expert. He had introduced in Chile a system of adjustable savings and mortgage loans linked to cost-of-living indexes, first observed by him while serving in Israel. After its successful application in Chile the system was in turn adapted for use in Brazil and in Singapore.[3]

Stemming the Drain of Professional Manpower

An acute problem in development is the well-known loss of professional manpower, popularly known as the "brain drain." It would be impossible to measure precisely the economic and social cost of this phenomenon, but there is no doubt that its retarding effect on the development of emerging countries is tremendous. Moreover, it has often ludicrously perverted the goals of international assistance, particularly of U. S. assistance. The United States, the chief beneficiary of the brain drain, has often unwittingly deprived developing countries of the very manpower it has helped to train.

For example, the Iranian Embassy in Washington found in a recent survey that more than half the Iranian students who study in the United States do not return home upon completion of their studies.[4] Taiwan's Education Ministry disclosed recently that of the more than 7,000 graduate students who went abroad from 1957 to 1963 only 7 per cent returned to the island.[5]

[3] *Jerusalem Post Weekly,* November 12, 1965; March 4, 1966.

[4] Habib Naficy, *The "Brain-Drain": The Case of Iranian Non-Returnees,* report presented at the annual conference of the Society for International Development, New York, March 17, 1966 (mimeo.). The Embassy estimated that there were 8,000 Iranian students in the United States in 1966.

[5] *Survey of International Development,* October 15, 1965.

Cooperation between developing countries cannot eliminate this steady drain of professional personnel but it can help to alleviate it by promoting the use of educational and training facilities in the developing countries themselves. Experience indicates that students who go to another developing country to study are far more likely to return home than are those who go to an economically advanced country. Increasing numbers of American, Asian and African educators are concluding that undergraduate studies should be and can be completed in the regions where the students live.[6]

Enriching Professional Experiences

As for graduate students and those already professionally active in the developing countries, one of their principal reasons for leaving appears to be lack of professional opportunities and status.[7] Mutual aid between developing countries makes it possible for these professionals to have broadening professional experiences, as well as opportunities for foreign travel and enhanced status, without abandoning their countries. This has apparently been the experience of Israeli experts working abroad. Thus mutual assistance seems to offer the professionals of developing countries an acceptable alternative to frustration or emigration.

The international organizations, of course, have offered opportunities of this kind for some years. However, temporary assignment on behalf of the expert's own country in a bilateral or regional program of mutual assistance is apt to engage stronger patriotic sentiments, and thus stronger commitment to the task at hand, than an assignment on behalf of an international agency.

The personally enriching experiences gained in mutual assistance efforts may therefore strengthen the bonds of professionals with their own countries and increase their effectiveness. These experiences also help to provide a link between the leaders of the developing world and widen their horizons.

[6] See, for example, *The Development of Higher Education in Africa,* United Nations Educational, Scientific and Cultural Organization, Paris, 1963, Ed.62/ D.20/A, p. 16.

[7] For a far-ranging discussion of the problem and possible solutions in India, Greece and Taiwan, see "Brain Drain," *Development Digest,* April 1966, pp. 27–46.

Broadening the Outlook of National Leaders

The prospects for modernization of the developing countries are often analyzed in terms of the education and ideological and psychological make-up of their professional and political leaders. It seems generally agreed that these individuals, whom George H. T. Kimble describes as the "high priests of the new order . . . apostles of the manifold graces of nationalism . . . the men with the keys to the kingdom, the chosen people," exert a strong, sometimes decisive, influence on the pace of development in their respective countries.[8]

No one who has visited and spoken with representatives of this "development elite," however, can fail to be impressed by their peculiar insularity, their disinterest and ignorance about each other. Well-educated French-speaking West Africans are almost sure to know and care a great deal more about the latest French political scandal than about the success or failure of democracy or of cooperative settlements in Nigeria; eloquent Guyanese radicals will speak admiringly, though probably without much knowledge, of "African socialism," but will be thoroughly ignorant of events in neighboring Venezuela; cosmopolitan Peruvians will no doubt be better informed about political and social developments in the United States than in Ecuador or Argentina.

This kind of orientation hinders the flow of information and experience between developing countries. It also tends to perpetuate old prejudices and to weaken measures for economic integration to which the leaders of these countries may be politically as well as intellectually committed.

Cooperation in the use of human and institutional resources helps to overcome these tendencies. In the process of sharing, contacts increase, information flows, prejudices are eroded and a community of interests is established. Some new frictions may also be created and new prejudices acquired, but the risks seem small compared to the

[8] See Kimble, *Tropical Africa,* The Twentieth Century Fund, New York, 1960, Vol. II, Chap. 22 (quotation, p. 362); Clark Kerr and others, *Industrialism and Industrial Man,* Oxford University Press, London, 1963; S. N. Eisenstadt, "Breakdowns of Modernization," *Economic Development and Cultural Change,* July 1964.

promise of a broader outlook that mutual assistance offers to the leaders of developing countries.

Mutuality and International Stature

The way a country is regarded by its own people and by the world at large can have a profound effect on the form and pace of its development.

The concept of the frontier surely had a sustained effect not only on the early social, economic and political development of the United States, but also on the actions of its leaders and on the way it was regarded in other countries. President Kennedy sought to build on this reputation in 1961 with his "New Frontier," and none who witnessed this brief moment in history will forget the impact that the concept of the "New Frontier" had on U. S. policies and on U. S. standing abroad.

Similarly, the pioneering concept in Israel has not only helped shape the social and economic character of the modern Israeli state, but as subsequent chapters show, has contributed immeasurably to Israel's ability to inspire nation-building activities in other countries. Much of Israel's prestige and influence abroad is linked to this concept.

National images and international stature are not created overnight. They are based in tradition and history, and countries endeavoring to radically transform their societies often find it difficult to shape or reshape their national images and international reputations. One path to such transformation is adoption by a developing country of the concept of mutuality in promoting economic and social development. Webster defines mutuality as "quality of reciprocity, interchange, interaction, interdependence." No definition could better describe the characteristic that the emerging countries can collectively acquire through programs of cooperation. As applied to relations between countries, it connotes generosity and concern for others, as well as recognition of the fact that no country has a monopoly on wisdom and knowledge.

Mutuality in relations between developing countries can be evidenced, of course, only by concrete acts of mutual assistance. However, like the concept of the frontier in the United States and pioneering in Israel, it can serve as a catalyst, influencing attitudes and itself generating further actions of mutuality. Its most important effect in the long run may be to help crack the walls of prejudice and suspicion that at present impede the development of constructive relationships between many countries, developing and economically advanced. It may, moreover, help to neutralize the damaging psychological effects that often arise from the donor-recipient relationship between the aiding countries and the aided.

Israel recognized this fact early in the operation of its program, and thus from the start, has stressed "cooperation," "mutuality," "reciprocity," rather than "aid" or "assistance" in its relations with partner governments. Israeli personnel carry this idea into their relations with the people of other developing countries, a fact that has no doubt helped Israel to establish friendly relations with many of these countries.

If mutuality can enhance relations between developing countries, it may eventually also exert a beneficial influence on relations between the economically advanced and the developing countries. In this sphere the corrosive effects of the donor-recipient relationship are particularly acute. The U. S. Senate Foreign Relations Committee recently acknowledged this fact by calling for "concerted efforts to move away from the giver-receiver relationships of aid, with all the psychological handicaps involved." [9] President Johnson's proposal in February 1966 to establish an "Exchange Peace Corps" represents at least a symbolic step by the U. S. Government to begin repairing the psychological damage which has been the by-product of more than two decades of aid-giving. "Our nation has no better ambassadors," the President said, "than the young volunteers who serve in 46 countries in the Peace Corps. I propose that we welcome similar ambassadors to our shores. We need their special skills and understanding, just as they need ours." [10] This idea is currently being applied on a pilot basis through a small "Volunteers to America" program for 100 young foreign volunteers, who are expected to teach their own lan-

[9] *The New York Times,* July 8, 1966.

[10] Excerpts from the President's "Message to the Congress Proposing Methods to Improve the Education and Health of Peoples Throughout the World," February 2, 1966.

guages and culture in U. S. communities or work alongside U. S. Volunteers in Service to America (VISTA).

Mutual assistance can place international relations between rich and poor countries on a healthier, more dignified basis. Though the cooperative program of a developing country may be small, it changes the country's status and contributes to its national prestige and maturity.

A Widening Network of Mutual Assistance

The evolution of mutual assistance is far from complete. Neither the ideology nor the international framework in which it can function is fully developed or understood. Nevertheless its characteristics and tools of operation continue to evolve pragmatically.

Of the independent bilateral programs of assistance between developing countries, those of Yugoslavia, Taiwan, Kuwait and Israel are probably the most significant. The fact that political considerations played a role in the initiation of these programs—as they have in the assistance programs of the economically advanced countries—does not detract from their ultimate worth. Except for oil-rich Kuwait, which between 1961 and 1965 extended almost $400 million in loans to its neighbors, these countries have assisted other developing countries primarily through the transfer of skills and experience, not capital. For the foreseeable future the sharing of these resources will continue to offer the best prospect for the growth of mutuality in the developing world.

Other emerging countries—even very poor ones—have also developed some forms of mutual aid. Ghana and Ethiopia have opened their limited academic facilities to scholarship students from other African countries. The United Arab Republic has sent teachers to Moslem countries in the Middle East and Africa, received students at its own academic institutions and offered training facilities to the Organization of African Unity. Argentina, Mexico and other Latin American countries have for years admitted thousands of students from neighboring countries to their state-supported universities, tuition-free or with only nominal tuition.

Most of the assistance between developing countries has thus far taken place under the auspices of regional or international agencies. The economically advanced countries have indirectly supported these programs through financial contributions to the agencies sponsoring them. The United States, moreover, has for years financed training activities of developing countries through its Third-Country Training Program. In the "Colombo Plan for Co-operative Economic Development in South and South-East Asia," member countries of the region, as well as economically advanced member countries, exchange information about training facilities and technical assistance requirements and work out bilateral arrangements for cooperation. Of the developing country members, India has been the largest contributor to this program, notably in supplying experts to Nepal.

In the Organization of American States the principal focus outside the political sphere has long been on the achievement of economic integration, which is outside the sphere of the present study. However, the OAS is also gradually developing interest in programs of sharing within Latin America. Regional training and research institutions, such as the Inter-American Institute of Agricultural Sciences, and the establishment of technical assistance programs, partially funded and staffed by the OAS, represent the beginnings of systematic cooperative endeavors in the use of the very considerable human and material resources of the hemisphere. New measures adopted by the American Presidents at their meeting in Punta del Este in April 1967 should speed this process. Israel's cooperation with the OAS has demonstrated, moreover, that regional organizations can play an important role in helping to stimulate and facilitate the transfer of skills and experiences between developing countries of different regions.

Three countries of the Near East—Turkey, Pakistan and Iran—have since 1959 carried out small-scale technical assistance programs within the framework of the Central Treaty Organization (CENTO); more recently they have taken steps to increase these and other regional activities through a new organization, Regional Cooperation for Development (RCD), which does not include their "big power" CENTO partners, Great Britain and the United States.

The far-flung United Nations organizations have thus far played perhaps the most significant role in promoting utilization of the skills and institutions of developing countries. As a matter of established policy, the agencies and programs of the United Nations employ increasing numbers of experts from developing countries to work in other developing countries. Likewise, UN agencies seek to utilize academic and other training institutions in the developing world for trainees from developing countries.

One UN program alone, the Expanded Program of Technical Assistance (EPTA), now a part of the UN Development Program, in 1965 employed nearly 1,000 experts from developing countries, over 30 per cent of its total expert staff. (See Table 13-1.) The same program also awarded almost 1,300 fellowships—more than one third of the total number awarded—for study in institutions of developing countries.

The many forms that mutual aid between developing countries has taken indicate the fluid, dynamic process at work. The origins, problems and potentialities of this process, however, can best be understood by examining in detail the experiences of a single country. Israel's program of cooperation with other developing countries has been selected for this examination.

The Choice of Israel

No one would claim that all of Israel's experiences in international technical cooperation are typical of mutual aid programs. Yet the choice of Israel's program for a probe in depth seems a logical one for the present study. Of all the emerging countries engaged in mutual assistance activities, Israel has the largest and most varied program. This fact, combined with the high reputation that its program has enjoyed, suggested that a closer analysis would lead to meaningful conclusions regarding the prospects and problems of mutual assistance between developing countries.

Although the characterization of Israel as a developing country is consistent with the United Nations classification and Israel's own definition, some might contest it. Indeed, it would be absurd to suggest that a developing country with a per capita gross national product of a few hundred dollars could emulate the effort of Israel, with a per capita gross national product of about $1,300.

In the context of this study, however, the time period and the pattern of Israel's growth are important, since the development process is viewed as a ladder on which countries climb upward, step by step. Israel stands somewhere midway in the development scale between the developed and the developing world. Unlike most of the economically advanced countries, Israel reached an advanced stage of social and economic development in decades, not centuries. The consistently high growth rate in its per capita gross national product of around 5 per cent per year between 1955 and 1965 characterized a rapidly developing economy. At the same time, problems of low labor productivity, inadequate secondary school facilities, imbalance in the labor force and incomplete social integration remained acute, and were directly or indirectly related to the economic downturn after 1965. Thus, while the nation-building process is far advanced, it is by no means concluded.

For many of the developing countries, Israel's "in-between" status represents the "next step" on the development ladder—far ahead of their present status but not so far as to appear beyond reach. This no doubt is one of the reasons for the symbolic significance that Israel seems to have attained in the emerging world.

Part I

Israel's Program of Cooperation

Chapter 2

The Setting

ISRAEL HAS BEEN engaged in a program of cooperation with developing nations on a significant scale since 1958. Under this program, by the end of 1966, some 9,000 men and women from over 90 developing countries had traveled to Israel for training, study or observation, and Israeli experts had carried out about 3,500 technical assistance assignments abroad. (The countries participating in the program and the program's growth since 1958 are shown in Figures 2-1 and 2-2.) The scale of Israel's efforts ranks high among the smaller countries engaged in this type of activity, and is unique for a country so young—independent for only 19 years. Before examining Israel's techniques and the lessons to be drawn from its cooperation program, however, it is desirable to review the historical setting in which the program developed.

Historical Background

Israel is a child of the United Nations. It came into being in 1948 as the only new political entity to emerge from the United Nations' valiant, if not always consistent, efforts to help Great Britain liquidate its troublesome mandate over Palestine. The United Nations has played an important role in its life since that time. Two truce agreements and eventually general armistice agreements, negotiated under UN auspices in 1949, put an end to the Arab-Israeli war, which had

FIGURE 2-1

ISRAEL'S PARTNERS IN COOPERATION

1958-1966

LATIN AMERICA

Argentina
Bolivia
Brazil
Chile
Colombia
Costa Rica
Dominican Republic
Ecuador
Guatemala
* Guyana
* Haiti
* Honduras
Jamaica
* Mexico
* Nicaragua
* Panama
* Paraguay
Peru
* El Salvador
Surinam
Trinidad and Tobago
* Uruguay
Venezuela

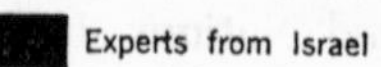
Experts from Israel and trainees to Israel

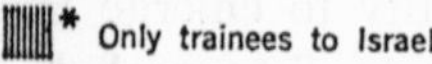
* Only trainees to Israel

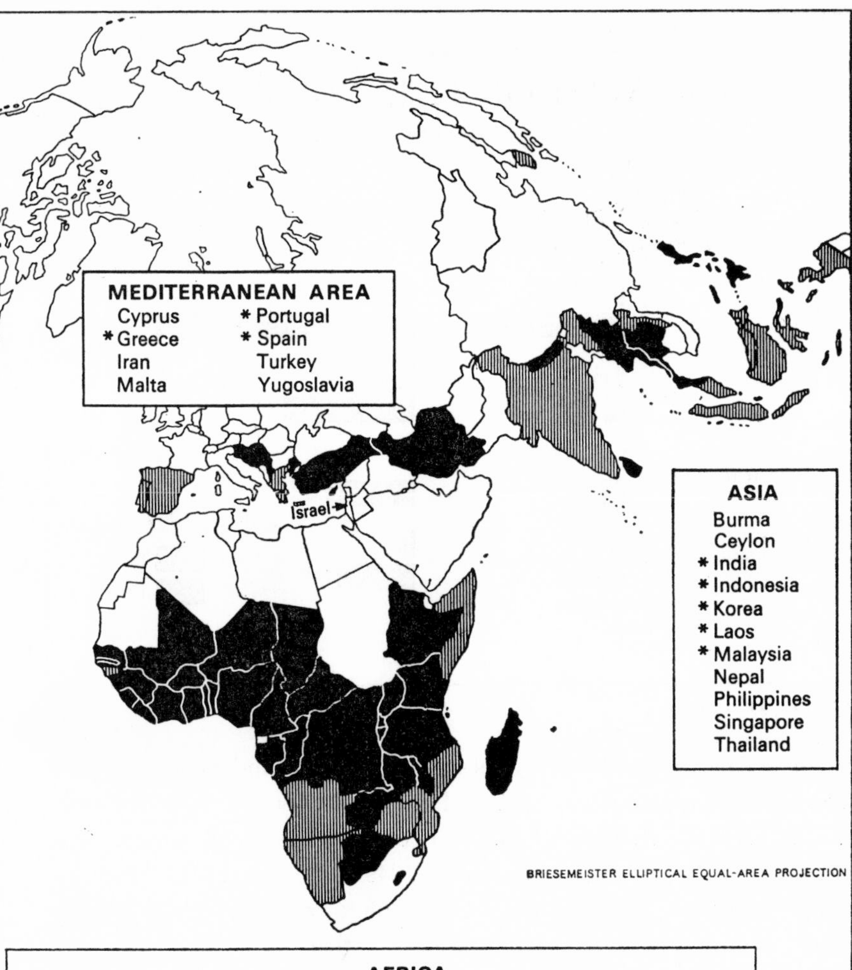

AFRICA

*Angola
Botswana
formerly Bechuanaland
Burundi
Cameroon
Central African Republic
Chad
Congo (Brazzaville)
Congo (Kinshasa)
formerly Congo (Léopoldville)
Dahomey
Ethiopia
Gabon
Gambia
Ghana
Guinea
*Guinea (Portuguese)
Ivory Coast
Kenya
Lesotho
formerly Basutoland
Liberia
Malagasy
Malawi
Mali
Mauritius
*Mozambique
Niger
Nigeria
*Rhodesia
Rwanda
Senegal
Sierra Leone
*Somali
*South-West Africa
*Swaziland
Tanzania
Togo
Uganda
Upper Volta
Zambia

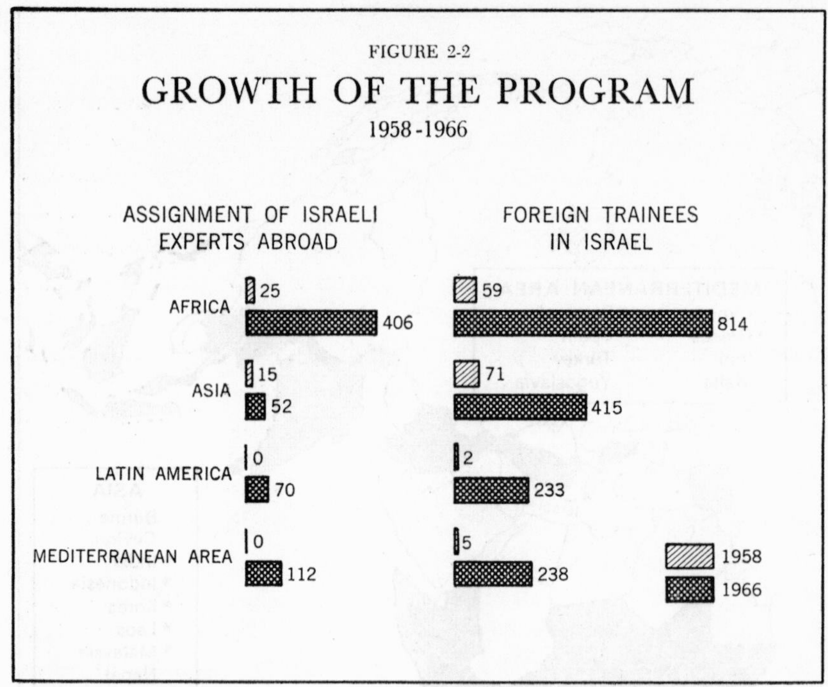

SOURCE: Table 5-1.

begun a year earlier with Israel's declaration of independence. The international organization assumed responsibility for and continues to care for Arab refugees of this war; dozens of Security Council and General Assembly resolutions since 1949 have sought to keep the shaky armistice structure from crumbling, and have sporadically aimed at bringing about a more lasting settlement.

The presence of the UN Truce Supervision Organization and the UN Emergency Force (stationed since 1956 in the Egyptian-held Gaza Strip) has prevented frequent border incidents from erupting into a new Arab-Israeli war.* All these circumstances emphasize not only the crucial political importance for Israel of the United Nations itself, but of the individual states that make up its membership. Sooner or later, Israel's leaders realize, each of these countries may be in a position to influence issues vital to Israel's welfare.

* This situation was abruptly changed, after this book had gone to press, by the renewed Arab-Israeli hostilities which broke out in June 1967.

Israel's Isolation[1]

Even in the mid-1950's the emerging countries of Africa and Asia knew little of Israel and its history. Except for Ethiopia, they had no traditional ties with or special interest in Israel. The situation was not helped by the fact that the Zionist movement was largely identified with the West. Many Asians and Africans, if they knew anything of Palestine, were mystified by the Arab-Israeli conflict and by earlier intermittent Jewish collaboration with the British mandatory government, which had culminated in World War II in the joint struggle against Hitler. They knew little of the Jewish struggle against British policy in Palestine, or saw it as another "colonialist" venture directed against the Arab inhabitants of Palestine. The very name "Israel" was a product of the Judeo-Christian tradition and thus of Western culture.

Israel's enemies lost no opportunity to portray it as a "tool of imperialism." The growing strength of Moslem communities throughout Asia and Africa strengthened these voices. Walter Eytan, the first Director General of the Israeli Foreign Ministry, summarized Asian attitudes in the following words: [2]

> Asia failed to see Israel as a people fighting desperately for its national resurgence. . . . Precisely because it lay outside the Judeo-Christian tradition [Asia] had never known anti-Semitism, [and] could not recognize instinctively the need and justice of a Jewish state.

The unhappy "Suez affair" of October 1956, which found Israel aligned alongside Great Britain and France, seemed to confirm the charges of its enemies, and Israel was in danger of political isolation from a large number of the new nations. Israel's former Ambassador to Burma, David Hacohen, has described the climate Israeli delegates found at an Asian socialist conference at that time: [3]

> The faces around us, even the faces of some devoted friends of Israel, were stern. . . . It was a wrathful atmosphere . . . when even our best friends were liable under pressure of circumstances to join our opponents

[1] This account is based largely on Walter Eytan, *The First Ten Years*, Weidenfeld and Nicolson, London, 1958, Chap. 8.

[2] *Ibid.*, pp. 167, 169.

[3] *Jerusalem Post*, August 8, 1965.

and to expel us unceremoniously from the organization we ourselves had helped to establish. . . .

After Suez, establishing friendly relations with the developing countries became for Israel not only a challenge, born of political necessity, but also a golden opportunity to broaden and normalize its international position. The freeing of Israel's tiny port of Eilat on the Red Sea—its "window to the East," previously blocked by powerful Egyptian guns—gave Israel a physical outlet to Asia and Africa that bypassed the Suez Canal, and facilitated development of contacts with the emerging countries. In this effort Israel was able to draw on two resources with which it was more amply endowed than many other new countries—skilled and well-motivated manpower and recent experience in development.

Early Contacts

Actually, Israel had not been wholly without contacts in other Asian and African countries before the formal inception of the program of mutual cooperation. Long before Israel's independence, two powerful organizations with largely the same leadership—the General Federation of Labor (Histadrut), and the Israeli Workers Party (Mapai)—had dominated Jewish political and economic life in Palestine. Their social-democratic orientation was the product of the well-developed socialist Zionist movements originated among European Jews in the late nineteenth and early twentieth centuries. Histadrut and Mapai were in the forefront of Israel's independence struggle, and maintained important contacts with labor and socialist circles abroad. These contacts continued after independence, and were particularly significant in Israel's early relations with the developing countries.

In many of these countries also, the labor movement had taken the lead in the struggle for independence. Even when political activity was forbidden, trade unionism enjoyed a certain legitimacy that colonial governments found difficult to suppress. On the international political front, the Socialist International and socialist parties in various countries provided points of contact with struggling leaders from the developing countries.

In Burma and to some extent in Ghana these semiofficial contacts through Histadrut and Mapai paved the way for Israel's assistance activities on a governmental level.

Burma—Milestone and Challenge

Relations with Burma go back to 1950, when three Burmese delegates to the International Trade Union Congress in Belgrade visited Israel on their return trip to Burma. They were impressed and surprised by the achievements of labor enterprise in Israel.[4] However, the possibility of organizing a program of technical cooperation between the two countries was not considered at that time.

Discussions at the Asian Socialist Conference in Rangoon in 1953 between Burmese officials and Israel's representative, the late Moshe Sharett, a leading member of the Mapai and then Foreign Minister, led to the establishment of diplomatic relations between the two countries. Israel sent as its first ambassador to an Asian country David Hacohen, who had been host to the Burmese visitors to Israel in 1950 and who brought to his task a deep commitment to the ideals of democratic socialism and long experience with Histadrut economic enterprise.

Armed with his rich experience as director of Histadrut's huge building and construction subsidiary, Solel Boneh, one of Israel's largest industrial enterprises, David Hacohen began to cement Israeli-Burmese relations. According to his account, technical cooperation began with the dispatch of a Burmese military mission to Israel in August 1954.[5] Arrangements were made for Israeli experts to advise the Defense Service Industries, the economic branch of the Burmese army, in a variety of nonmilitary fields; in the military sphere Israel provided training for air force ground crews and other army technicians. Premier U Nu's visit to Israel in the late spring of 1955 led to even closer cooperation, including the planning of large-scale agricultural programs.

[4] Mordechai E. Kreinin, *Israel and Africa—A Study in Technical Cooperation,* Praeger, New York, 1964, pp. 13–14.

[5] David Hacohen, *Yoman Burma* (Burmese Diary), Am Oved, Tel Aviv, 1963, p. 269.

Ghana—The Next Step

Government-to-government relations and Histadrut collaboration began in Ghana at about the same time, coinciding roughly with Ghana's achievement of independence in 1957. Israel's delegation to Ghana's independence celebration included David Hacohen and Pinchas Sapir, then Minister of Commerce and Industry, member of the Executive Committee of Mapai and former director of the national water company, a vitally important enterprise owned jointly by Histadrut, the Government of Israel and the Jewish Agency.

While in Ghana, the Israelis, like other visiting delegations, were handed a list of Ghana's needs for assistance. They took the list seriously and later that year the first project, the Black Star Shipping Line, a joint venture between the Government of Ghana and Israel's publicly owned Zim Navigation Company, was established. In the same year, John Tettegah, then Secretary General of Ghana's Trade Union Congress, visited Israel, and decided that Ghana's loosely organized and ineffective trade union movement should be reorganized along the lines of Histadrut. For several years a number of Histadrut trade unionists worked with Tettegah and his successors as advisers to Ghana's Trade Union Congress. Simultaneously, Ghana-Israel trade began to flow, and numerous technical assistance activities were started. One Israeli official described this "honeymoon" period of Israel-Ghana relations as the time when Ghanaians "expected Israel to accomplish everything the United Kingdom couldn't or wouldn't accomplish."

Israel's approach had been that, like the other developing countries of Asia and Africa, it had risen from the ruins of imperialism, but had been able to accomplish prior to independence much of the political, social and technological growth that newly independent nations generally have to telescope into a brief period. It therefore had much to share with the other countries. Its strong socialist parties and socialist-inspired economy particularly equipped it to assist these countries, many of whose leaders also professed a socialist orientation and favored public enterprise. In addition, Israelis were moved by deep, genuine sympathy for other struggling new countries. Their youthful enthusiasm and sincerity made up for their lack of experience as dispensers of technical assistance, and had a marked infectious effect on their cooperation partners. Burma's Premier U Nu reflected some of this special emotional dimension when he reputedly told an American Senator, "The Americans are prepared to aid in those fields which *they* consider useful; the Israelis, on the other hand, aid in those fields which the *Burmese* consider important." [6] (Emphasis added.)

This, very briefly, is how Israeli cooperation with developing countries began—somewhat unplanned, but with passion and eagerness on the part of the nations involved.

Import and Export of Knowledge

Since independence, Israel itself has been the beneficiary of foreign technical assistance, some of it in the very areas in which it now offers expertise to others.

The United States spent about $15 million on technical assistance for Israel from December 1951 to June 1962. More than 600 Israelis were trained under this program, largely in the United States, and 340 U. S. technicians went to Israel in support of some 70 projects in agriculture, irrigation and water technology, industry and transportation.[7]

From 1950 to 1964 the United Nations and its specialized agencies spent over $5 million on experts and fellowships for Israel.[8]

There is a relation between knowledge imported into Israel (in the form of United States and United Nations experts and foreign training grants) and knowledge exported by Israel in its own program of cooperation with developing countries. This is not to imply, however, that Israel has merely served as a relay for techniques developed in other lands. Rather, Israel has absorbed Western technology and

[6] Unpublished memo by A. Sprinzak, former leader of the Israeli agricultural assistance team in Burma, to the Ministry for Foreign Affairs, Jerusalem, May 7, 1961.

[7] Uzi Peled, *Evaluation Survey of Israel Participants in the AID Training Program,* The Israel Institute of Applied Social Research, Jerusalem, 1962, p. 2; and "Investment in Progress," U. S. Information Service and Israeli Ministry of Finance, December 1964, p. 12 (pamphlet); *Mutual Security in Action—Israel,* U. S. Department of State, Washington, Publication 6935, June 1960, pp. 7–13.

[8] "The UN Technical Assistance Program in Israel," Office of the UN Resident Representative, Jerusalem, October 24, 1964 (press release).

adapted it to the needs of the developing countries. A striking illustration of this process can be seen in the evolution of Israel's work in agricultural extension.

Israel's Agricultural Extension Service, developed with extensive U. S. help, follows the basic U. S. approach of a unified service, with close cooperation between research and practical extension work. However, in Israel adult male farmers receive priority over youth, since the acute immediate needs outweigh the long-range benefits to be derived from training future farmers. Also, extension officers visit farmers almost weekly, instead of four or five times a year, as in the United States.

Based on this modified U. S. model, Israel developed a highly efficient extension service, which in turn became one of its largest training institutions for students from developing countries. From 1960 to 1965, 71 training courses, in which 1,500 trainees participated, were given under the auspices of the Agricultural Extension Service.[9] Similarly, programs in agricultural extension are among the most successful Israeli-supported projects abroad.

A recent survey undertaken as part of this study indicates that a sizable number of the experts and instructors who have served in Israel's program had received training in technical assistance programs abroad.[10] This illustrates how the now-terminated United States program and the continuing United Nations program have achieved a significant chain reaction or "multiplier effect" in Israel, and through Israel in other countries, thus broadening the total impact of this assistance. Henry Chalfant, former U. S. Mission Director in Israel, alluded to this fact when he wrote: [11]

> Israelis selected for training abroad were carefully chosen with a view to returning to Israel as disseminators of skill and knowledge to others. This "multiplier effect" is an essential element of any program of technical assistance. . . . The high quality of the trained Israeli is further attested to by the fact that Israel is now and has been in recent years transferring these acquired skills and knowledge to less fortunate people through a technical assistance program of her own.

[9] *Israel's Programme of International Cooperation*, Ministry for Foreign Affairs, Jerusalem, 1966, p. 82 (mimeo.).

[10] See footnote 2, Chapter 4 for a description of this survey.

[11] Quoted in Peled, *op. cit.*, pp. 2–3. This aspect of technical assistance is examined more closely in Chapter 1 of the present study.

Though its needs for foreign expertise have declined and changed in character over the years, of course, Israel continues to require—and to receive—foreign assistance. The UN technical assistance program to Israel, for example, maintained a fairly steady expenditure level of $300,000 to $400,000 per year through 1962.[12] Since then it has declined only slightly and in 1965 and 1966 it was estimated at about $250,000.

Principles of the Program

Israel's experience as the recipient of assistance has had a definite influence on its own policies in the operation of assistance programs in other countries. Although the program of cooperation with developing countries grew from small beginnings and almost without advance planning, it quickly developed its own characteristics and operating principles.

Unlike the United States, for example, Israel never establishes self-contained assistance "missions" abroad, nor does it set up commissaries or acquire blocs of houses for Israelis on foreign assignments. Even in countries where there are 30 or 40 Israeli experts, the Israelis work in the offices of or on the sites of the projects to which they are attached, and often live on the sites of projects. These practices lessen the likelihood that Israeli experts will be isolated from the environment in which their local colleagues operate. Israelis are also keenly aware of the importance of language as a tool for effective transfer of knowledge, both in training courses in Israel and for experts working abroad. It is inconceivable that Israelis would turn down a host government's offer to provide language instruction for their experts, as U. S. representatives reportedly did at one time, when the Government of Israel offered to provide one-month intensive Hebrew courses for American experts working in Israel.

Having been on the receiving end themselves, Israelis may also have developed a particular sensitivity to the feelings of people from

[12] "The UN Technical Assistance Program in Israel," Office of the United Nations Resident Representative, Jerusalem, October 24, 1964, p. 1 (press release).

developing countries. This is illustrated by the remark of an Israeli nurse who had served in Burma:[13]

> When foreign advisers came to Israel and told us that something was not right, we used to get offended. Consequently my approach in Burma was to teach by doing rather than by ordering and to keep showing how things are done in Israel without insisting on quick changes.

The Israeli program of cooperation differs importantly from assistance programs of developed countries in the provision of capital. Because of Israel's limited financial resources, the architects of Israel's program ruled out competition with more affluent countries in extending loans or making capital grants. This policy remains in effect, and tends to restrict Israel's activities in most countries to technical assistance. Thus, of necessity, Israel avoids the serious errors that result when technical assistance is treated "simply as an adjunct to capital aid."[14] It has been far from easy for Israel to operate within the restricted sphere of technical assistance, however, and many knowledgeable Israelis think that the lack of capital resources has seriously hampered the program. (See Chapter 3 for further discussion of the financing of Israel's program.)

Preference for Training

Partly because of the scarcity of capital, the emphasis of Israel's program has been on training, as can be seen from Foreign Ministry statistics showing that during 1965 a record number of more than 5,000 trainees attended Israel's sponsored courses in Israel and abroad, compared to about 650 assignments of Israeli experts to projects abroad. Another reason for concentrating on training is that it is easier to arrange than are other types of projects. Finally, Israelis are convinced that intensive, concentrated training can foster new attitudes that are "indispensable . . . in the assumption of difficult development tasks."[15] The recent trend toward expansion of Israel's on-the-spot training programs abroad reflects all of these reasons, for

[13] Kreinin, *op. cit.,* p. 9.

[14] See Angus Maddison, *Foreign Skills and Technical Assistance in Economic Development,* Development Centre, OECD, Paris, 1965, p. 12.

[15] *Israel's Programme of International Cooperation,* p. 78.

these programs enable Israel to reach large numbers of people at little additional expense. (See Chapter 10.)

The Integrated Project

Israel's emphasis on training is even more pronounced than the participation figures cited above indicate, for many projects in which Israeli experts are active are supported by training programs, either on the spot or in Israel, in keeping with what the Israelis refer to as the "integrated project" concept. In this way, training programs reinforce and facilitate the work of the experts. When the training takes place in Israel, trainees are exposed to Israeli attitudes in a concentrated way, and, upon their return to their homelands, are presumably more receptive to the work of the experts than they would have been without this exposure. A publication of the Israeli Foreign Ministry explains the concept as follows: [16]

> . . . during the period of the expert's mission in the country concerned, local personnel are being trained in Israel in the relevant field so that, on their return, they can be "integrated" within the project which has meanwhile got under way. This system achieves a dual objective. For one, it facilitates the efficient implementation of the project by local staff, for the returning cadres have had the opportunity to become familiar with Israel operational methods . . . The second advantage of the integrated project is that it ensures the availability of suitably trained staff to take over the responsibility of the project on completion of the Israeli expert's assignment. Since Israel has no interest in maintaining a long-term influence over foreign ventures, this is of paramount importance to the continuation of an operation after its experts have withdrawn. From the standpoint of the country concerned, the planned take-over by its own nationals with the minimum possible delay of a project initiated in collaboration with visiting experts represents a concrete step in its development. From Israel's point of view, it means the quick release of its technicians for vital development tasks at home.

The principle of combining training in Israel with operations abroad was actually incorporated—and on a fairly grand scale—into Israel's first technical assistance program in Burma. The specific project was to develop Burma's arid zone of Namsang in the Shan states by settling groups of Burmese army veterans there. After Israeli experts had surveyed the region, 100 Burmese ex-servicemen and their fam-

[16] *Ibid.*, p. 5.

ilies, who were to be the cadre of the resettlement program, were brought to Israel to live for a year in various Israeli settlements. After they returned to Burma, a team of four Israeli experts joined them and worked with them to develop villages and crops in their new lands. The results of this experiment were mixed, as far as the attitudes of the new settlers were concerned, but on the whole the integrated project approach proved effective.

An integrated project still under way is the program for combating blindness and eye diseases in Liberia. Under this program, discussed in greater detail in Chapter 8, an Israeli physician went to Liberia in 1959 to establish an eye hospital. While the hospital was being readied, two Liberian nurses went to Israel for six months' specialized training in ophthalmological nursing and returned in time to enter on duty in the newly opened hospital. Another Liberian nurse was trained on the spot in Liberia. A Liberian physician went to Israel for two years of advanced studies in the Department of Ophthalmology of the Hebrew University's Medical School and upon his return was able to replace one of two Israeli physicians working in Liberia. It was hoped that by 1966 the remaining Israeli physician could be replaced by another Liberian physician trained on the spot.

Teamwork

The team approach is another working principle in Israel's program. In the early days, when the Israelis were establishing their identity on the international assistance scene, they paid little attention to the organizational effectiveness of their activity. The tendency, in fact, seemed to be to scatter experts over as wide an area as possible. Some of this tendency remains, but there is growing recognition of the need for greater concentration of effort through the team approach.

For example, a country requesting assistance in preparing young people for agricultural settlement, perhaps combined with army service after the pattern of Israel's Fighting Pioneer Youth (Nahal),[17]

[17] Nahal was formed in 1948, shortly after the establishment of the State of Israel, to enable young people to combine their army service with pioneering and agricultural work in exposed border settlements or new settlement areas. (For further discussion of Nahal programs for developing countries, see Chapter 7.)

will normally be offered a team of 5 to 10 people, consisting of a leader who combines agricultural with army experience, agricultural instructors with some army experience, a heavy equipment operator, an agricultural planner and an agronomist. Nahal teams organized along these lines were operating in 10 African and 2 Latin American countries in 1966.

A different type of team was used in a joint marketing venture in Tanzania, where Israel supplied a managerial team consisting of the general manager, deputy general manager, commercial manager and several other key officials. As the project progressed, local personnel gradually took over executive responsibilities, replacing the Israeli team.

Israelis prefer the team approach to scattered individual experts for several reasons. They have found that team members reinforce each other, and thus can more easily overcome operational difficulties, and that teams can cope better with psychological and social problems of adjustment encountered by experts and their families. They have also learned that their effectiveness in a country is not necessarily a function of the number of projects scattered throughout the land, but rather of the quality of projects and their clear identification with the Israeli presence. Israeli officials estimate that about 80 per cent of their experts abroad are working as members of identifiable Israeli teams.

The Open Door

Israel, as a rule, accepts trainees and requests for technical assistance from any developing country, regardless of its political attitudes. There have been numerous trainees in Israel, for example, from India, Malaysia and Iran, countries that do not maintain normal diplomatic relations with Israel. Several African countries also have sent trainees to Israel and accepted Israeli experts on their soil, but for reasons of politics or economy have chosen not to establish diplomatic representation in Israel. The Israelis are by no means insensitive to the question of normalizing diplomatic relations with these countries, but they apparently have concluded that, in general, refusal of technical assistance is not the way to change the situation. However, in 1963, when a local government body in India applied for Israeli technical experts, the request was reportedly turned down because the Government of India refused to submit an official request.

The Israelis seem to feel that contacts at the technical level will demonstrate the value of normal relations, win friends for Israel and eventually lead to improved relations at the political level. Their basic criteria for establishing a technical assistance program are: the effect of the assistance on the development of the recipient country; Israel's ability to supply the aid sought; and the conditions in the recipient state, including its capacity to provide counterparts, trainees and enough money for successful completion of the program.

They prefer programs that can reach fruition fairly quickly and that require at the outset minimal resources on the beneficiary's part, but that will create the basis for further development, with little or no help from the outside.[18]

Official statements of principles do not, of course, tell the whole story of complex political, economic and social processes. Israel's program is no exception to this rule. From this list of criteria, for example, we learn nothing of the political pressures that in Israel, as in other countries, influence the selection of programs; of the ever-present financial restraints; of the economic considerations that sometimes weigh in the balance. Though these generally restrictive factors operate to some extent in the programs of all nations, it is to Israel's credit that they apparently have not seriously infringed upon its "open-door" policy.

Israel has applied its "open-door" policy in the economic, as well as in the political, sphere. It has shared its experience in developing potentially competitive foreign industries and has offered liberal procurement provisions in the few foreign loans it has made.

Israel's policy on citrus is the outstanding example of its economic "open door." Citrus has long been Israel's major agricultural export product, and in 1965 accounted for about one sixth of total export earnings.[19] Nevertheless, for some years Israel has had experts advising on development of citrus crops in a number of Asian, African

[18] *Programme of Cooperation with Developing Countries, 1961–1962*, Department for International Cooperation, Ministry for Foreign Affairs, Jerusalem, 1963, p. 4.

[19] *Statistical Abstract of Israel, 1966*, Central Bureau of Statistics, Jerusalem, p. 255.

and South American countries. Some of these countries—Ecuador and Ceylon, for example—are not soon likely to become Israel's competitors in the world citrus market; others, however—such as Uganda and Israel's Mediterranean neighbors, Greece and Turkey—are already, or could easily become, citrus exporters to Israel's European markets.

When the question of assisting in the development of citrus crops in these countries arose, it triggered a spirited debate within the Israeli Government and within the powerful Citrus Growers' Association. But the decision was to go ahead, and since then Israelis have trained Ugandans in citriculture, advised Greeks on combating citrus viruses, and offered to help improve Turkey's citrus-marketing organization.

Good Will Abroad

The reasoning behind this decision was that Israel had no monopoly on knowledge and that these countries could, and undoubtedly would, get their advice elsewhere, if Israel refused to help them. Furthermore, it was felt that refusal to assist in a field of knowledge in which Israel had known competence would be regarded as a selfish act and therefore would damage Israel's reputation and political relations. Finally, since these countries were going into the citrus business regardless of Israel's help, the Israelis realized that early friendly contacts and cooperation might lead to useful arrangements at a later stage.

Similar reasoning also applied to Israel's willingness to assist Greece in improving its poultry industry, although for some years Israel had actually been exporting small quantities of eggs to Greece.

Israeli officials make no claims to exceptional virtue in explaining their policy, for they are convinced that, in these cases at least, international morality happily supported the goals of practical politics. Their policy has not produced any major domestic crises in Israel, and it has won them much good will abroad. It has also led to friendly professional contacts, through which Israel, in one case, was able to obtain material that it needed for its own agricultural development.[20]

[20] Israel's policy in this respect differs from that of the United States, which maintains some restrictions on providing assistance for the development of major U. S. agricultural crops, such as cotton.

Sharing the Burden

The scarcity of financial resources, previously discussed, is a major reason for the burden-sharing principle in the Israeli program. In addition, however, Israeli policy makers believe that "If you give people something for nothing, they will not appreciate it and your efforts will be lost."

There are obvious political risks involved in adhering firmly to this principle, and on occasion assistance offered on this basis has been refused. What is remarkable, however, is that it has so often been willingly accepted. This willingness is exemplified by the remark attributed to one head of government that he would get money for an Israeli-backed project, "even if I have to steal it." Though burden-sharing strengthens the partnership, lack of funds in a developing country can become a serious handicap, if not an insurmountable barrier, to implementing otherwise sound projects.

Education by Doing

Because of financial limitations and the consequent importance of making the best possible use of available resources, the Israelis have given great attention to practical and demonstration work.

"When I hear, I forget; when I see, I remember; when I do, I know," was the way a 63-year-old Israeli farmer working in a remote area of Ethiopia explained the principle of demonstration to a visitor. As an ingenious experimenter and innovator (who, among other things, taught his young wards to fashion a primitive but effective plow out of local scrap iron) he demonstrated, furthermore, the close relationship between "doing" and adapting to local conditions.

"Experts who work in the field and teach by personal example have the greatest success," states one of nine "principles of mutual cooperation" contained in an Israeli Foreign Ministry pamphlet. Other relevant "principles" are: "Knowledge and experience must be adapted to suit local conditions." "What really matters in any development scheme is: can it reasonably soon become a practical reality." [21]

Israel's preference for "doing" is reflected in the types of projects

[21] "Sharing," Jerusalem (no date), p. 15.

it undertakes abroad and in the curriculum and design of Israeli-based training programs. A 4-months' course in "Labor Studies and Cooperation" conducted in 1965 at the Afro-Asian Institute in Tel Aviv provided for 1 month of visits and actual work away from the Institute, 60 hours of field trips to labor and cooperative enterprises and institutions and additional field trips for specialized study groups. Other training courses—in public administration, agricultural extension and utilization of water under arid conditions, for example—allotted from one fourth to one half the training period to practical work of some kind.[22]

Mutual Benefit

While mutual benefit is one of the principles of the cooperation program frequently cited by Israelis, it is also one of the most elusive. To understand this principle, it is helpful to remember the Israeli insistence on practicality.

The political application of the principle can be readily understood. Friendly relations and understanding (if not support) in international forums, which in part at least can be traced to Israel's program of technical cooperation, represent tangible benefits for both Israel and its partners. But while Israelis are appreciative of the political benefits, they prefer to emphasize a different kind of mutual benefit—that of exchange of knowledge and experience. "The day will come when Peruvians will teach Israelis a lesson in cooperation," declared Israel's Ambassador Netanel Lorch at the inauguration of an Israel-sponsored training course in northern Peru.[23] And the first and third of the nine "principles of mutual cooperation" echo the same thought: "There are no backward peoples, only backward conditions" and "Developing countries can learn from each other." [24]

This is the mutual benefit aspect that still is so elusive when applied concretely, and many Israeli officials say candidly that thus far it

[22] *Program of Studies, Tenth International Course,* The Afro-Asian Institute for Labour Studies and Cooperation, Tel Aviv, 1965; Aryeh Semo, "The Training of Senior Officials for African Countries," *Public Administration in Israel and Abroad, 1961* (annual, Israel Institute of Public Administration, Jerusalem), p. 66.

[23] *El Correo,* Piura, Peru, October 25, 1965.

[24] "Sharing," p. 15.

hardly exists in Israel's relations with developing countries, that the assistance process is still pretty much a one-way street. Nevertheless, the espousal of the principle has considerable psychological importance, for it negates the traditional paternalism inherent in the donor-recipient image and puts the program in the context of a partnership. Knowledgeable Israeli officials believe that a two-way flow between Israel and other developing countries will gradually increase.

Furthermore, the Israelis realize that the program has indeed been one of mutual benefits in terms of its important political, economic and psychological consequences for Israel. They believe that it has promoted Israel's self-respect and self-confidence, counteracted some of the charges of Israel's adversaries and laid the basis for friendly international relations—that more than any other single factor, it has "opened the world" for Israel.

Chapter 3

Administration and Finances

THE ESSENTIALS of effective technical cooperation are motivation, imagination, worthwhile experience that can be transmitted, skilled personnel, organization and money. At the start of its program Israel had an abundance of the first three elements, a fair supply of personnel and little organization or money. The expansion of its efforts has necessitated the development of tighter organization and more precise fixing of responsibility for administration and policy guidance. This chapter describes the administrative and financial machinery that has evolved to keep the program operating.

Israel's cooperation activities were initially carried out as part of the regular work of the Foreign Ministry, with three or four people assigned to it in the Office of the Director General. Today most of the program falls under the jurisdiction of a special Department for International Cooperation (known by its Hebrew acronym, "Mashav"), of the Ministry for Foreign Affairs. The Ministry's Economic Department, in consultation with the Ministry of Finance, oversees the few loans that have been extended to developing countries and gives policy guidance for joint ventures and commercial operations of public companies abroad. The Foreign Ministry delegates responsibility for the professional aspects of its cooperation activities to other ministries, institutions and organizations.

The Department for International Cooperation (Mashav)

The rapid and somewhat unplanned growth of Mashav to the largest single department of the Foreign Ministry (with some 60 employees, down from a peak of 80) has disturbed government critics and confounded efficiency experts. Yet the fact is that a program on the scale of Israel's must have people to administer it.

Mashav, although only a department within the Foreign Ministry, was semiautonomous until 1965, as far as administration and operation were concerned. It differed in this respect from other departments of the Ministry, which are organized along either geographic or functional lines and are fiscally and administratively centrally coordinated. The relationship of Mashav to the Ministry for Foreign Affairs was comparable to that of the U. S. Agency for International Development (AID) to the U. S. Department of State. At the beginning of 1966, however, in an attempt to tighten and streamline operations, Mashav's semiautonomous status within the Foreign Ministry was abolished. Figure 3-1 shows its present organization.

As indicated in the chart, functional and area officers operate along parallel lines under the over-all direction of Mashav's Director. They receive routine policy guidance from the political officials of the Ministry, but general policy direction flows through Mashav's Director. The functional and area officers in turn give guidance to operating agencies or officials—course directors, team leaders, other Ministries and institutions and Israeli diplomats abroad. They also participate in the selection and briefing of experts and training personnel, and keep abreast of all programs in their geographic areas and functional specialties.

Divided Responsibility

While Mashav has over-all control and holds the purse strings, substantive control over content and day-to-day operations rests with

FIGURE 3-1

ORGANIZATIONAL STRUCTURE OF THE DEPARTMENT FOR INTERNATIONAL COOPERATION, 1966

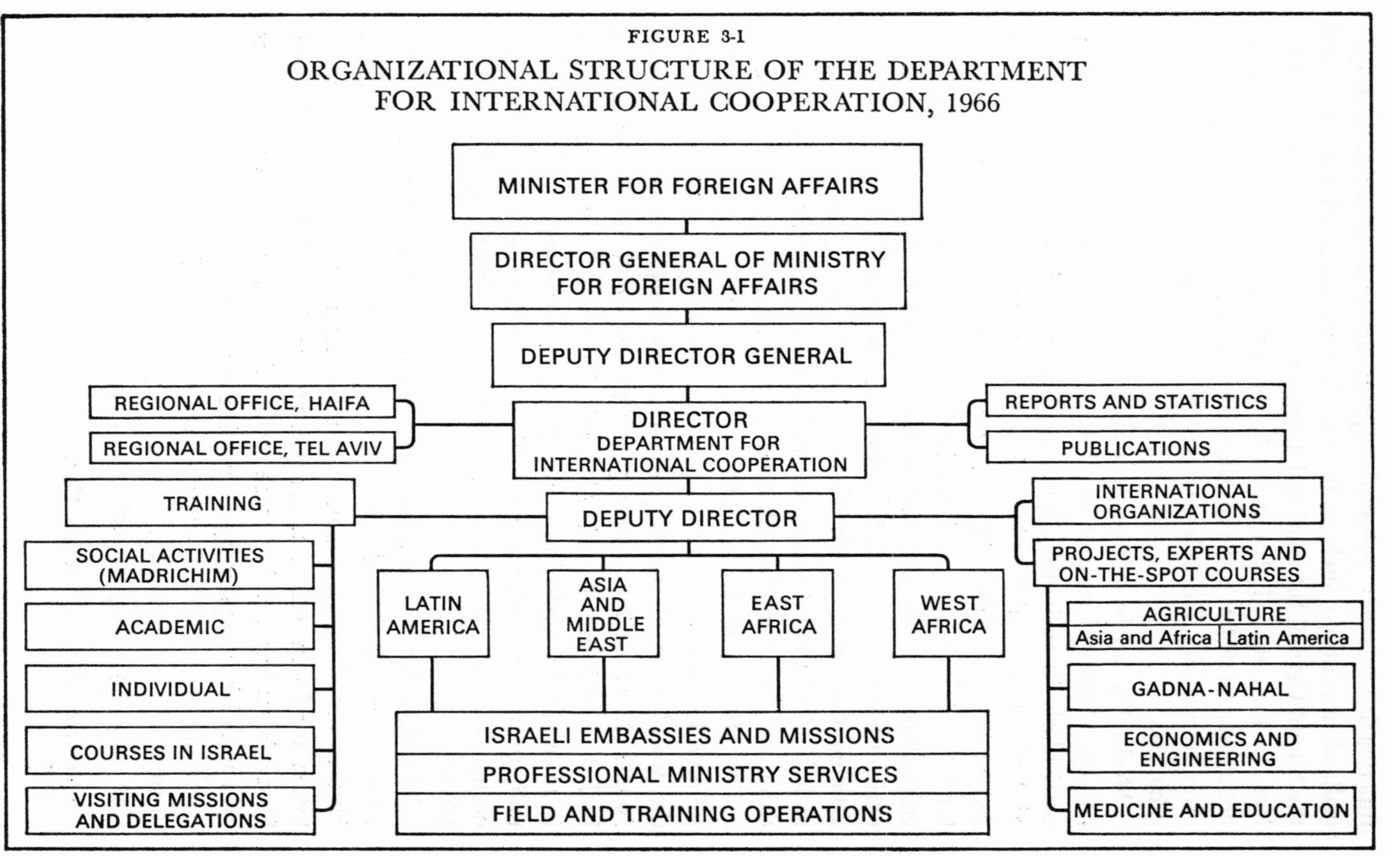

functional Ministries, primarily Agriculture and Defense, and specialized institutions such as the Israeli Institute of Productivity and the Mount Carmel International Training Center for Community Services. In fact, the Ministries of Agriculture and Defense, which together account for a large share of Israel's cooperation program, exercise considerable independence in running their segments of the program.

Moshe Dayan, Israel's colorful former Minister of Agriculture, took an active personal interest in all aspects of the cooperation program, particularly its agricultural projects. Under his direction, the Ministry of Agriculture established the Foreign Training Department of the Agricultural Extension Service, responsible for Israel-based agricultural training courses, and another department that supervises agricultural projects abroad. Various independent bodies connected with agricultural programs, such as the Rehovoth Center for the Study of Foreign Countries, which advised and briefed agricultural experts, and the Agricultural Development Company, have lately been liquidated and their functions absorbed by the Ministry of Agriculture.

The Ministry of Defense has a Department for Cooperation and Foreign Liaison, with a 20-man staff specializing in different areas of the world. One of the Department's functions is the operation of Israel's Nahal-Gadna cooperation program with foreign countries, both in Israel and abroad. Although the Nahal-Gadna work abroad is primarily in agriculture and youth development rather than in military training, virtually all Nahal-Gadna experts, regardless of occupation, go abroad as military officers, responsible to the Defense Ministry.

The Histadrut Labor Federation also has a share in managing the cooperation program. It runs the Afro-Asian Institute for Labour Studies and Cooperation, and has much influence on the sister institution for Latin America, the Center for Cooperative and Labour Study. Histadrut also has some technical assistance agreements of its own with labor organizations in other countries.[1]

Friction, jurisdictional disputes and some inefficiency are inherent in such divided authority. Although not always responsible, the Foreign Ministry's Department for International Cooperation, as the

[1] *Jerusalem Post*, October 10, 1964.

agency nominally in charge, has borne the brunt of public criticism for shortcomings that have come to public attention. Such criticism, however, has been directed largely at questions of administration and operating efficiency and not at the program as such, which in fact enjoys broad public support.

Partly in response to the criticism, Aharon Remez, Mashav's free-wheeling founder and dynamic first Director, was replaced late in 1964 by David Golan, a talented economist and Finance Ministry official, who headed the program until early 1966. His leadership was efficient and businesslike, but without the fire and inspiration of Remez. Golan has been succeeded by Eytan Ron, a Foreign Ministry official with considerable experience in Africa. During Golan's administration and subsequently some streamlining was accomplished, but the basic pattern of decentralized functional operation remains unchanged. Proposals for setting up a separate foreign cooperation agency, independent of the Foreign Ministry, and giving it full operational control over all programs have thus far been rejected.

Israeli officials evidently believe the program is too sensitive and politically important to be separated from the Foreign Ministry; well-established interests outside the Ministry are equally adamant in arguing that they must retain their share of control. Experience elsewhere, notably in the United States, indicates that no solution is likely to be entirely satisfactory.

Costs and Cost-Sharing

Funds for the operation of Israel's cooperation program are provided by the Israeli Government, the partner governments, international organizations and, to some extent, private sources. Because of this fact total costs are difficult to assess. The official Mashav budget estimate for 1966–67 is 10 million Israeli pounds ($3.33 million at the official exchange rate of $1.00 = IL3).[2] Foreign Ministry officials, however, confirm that the official budget estimate has in the past usually been exceeded by about IL5 million ($1.66 million). Mashav budgetary allocations for 1966–67 therefore probably totaled about

[2] *Jerusalem Post,* March 25, 1966. The Israeli budget year begins April 1 and ends March 31.

TABLE 3-1 *Official Expenditures of the Department for International Cooperation, 1961–1963*
(In Thousands of U. S. Dollars)

Type of Expenditure	1961	1962	1963
Total	$3,118	$4,675	$5,616
Training in Israel	1,550	2,061	2,479
Activities abroad [a]	802	1,580	2,336
UN multilateral assistance	256	296	331
Payments to nongovernmental organizations and corporations for services	10	35	110
Investments	350	400	77
Administration and overhead in Israel	100	133	234
Other	50	170	49

SOURCE: Ministry for Foreign Affairs, Jerusalem.

[a] Represents mostly salaries and expenses of experts, but also includes the partial financing of projects in Upper Volta, Kenya, the Mekong River Project, Guinea and on-the-spot training courses.

IL15 million ($5 million). Detailed breakdowns of expenditures are available only through 1963. (See Table 3-1.) After 1963 the program began to level off—in terms of expenditures, but not activities.

In addition to the funds supplied by the Foreign Ministry, some contributions to the program are made by the Ministry of Defense and by Histadrut. The Defense Ministry absorbs some of the personnel costs of operating Israel-based Nahal-Gadna training courses, as well as expenditures incurred for strictly military assistance. Histadrut continues to contribute to the financing of the operation of the Afro-Asian Institute for Labour Studies and Cooperation and of some trade-union related seminars and training visits. It is difficult to know how much these and minor contributions from other Israeli sources add to Israel's total investment in the program, but estimates made in connection with the present study ranged as high as 30 per cent.

Contributions from Beneficiary Countries

As indicated in Chapter 2, Israel's program operates on the principle of "sharing the burden." The largest non-Israeli contribution to the cost of the program therefore comes from the various beneficiary countries themselves. Aside from furnishing the capital equipment needed for particular projects, the partner countries normally pay transportation, salary and housing costs of Israeli experts abroad and international travel costs for trainees coming to Israel. There is, however, no fixed pattern regarding these contributions by beneficiary countries; they depend on the country's ability to pay, the political priority of the project for Israel, Israel's own budgetary situation and other factors.

On only two items is financial responsibility fairly uniform: Israel usually bears the cost of training courses, local travel and subsistence for trainees in Israel and the host country pays local travel costs of Israeli experts abroad.

The policy in regard to payment for international travel is more varied. While Israel normally does not pay travel costs of trainees to Israel, there are many exceptions to this rule.[3] Similarly, Israel's policy that host governments cover international travel expenses of experts and their families is often not complied with. Particularly for short-term experts, Israel often pays all or part of the travel expenses.

In a report to the OECD Israel explained its position on travel costs as follows: [4]

> Travelling expenses (i.e., international travel) for either trainees or experts are usually borne by the beneficiary country, and only in exceptional cases does Israel cover them. . . . In most of its bilateral agreements for technical assistance the Government of Israel, as a matter of principle, declines to commit itself to paying salaries and travelling expenses of the experts seconded. Yet, whenever it is unavoidable, it is willing to supplement the salaries paid by the beneficiary countries and/or pay travelling expenses.

Most nations and international agencies engaged in foreign assistance require some contributions from recipient countries, especially for local costs; what is different in Israel's program—and apparently

[3] It was found in field interviews in connection with this study that in a typical training course of 36 participants, held in 1964, the international travel of 12 of the trainees was financed by sending governments; of 8, by Israel; and of 16, by an international organization.

[4] *Programme of Cooperation with Developing Countries, 1961–1962,* Department for International Cooperation, Ministry for Foreign Affairs, Jerusalem, 1963, pp. 39–40.

TABLE 3-2 *Provisions for Paying Salaries, Housing and International Travel in Technical Assistance Agreements Between Tanzania and Selected Cooperating Countries, 1965* [a]

Cooperating Country	Payment of Salaries of Experts	Housing	Payment of International Travel Costs of Experts	Payment of International Travel Costs of Trainees
West Germany	Cooperating country	Tanzania	Cooperating country	Cooperating country
Yugoslavia	Cooperating country 35% Tanzania 65%	Tanzania	Tanzania normally	Tanzania
Scandinavian countries (joint project)	Cooperating country	Cooperating country	Cooperating country	[b]
Sweden	Cooperating country	Tanzania	Cooperating country	[b]
Israel				
Under 3 months	Cooperating country	Tanzania (50% if in hotel)	Cooperating country	[b]
Over 3 months	Tanzania	Tanzania	Tanzania	Tanzania
Seconded staff [c]	Tanzania	Tanzania	Tanzania	[b]

SOURCE: Field interviews.

[a] It should be noted that while these agreements represent a general framework, in practice the terms are flexibly applied. For example, salaries of the members of one of Israel's long-term teams in Tanzania are paid by Israel—the terms of the umbrella agreement notwithstanding.

[b] Not applicable.

[c] Experts lent to a foreign government to perform regular staff functions.

in Yugoslavia's as well—is the extent to which recipient nations have accepted the burden-sharing principle. Tanzania, for example, in concluding five technical assistance agreements, accepted more obligations in agreements with Israel and Yugoslavia than with the other three countries involved. (See Table 3-2.)

The variety of (as well as consistencies in) funding arrangements in agreements and contracts between Israel and partner countries can be gauged by comparing some of the terms of technical assistance agreements between Israel and four other countries, shown in Table 3-3. For example, in every case salaries of long-term experts are paid by host governments and salaries of short-term experts by Israel; housing of trainees in Israel is provided by Israel but their interna-

TABLE 3-3 *Provisions for Paying Salaries, Housing and International Travel in Technical Assistance Agreements [a] Between Israel and Upper Volta, Ghana, Tanzania [b] and Ecuador,[c] 1965*

Item to Be Paid	Provisions for Payment			
	Upper Volta	Ghana	Tanzania	Ecuador
Salaries				
Long-term experts	Upper Volta	Ghana (over 1 year)	Tanzania (over 3 months)	Ecuador
Short-term experts	Israel (under 2 months)	Israel	Israel	Israel (under 3 months)
Housing				
Long-term experts	[d]	[d]	Tanzania and Israel (50% each)	[d]
Short-term experts	Upper Volta	Ghana	Tanzania and Israel (50% each)	[d]
Trainees in Israel	Israel	Israel	Israel	Israel
International travel				
Long-term experts	Upper Volta	Ghana	Tanzania (over 3 months)	Israel
Short-term experts	Upper Volta	Ghana	Israel (under 3 months)	Israel
Trainees in Israel	Upper Volta	Ghana	Tanzania	Ecuador

SOURCE: Technical assistance agreements between Israel and Upper Volta, Ghana, Tanzania and Ecuador.

[a] It should be noted that while these agreements represent a general framework, in practice the terms are flexibly applied. For example, the salaries of the members of one of Israel's long-term teams in Tanzania are paid by Israel—the terms of the umbrella agreement notwithstanding. It should also be noted that salaries of Israeli experts paid by recipient governments are often supplemented by Israel.

[b] The term "expert" as used in the agreement with Tanzania does not include personnel on secondment (on loan for the performance of staff duties) to the Government of Tanzania. Salaries of seconded personnel are largely paid by the Government of Tanzania.

[c] This agreement covers technical assistance in agriculture only. It provides for four long-term and two short-term experts and one trainee in Israel. It anticipates similar arrangements in the future.

[d] Not available.

tional travel is paid for by the sending governments. Apparently, the only permissible generalization is that by and large the principle of "sharing the burden" has been accepted by Israel's partners in technical assistance, especially with respect to two high-cost items—salaries of long-term experts and international travel for trainees coming to Israel.

International Participation

While Israel has jealously guarded the largely bilateral character of its efforts, it has also progressively expanded its cooperative relationships with technical assistance programs of international agencies. These relationships are politically important for Israel, and have also served to enlarge the scope and financial support for Israel's activities.

Participation by the international organizations began with support of occasional training programs in Israel. It has grown over the years and now includes on-the-spot training courses and other projects abroad. One of the earliest internationally supported programs in Israel was the training course for medical students from developing countries, initiated in 1961. The World Health Organization provides tuition scholarships to more than half of the students, while the rest of the expenses are borne by Israel and sending governments. Similar tripartite arrangements were also worked out with the United Nations Special Fund on the establishment and operation of the multipurpose agricultural training center in Upper Volta [5] and with the UN Technical Assistance Board in the construction of housing projects in Guinea.

Most international organizations value highly the Israeli training efforts for developing countries, and have sponsored trainees for individual study tours and as participants in courses. Some, including the United Nations Educational, Scientific and Cultural Organization (UNESCO), The Food and Agricultural Organization (FAO), the United Nations Children's Fund (UNICEF) and the International Atomic Energy Agency (IAEA), have sponsored or cosponsored seminars and training courses in Israel.

The Government of Israel, in turn, has consistently participated in multilateral technical assistance activities of UN agencies. It responds to requests from them for the services of Israeli experts, and has made voluntary contributions to international programs over and above its normal assessments. An outstanding example of this type of cooperation is Israel's participation in the international project for the de-

[5] See Chapters 6 and 13.

velopment of the Mekong River area, sponsored by the UN Economic Commission for Asia and the Far East. Israel has contributed over $500,000 in materials and personnel services to the project, including the establishment of model farms in Laos and Cambodia.[6] However, Israel's most comprehensive cooperative arrangements are with the Organization for Economic Cooperation and Development (OECD) and the Organization of American States (OAS).

The relationship with the OECD started in 1961 and has steadily expanded, to the apparent satisfaction of both parties. The OECD has drawn on Israel for expertise to assist in the development of some of its own member countries, and has financed numerous seminars and study missions in Israel. A 1964 seminar on "Regional Development and Accelerated Growth," for instance, brought together top planners from Greece, Portugal, Spain, Yugoslavia and Israel. A totally different kind of activity was an OECD-financed contract with Israel's Agricultural Development Company (International) to assist Greece in preparing a comprehensive 10-year development plan for the island of Crete.[7] In another OECD-sponsored project Israel's Settlement Study Center of the National and University Institute of Agriculture is assisting the Faculty of Architecture of Turkey's Middle East Technical University to develop a department of regional planning and to conduct related research of interest to the university and to the Turkish Government.

Israel's cooperation with the OAS began with an agreement in October 1962 to conduct training courses for 200 Latin Americans over an 18-month period. This was part of a newly launched Extra-continental Training Program for the OAS that was designed to enlist the participation of countries outside the hemisphere. The trainees who went to Israel were jointly selected by the OAS and the Israeli Government; the OAS paid their travel to and from Israel plus $100 for clothing and books, while Israel bore the cost of training and maintenance in Israel.[8] According to the OAS, Israel's contribution to

[6] Ministry for Foreign Affairs, Jerusalem; and *Jerusalem Post Weekly,* March 25, 1966.

[7] The plan, prepared by a 43-man team of Greek and Israeli experts, is in line with Israeli approaches to regional development described in Chapter 6.

[8] OAS Press Release, C-462/62, Washington, October 18, 1962. Under more recent arrangements, Israel pays the book and clothing allowance.

this extracontinental training program exceeded that of all the participating European countries. In 1963–64 nearly half of the trainees under the program went to Israel. In addition, Israel pledged $72,000 in expert and training services in Latin America as its contribution to the OAS Special Fund for Development Assistance, the first nonmember of the OAS to make such a pledge. In July 1964 the training agreement was extended for two more years, but the number of trainees had already reached more than 200. In 1966, therefore, an open-ended two-year agreement was signed, which is still in force.

Since 1964 the OAS has contributed to the cost of on-the-spot training courses conducted in Latin America by Israel. In 1965, based on the successful experience with an Israeli team in Venezuela, the OAS agreed to finance three mobile interdisciplinary teams of Israeli experts, to promote comprehensive rural development throughout the hemisphere.[9] An additional Israeli team is being stationed in Central America, in accordance with a 1966 agreement between Israel, the OAS and the Inter-American Development Bank. The Bank is underwriting the major maintenance costs of the team.

Participation of Nongovernmental Groups and Third Countries

A number of nongovernmental groups and, to a lesser extent, governments of third countries also participate in Israel's program.

The Afro-Asian Institute for Labour Studies and Cooperation, in Tel Aviv, has since its inception received support from various foreign labor organizations. From 1960 to 1962, for instance, the U. S. American Federation of Labor–Congress of Industrial Organizations provided $300,000 in scholarships, and individual U. S. unions and British, Swiss, Dutch and Scandinavian labor organizations have made smaller contributions.[10] Similarly, the Mount Carmel International Training Center for Community Services, in Haifa, established close

[9] Exchange of letters between Jose A. Mora, OAS Secretary General, and Avraham Harman, Israeli Ambassador to the United States, July 1 and 10, 1964; November 4 and 9, 1965; and February 18 and 23, 1966. (Unpublished resumé of cooperation activities of the Ministry for Foreign Affairs, Jerusalem, January 1967. For discussion of the team experience in Venezuela, see Chapter 6.)

[10] Henry C. Fleisher, "The Shaping of Afro-Asian Leaders," *AFL-CIO American Federationist,* November 1963.

relations with Swedish women's groups, with the active encouragement of Mrs. Inga Thorsson, Sweden's former Ambassador to Israel and a former President of the Swedish Socialist Women's Federation. These groups contributed $250,000 to the work of the center in 1963 and have sponsored lectures and other activities at the center. The International Council of Social Democratic Women and the Government of Sweden (via UNESCO) have also provided some scholarship support for the center.[11]

Occasionally third governments have provided support for Israeli projects abroad through assistance to recipient governments. For example, the U. S. Agency for International Development (AID) has helped with equipment for Israel-aided youth projects in the Central African Republic, Dahomey and Costa Rica;[12] France has assisted youth projects in the Ivory Coast; and Great Britain and West Germany have reportedly given assistance to projects elsewhere in Africa.[13] Details on the extent of this type of cooperation are not readily available, but since the United States and all of these European countries have their own assistance programs and, like Israel, continue to promote the bilateral character of their programs, it is unlikely that the scale of support for Israel's program from these sources is very large.

Comparative Costs—Israel and Other Countries

Israelis say that the costs of their operations abroad are far lower than the costs of comparable operations of developed countries. One Israeli journalist, for example, upon completion of an African journey, reported:[14]

> Israel allots about 5 million dollars yearly to assistance to developing countries. This looks puny in comparison with the sums others spend, but

[11] *The International Training Center for Community Services* (Mount Carmel, Haifa), Ministry for Foreign Affairs, Jerusalem, and the Municipality of Haifa, November 1964 (pamphlet); and unpublished information from Ministry for Foreign Affairs.

[12] See Chapter 7.

[13] *Jerusalem Post,* November 29, 1963; *Maariv* (Tel Aviv), February 3, 1964.

[14] Arieh Eshet, "Israel-African Economic Relations," *Davar* (Tel Aviv), December 12, 1964.

> it seems that the productiveness of the American dollar or the Russian ruble is tens of times lower than the productiveness of Israel's currency.

David Golan, the former director of the Department for International Cooperation of the Ministry for Foreign Affairs, more modest in his estimates, told a group of U. S. visitors that Israel gets twice as much in return for its foreign aid dollar as does the United States.[15] How valid are these claims?

Salaries of Israeli experts abroad range from $6,000 to $9,000, but the total cost of maintaining an expert with his family ranges from $11,000 to $13,000.[16] Maintenance costs for European experts in developing countries are about the same as for the Israeli experts, but maintenance costs for experts from the United States are about twice as much. (See Table 3-4.)

The cost of training in Israel, based on a comparison of data from various sources, appears to range from $330 to $660 per trainee-month for short-term courses, and from $220 to $330 per trainee-month for long-term studies. While expenses for short stays are understandably higher than for those of longer duration, the great cost variation for training in Israel is primarily a function of the type of course and accommodation provided. Long-term training benefits from economies over time, as well as from relatively low fees (and high government subsidies) at academic institutions where most of the students are enrolled.

The figures cited in Table 3-4, though not strictly comparable, suggest that both short- and long-term training in Israel in the early 1960's cost less than in the United States but more than in Europe. Thus while the available evidence indicates that operating costs of Israel's program are lower than comparable U. S. efforts, they are not nearly so low as has sometimes been suggested.

[15] *Jerusalem Post*, July 27, 1965.

[16] According to information received from Israeli Government sources and in field interviews, the majority of Israeli experts are paid between $6,000 and $7,000. Long-term experts receive no housing allowances, unless the cost of housing exceeds 20 per cent of their salaries, but under certain conditions they do draw a one-time furniture allowance of up to $800 and allowances to buy a refrigerator, stove or air conditioner, if needed. Other fringe benefits include a social insurance contribution of 18.5 per cent of salary and one month's vacation per year. There are no "hardship allowances" for Israeli experts.

TABLE 3-4 *Comparative Costs of Technical Assistance Programs, Israel and Other Countries, 1962*

Country	Cost per Person per Year
	Technical Assistance Experts
Donor	
United States, Canada and multilateral agencies	$25,000
European and other developed countries	12,000 [a]
Israel	12,000
	Students [b]
Host	
United States and Canada	$3,300
Other developed countries	1,100
Israel	2,500
	Trainees [c]
Host	
United States and Canada	$6,000
Other developed countries	4,000
Israel	5,000

SOURCES: Israel—estimated by author; other countries—Angus Maddison, *Foreign Skills and Technical Assistance in Economic Development,* Development Centre, OECD, Paris, 1965, pp. 62–64.

[a] Maddison's actual estimate for European technical assistance experts is $7,500 but this includes a large number of low-paid teachers, a category that does not exist in Israel's program. In order to make the figures more comparable, Maddison's cost estimate for so-called "capital aid experts" has been used for European experts.

[b] Includes maintenance, fees and travel in host country. Does not include government subsidies at academic institutions.

[c] Though cost is given per annum, the average stay is much less. Maddison assumes an average stay of 6 months. Average stay of trainees in Israel is about 3 months.

Total Cost of Program

It is difficult to obtain precise figures on the total cost of Israel's program, in part because of the many sources from which financial support is drawn.

David Golan estimated in 1965 that the total amount of assistance generated is four to five times greater than the 10 million Israeli pounds ($3.3 million) officially budgeted that year for the purpose.[17] On this basis, total expenditures in 1965 would have ranged from $13

[17] *Jerusalem Post,* July 27, 1965.

to $17 million.[18] If it can be assumed that all of Israel's expenditure was about 80 per cent more than the Foreign Ministry's budget estimate (as explained earlier in this chapter), then Israel's own contribution to the program from all sources in 1965 was about $6 million, or less than half the total amount expended. The balance was contributed from external sources, primarily partner governments and international organizations.

Assuming that at least 50 per cent of Israel's own expenditures were in local costs (see Table 3-1), the cost to Israel in 1965 in hard currency would appear to have been around $3 million, or less than 1 per cent of Israel's capital transfers abroad during that year.[19] This outflow, however, was compensated at least in part by hard-currency remittances of Israeli experts abroad and by trainee spending in Israel over and above the government-provided maintenance. Thus the net effect of the program on Israel's precarious balance-of-payments position appears to have been negligible.

Israel's achievement in having more than half its effort financed from non-Israeli sources is probably unique in the tangled history of postwar technical assistance operations. This shows how a small country, short of capital, but with the will and the objective capacity, can generate a sizable technical assistance program with little capital investment and negligible effect on its balance-of-payments position. It also is a tribute to the determination and ingenuity of Israel's officials and the special quality of the experts and instructors who have helped to shape the program.

[18] In this connection, it is of interest to compare expenditures for Israeli and OECD assistance programs. The Development Centre of the OECD, in a 1965 study, estimated that expenditures for bilateral technical assistance of the 21 OECD member countries combined in 1963 were about $850 million. (Angus Maddison, *Foreign Skills and Technical Assistance in Economic Development*, Paris, p. 84.) Expenditures from all Israeli sources for Israel's assistance program in that year were probably in the neighborhood of $7 million, or less than 1 per cent of the spending for technical assistance of major donor nations outside the Sino-Soviet sphere.

[19] *Statistical Abstract of Israel, 1966,* Central Bureau of Statistics, Jerusalem, pp. 218–19.

Chapter 4

The Human Equation

"*Tushiya, ikhpatyut,* and 'the sky is the limit'" characterize the people working in Israel's cooperation program, according to Aryeh Eliav, who headed Israel's first, highly successful, team of planners and other experts in Iran. *Tushiya,* in modern Israeli usage, means "the ability to size up a situation and start taking action before the propitious split-second passes, . . . the ability to improvise"; *ikhpatyut* can be defined as "give-a-damnedness, . . . the state of being personally concerned and involved"; and "the sky is the limit" expresses an undaunted optimism about the future in the face of difficulty.[1]

These qualities constitute a very special *attitude toward development,* which helps explain why Israel's program continues to enjoy an excellent reputation after eight years of operation, despite some problems and weaknesses discussed later in this book. Many observers of Israelis at work abroad or training foreigners in Israel have spoken highly of their "spirit"; some have stressed their practicality and informality in getting the job done; others have emphasized their

[1] Moshe Kohn, "You Reach a Stage Where They Don't Have to Tell You," *Jerusalem Post,* July 30, 1965.

dogged determination and personal concern. In fact, they were all talking about the same thing—an attitude embodying *tushiya, ikhpatyut* and "the sky is the limit." The promotion and encouragement of such an attitude toward development is the prime socioeconomic (as distinct from political) goal of Israel's program.

The Roots of the Past

This attitude and the mystique of nation-building, discussed in Chapter 5, have their roots in Israel's own often painful process of growth—characterized by speed in establishing settlements, in bringing in large numbers of immigrants, in training and mobilizing manpower; social idealism, growing out of genuine concern for human beings and a desire to build a better society within a revitalized nation, which was basic to Israel's pre-independence history; and pragmatic experimentation, which has been essential to the evolution of Israel's cooperative structure, its mixed economy, its work- and education-oriented army.

Those so inclined may see this transference to the developing world of the qualities and attitudes born of Israel's travail and rebirth as a manifestation of Israel's destiny. Others may simply conclude that by a felicitous coincidence Israelis have evolved approaches to development that are valued in many of the newly developing countries. All will agree that the Israeli expert or training instructor, with his attitudes and human qualities, gives to Israel's program a very special character.

Characteristics of the Experts [2]

Most of Israel's foreign experts are drawn from Israeli Government departments, academic institutions or publicly controlled organizations, including principally the Solel Boneh Construction Company,

[2] Data in this and subsequent sections of this chapter are drawn in part from a special survey of experts and instructors, conducted in 1965 in connection with this study by the Israel Institute for Applied Social Research in Jerusalem. It included interviews with 114 experts who had returned from foreign assignments, 57 experts then serving in Tanzania and Ghana and 28 full-time group leaders

Water Development (International), Tahal Water Planning Ltd. and the Jewish Agency for Israel. But the special survey of Israeli experts and training instructors also revealed that one third of the experts interviewed were or had at one time been members of a *kibbutz* (collective settlement) or a *moshav* (cooperative village).[3] This relatively high proportion (only 8 per cent of Israel's population currently lives in a *kibbutz* or a *moshav*) has no doubt contributed to the dominant image of pioneering in Israel's work abroad.

Another interesting fact revealed by the survey is the youth of the Israeli experts. Two thirds of those questioned were 26 to 45 years old, indicating that they probably began their professional careers after Israel had achieved its independence. An even larger proportion, the survey shows, were either born in Israel or came to Israel prior to independence in 1948.

These facts help to explain the Israeli expert's image at home and abroad, since speed, pragmatic improvisation and an underlying base of social idealism were the conditions both of Israel's rapid growth and of the experts' own professional training and early work experience. It is not surprising, therefore, that Israelis working in developing countries tend to see in them their own country as it was only a few decades ago.

Experts, asked by the interviewers in the special survey to describe behavior patterns characteristic of Israelis working abroad, said:

> When we didn't find the right tools, we used similar ones and modified them; or, having no alternative, we used tools never intended for such work. . . .
>
> We worked with the local people and wore the same work clothes they

and tutors in Israel-based training courses for students from developing countries. The 114 returned experts represented a sample drawn at random in a ratio of 1 to 3 from lists supplied by 4 major Israeli suppliers of experts for service abroad: the Ministry for Foreign Affairs, Solel Boneh Construction Company, Water Development Company (International) and Tahal Water Planning Ltd. The experts interviewed in Ghana and Tanzania included all of the Israeli experts then serving in those countries. The group leaders and tutors interviewed in Israel represented 70 per cent of the instructors at eight principal institutions for trainees from abroad. The survey is referred to hereafter as "special survey."

[3] The actual proportion of Israel's experts who had been *kibbutz* and *moshav* members is probably higher, for former advisers to national service (Nahal) and youth movement (Gadna) projects—many of them *kibbutz* members—could not be included in the survey.

did. We treated them as we treat our workers in Israel. We let them come into our hut, which no Englishman would do. . . .

Work schedules aren't a holy matter. If necessary, one works at night. . . .

The ability of the Israeli experts to identify from personal experience with the problems and aspirations of people in developing countries is undoubtedly one of their principal assets, an asset not possessed by most experts from economically advanced countries. All other considerations aside, it is also a persuasive argument in favor of using experts from developing or recently developed countries to assist other developing countries.[4]

Dominant Motivations

The capacity to see problems through the eyes of those being helped does not necessarily imply that the Israeli experts are primarily missionaries or idealists. The responses to the special survey indicated that the principal motivation of more than a third of the experts is the desire to make a contribution to the receiving country or to perform a service for Israel, while most of the rest see in their assignments an opportunity to broaden their own professional experience, earn a good salary or see new places. The more altruistically oriented minority, however, undoubtedly influence their colleagues and contribute significantly to the over-all image of Israel's program.

The question of professionalism cuts across motivational considerations, for many of the experts whose motives were primarily altruistic evidently thought of their contribution more in professional than in political terms. The survey strongly suggests that professional factors were clearly the most important in the spectrum of considerations influencing the decisions of the experts to take foreign assignments. (See Table 4-1.) The words of an Israeli water engineer in Iran, whose homesick family was anxious to return to Israel, are illustrative: "Israel is the holy country, you know. Full of holes. Will I get the chance to dig 200 new wells if I go back to Israel now?"[5] The strongest related evidence from the survey was the finding that the more

[4] See Chapter 1 for additional discussion of this point.

[5] "Iran—A Study of Development," *Near East Report,* Supplement, January 1966, p. A-24.

TABLE 4.1 *Motivations of Israeli Experts Accepting Foreign Assignments*

Order of Motivation	Number of Experts in Survey	To Contribute Something				To Obtain Something				Other Motivations
		Total	Professionally	To Israel	To Receiving Nation	Total	See New Places	Expand Own Professional Experience	Earn More Money	
Strongest										
Number	167	66	33	11	22	78	22	32	24	23
Per cent	100	40	20	7	13	46	13	19	14	14
Second strongest										
Number	167	75	26	22	27	72	27	24	21	20
Per cent	100	45	16	13	16	43	16	14	13	12

SOURCE: Special survey (see text, footnote 2, this chapter).

an expert gained professionally in his mission abroad, the greater his apparent satisfaction with the experience as a whole. While the majority of the experts were satisfied with their experience abroad, more than four fifths of those whose work had been professionally rewarding were satisfied.

Another interesting finding bearing on the question of motivation was that the percentage of experts motivated by a desire to contribute was higher among those over 35 years of age than among those 26 to 35 years old. While our sample was too small to draw definite conclusions from this finding, it does suggest that the older, more experienced professionals going abroad may be somewhat more altruistically motivated than their younger colleagues.

Somewhat surprising—in light of the pronounced ideological base of these institutions, especially the *kibbutz*—was the finding that *kibbutz* or *moshav* membership seemed to have no relation to the experts' motivations. The reason it apparently did not may be that some had left or were planning to leave their settlements for good, and therefore had strong incentives to improve their material and professional positions.[6] Others, who were still members, may have been attracted by the opportunity to leave the limited environment of the settlement for a while, and travel in the world.

Approach to Work

Regardless of motivations, the special survey seems to bear out the characterization of the Israeli experts as generally hard-working, devoted to their jobs and intent on transmitting their knowledge to the people of the host countries.

For example, almost three fourths of the respondents to the survey said that they had worked harder abroad than in their jobs in Israel, and a somewhat larger proportion said they had worked without much preplanning, or had made considerable changes in plans as they went

[6] Moshe Dayan, Israel's former Minister of Agriculture, once described former *kibbutz* members as possessing "three matchless qualities" for service in Africa: ". . . the idealism that brought them to the *kibbutz* originally, the agricultural experience they have amassed, and the fact that they do not have a *pruta* [Israel's penny] to their name, which means they are willing to stay on till they have saved up some money." (*Jerusalem Post,* November 29, 1963.)

along. Many gave personal demonstrations of methods they had learned and felt would be effective under new conditions.

The following are samples of comments of the experts interviewed:

> An engineer: "I had a set formula for mixing materials which I had learned and used in Israel. But it was not suitable for conditions in Ethiopia, so I changed and demonstrated my own personal experience. This was accepted."
>
> A horticulturist: "I gave courses in pruning, taught how to graft in the nurseries and demonstrated spraying with preventive materials and oils for the promotion of growth."
>
> A farm manager: "I explained details of farm administration, including the need for record-keeping, and demonstrated methods of cotton cultivation. . . . At first the farmers did not believe that new methods, such as watering the crops during the dry season, would increase their profits, but after the harvest, they were convinced."

Cultural and Language Problems

Most Israeli experts apparently did not breach the social barriers that customarily divide foreigners (particularly whites in Africa) from the local population. In answer to the question whether they had made friends with local people whom they met outside working hours, almost two thirds of the respondents said they had made few, and one out of every seven admitted that he had made none. In contrast, two thirds said they had socialized frequently or at least occasionally with foreign experts from other countries. This pattern of behavior should be no surprise to those who know conditions in developing countries. Indeed, since Israelis receive little logistic support from their embassies and use local housing and provisions, they are probably less isolated from the local population than are experts of some other countries.

Differences in language are probably the chief barriers to normal social relations. In this respect Israeli experts may be better off than those from many other countries, but, even so, the special survey revealed that about one out of three of the experts questioned had to use interpreters in the course of his work. In recognition of this problem, the Foreign Ministry recently began to provide language training for some experts prior to their going abroad.

Career Versus Temporary Service

Israeli experts working on long-term projects are usually hired for a specific project or mission and given two-year contracts. Those on short-term missions are usually temporarily detailed from their regular jobs in Israel. Officials responsible for the program hope to continue the present arrangement, as they are skeptical of the concept of a foreign career service for Israel's experts. They believe that the goal of technical assistance should be the end of technical assistance, and that no Israeli abroad should ever be suspected of wishing to perpetuate his job. In their opinion, the image of Israel's program would suffer if it were "professionalized," as would the performance of the experts removed for long periods from normal professional pursuits and from the Israeli environment.

Most of the experts interviewed in the special survey had served in only one country, and few thought of their work in the technical assistance program as a permanent career. Israeli officials report that recently some long-term experts have gone out for a second tour of duty. If this should become a general pattern, it might fundamentally alter the prevailing philosophy of Israel's program.

The concept of mutual benefit—learning from each other—which is basic to the total philosophy of the Israeli program, would be seriously hampered if the Israeli experts were to be more or less permanently stationed abroad. Under the present arrangements, on the other hand, they are not permanently uprooted, and, upon completion of their assignments, can take back with them insights and experiences beneficial to themselves and to their own society.[7]

The absence of a career service presents continuing recruitment problems, of course, and significantly increases the management burdens of the Foreign Ministry. For years the Ministry has walked an uneasy tightrope between centralized recruiting and administrative control and decentralization. In the early period, foreign expert assignments apparently were made largely by Ministry officials on the basis of personal acquaintance, provided the candidate received the approval of an interdepartmental professional committee. This system was satisfactory as long as the number of experts sent abroad was

[7] See Chapters 2 and 12 for additional discussion of this point.

small. With about 650 experts a year now going on missions or working on long-term projects abroad, it is obviously no longer feasible. Most recruitment responsibilities and also some of the administrative duties have been shifted to special semiautonomous bodies under the control of the various responsible ministries. The administration, including recruitment of personnel, of operations for which joint Israeli-foreign firms have been established has always been outside the Foreign Ministry's jurisdiction.

Nevertheless, recruitment difficulties persist, for in the absence of a career service every new project or replacement of an expert on a going project requires a new recruitment effort. A modest reserve pool of interested candidates in the various professions does exist, but evidently it has not been sufficient to meet the growing needs.

Obstacles to Effective Accomplishment

Local political conditions and sensitivities, lack of funds and equipment and difficult conditions for training were the most serious problems—in order of importance—encountered by the experts abroad, according to the special survey. They are, of course, not peculiar to Israel's program. They are present to some degree in most development work. The survey findings suggest that specific attention should be given to these problems when new projects are under consideration. Lack of capital is a much more serious impediment to Israel's program, which consists largely of technical assistance, than, let us say, to U. S. programs, in which technical and capital assistance usually are combined. One Israeli expert stationed in an African country put it this way when interviewed in the special survey:

> In my field of work the help given by the United States was much more effective, for a full research group was brought in with all its equipment and its own administration. This made it possible to carry out large-scale projects with the greatest efficiency, because it avoided the difficulties of a weak local administration and shortage of money and equipment.

Asked to describe their major sources of satisfaction and of disappointment with the program, the largest number of respondents expressed satisfaction over their professional accomplishments or opportunities, but, as might be expected, there was dissatisfaction over some aspects of Israel's administration of the program. These included what some experts felt was lack of concern, insufficient briefing before they left Israel and inadequate support abroad.

Only about a third of the respondents felt they had received adequate preparation for their work assignments before leaving Israel, and only about one in seven said he had received adequate background information on his country of destination. A third of the experts said they had received no general information at all. This situation has been somewhat remedied, as the hazards of sending people abroad without adequate preparation have become apparent to Israeli officials. In the early days the primary concern of the small overworked staff handling the program in the Foreign Ministry was to "get the man for the job"; the rest was left pretty much to the expert's own initiative and discretion. The tendency to worry primarily about filling the job was likely to be even stronger if the employer was one of the quasi-public companies rather than the Foreign Ministry.

By now the Department for International Cooperation of the Foreign Ministry has produced several "fact books" on various geographic regions, and some of the government-supported institutions dealing with experts, such as the Israeli Productivity Institute, have prepared other types of briefing materials.

Before leaving for foreign assignments all agricultural experts also attend briefing sessions of one or two days conducted by the Ministry of Agriculture, which also maintains contact with agricultural experts serving abroad. There is a similar arrangement for National Service (Nahal) and Youth (Gadna) specialists who go abroad under Defense Ministry auspices. In most other specialties, however, no regular provision has been made for orientation and continuing assistance while abroad, except for the short political briefings all government-sponsored experts receive at the Foreign Ministry prior to departure.

Aside from administrative shortcomings, there may be a psychological reason for the sparse attention to orientation and continuing support of experts while abroad. Israel's own development has been marked by "muddling through" many a difficult situation, by virtue of sheer optimism, nerve, ingenuity. These aspects of Israel's program may therefore be unconsciously neglected by responsible officials because of the belief that the "right man" will somehow manage. The usually good image of Israeli experts seems to support this belief, but the special survey indicates that behind the good image may be defects of morale and achievement that could be avoided with better preparation of the experts and more attention to their needs while serving abroad.

Contributing to the morale problem, no doubt, is the expert's lack of assurance that while he is away he will not lose out on professional opportunities at home. This is probably equally true of noncareer foreign experts of other countries. It does not apply to Israelis who are members of communal or cooperative settlements, where there is no problem of job security and where career aspirations are regarded in a different light. It does, however, apply very decidedly to the majority of Israel's experts who are not *kibbutz* or *moshav* members. Most experts who have gone abroad have received some assurance from their employers of jobs on their return to Israel. In the past most employers have been happy to retain competent personnel, but should the recent economic slump in Israel continue, this might change. In any event, assurance of work is not assurance of opportunity and of consideration for advancement. Because of these problems of job security, many first-rate people who might otherwise be candidates for foreign employment are lost to Israel's program.

Some officials believe legislative action is needed to insure seniority rights of experts, provide additional incentives through import privileges or tax adjustments and give the government authority to obtain temporary release of needed experts from domestic jobs. Others concerned with the manpower problem contend that in many specialties service abroad should be voluntarily accepted as an integral part of an agency's or institution's career development policy, from which both employers and employees would benefit. They cite as an example Professor Isaac Michaelson's Ophthalmology Department at the Hadassah Hospital in Jerusalem, where rotation of eye specialists for service abroad has clearly benefited both the specialists and the hospital.[8]

The Jewish Agency Settlement Department, in a variant on this system, until recently required professionals entering the department to agree to serve abroad if needed. *Kibbutzim,* which, as indicated

[8] See Chapter 8 for detailed discussion of the program.

earlier in this chapter, supply a disproportionately large number of experts, particularly in agriculture, have long made a quota of their members (usually 7 per cent) available for various types of public service as a patriotic duty. Many responsible government and other public positions, as well as educational activities among Jewish youth in Israel and abroad, are sustained from this quota. Service in Israel's program of cooperation is recognized as legitimate public service, and the program therefore benefits to some extent from the quotas, but they are often insufficient to meet the demand for foreign experts with a *kibbutz* background. Sometimes *kibbutzim* are persuaded to supply experts outside the quota, but because of their own acute labor shortage, many resist such demands.

Unless Israel's economic difficulties change the picture drastically, some measures to deal with problems of job security and morale seem necessary, or the supply of experts—particularly of those with experience, available for long-term assignments—is likely to decline.

Instructors in Training Programs

No discussion of the human equation in Israel's cooperation program would be complete without special attention to the instructors in the training courses conducted in Israel. Superficially, these instructors have much in common with the experts who are active abroad. Their major goal is the transfer of knowledge and the development of cordial, fruitful relations with their foreign guests. Actually, however, the domestic locale casts them in roles totally different from the roles of the experts who serve abroad, and even of the instructors in "on-the-spot" training courses conducted abroad. The expert or instructor abroad is close to the actual conditions of the developing country, whereas the instructor in Israel must rely on visual and practical reference to the Israeli scene. Moreover, the instructor—in contrast to the expert abroad—operates within his own environment, and his trainees are the strangers. The major emotional and psychological barrier he must overcome, therefore, is his students' strangeness to Israel and—in the multinational courses—to each other. Much of the responsibility for overcoming this barrier rests with a small full-time training staff.

There are four broad categories of instructors in Israel's program—tutors, visiting lecturers, on-the-job instructors and so-called "*madrichim*" (group leaders). Only the first and the last of these are full-time instructors who take a group through its entire training cycle.

Most short courses and training seminars, which together constitute the bulk of the training program in Israel, utilize at various stages of instruction all four types of personnel. Long-term courses and individual training programs are usually closely related to existing domestic institutions, such as the Hebrew University or the Haifa Technical Institute, and for the most part utilize the available academic staff of these institutions plus a few "group leaders." The functions of the on-the-job instructors, the visiting lecturers and, to some extent, the tutors resemble generally the customary tasks of such personnel in the technical assistance programs of other countries. The *madrichim,* on the other hand, are quite different from the escort officers or course administrators in other countries. They occupy a very special place in Israel's program, and undoubtedly have contributed significantly to the favorable image most short-term trainees take home with them from courses in Israel.

The Madrich-Educator

The *madrich* employed in Israel's technical assistance program is in many ways another version of the *madrich* prominent in Israel's numerous youth movements and youth programs. The concept of the *madrich,* his place in the group, his techniques, his attitudes and the special charisma which attaches to him are not the creation of today or of a decade ago. They represent the evolution of a concept through four decades, in which the Socialist-Zionist youth movements stood in the forefront of the pioneering process in Palestine and later in Israel. The literature on the problems, character and goals of the youth *madrich,* particularly in Youth Aliyah, the program under which since 1934 more than 100,000 youngsters have been brought to Israel and educated there, clearly establishes these origins.

The *madrich* has played a crucial role in the successful absorption and education of Youth Aliyah newcomers to Israel, according to Dr. Chanoch Rinot, formerly Director General of Israel's Ministry of

Education, who has studied the Youth Aliyah system in depth.[9] He not only represents the stable, authoritative link between the newcomer and his strange new surroundings, but he also quickly becomes the principal interpreter of that new environment, the channel through which the environment influences and changes the attitudes of the newcomer. The tasks of the ideal Youth Aliyah *madrich* are twofold —teaching and *hadracha* (guidance). Since both processes are regarded as inextricably related and essential to a successful educational experience, *madrichim* are expected to combine them in their work.

Most Youth Aliyah groups receive their initial training in *kibbutzim*, and the *madrichim* are usually drawn from the host settlement. In the past, many of these were not professional educators, although the trend more recently has been toward professionalization. What counted and still counts most, however, is that the *madrich's* personal qualities as a human being express in personal terms the best values of his society. Because the *madrich* must be totally involved with his group, he must spend as much time with it as possible, including evenings and weekends. He must learn to identify with the aspirations and problems of his students, in order to accomplish successfully his mission as the chief link between the newcomers and Israel. Rinot writes:[10]

> The spirit of the environment, the collective and democratic life, require a friendly atmosphere and simple relationships between *madrich* and student. Naturally, the youngsters will call the *madrich* by his first name. Simplicity in dress, eating together, and the social life of the kibbutz demand informal contact. The influence of the environment is strong, and one who does not identify with it, cannot educate in it. . . .
>
> Once the *madrich* identifies with his group, he can properly represent its interests to the local community. . . . His mission requires a double loyalty, both to the adult society and to his young charges. This dual role is not easy, and in case of conflict, his conscience must decide.

With minor changes, the tasks and techniques of the group leader assigned to training courses for students from developing countries are those of the Youth Aliyah *madrich* described above. The *madrich*

[9] This discussion is based largely on Chapter 3, "Madrichim and Training," of Dr. Rinot's [formerly Reinhold] study, *Noar Boneh Beito* (Youth Builds Its Home), Am Oved Publishers, Tel Aviv, 1952/53.

[10] *Ibid.*, pp. 96–97.

stays with his group most of the time and often doubles as a teacher in the classroom; his relations with the group are informal; he is perceptive, well-informed, and ideologically identified with his environment and society. It is undoubtedly no coincidence that in the special survey two thirds of the *madrichim* and tutors involved in Israel-based training programs had a *kibbutz* or *moshav* background, compared with only one third of the experts who had worked abroad. Many among them also had had previous experience as *madrichim* working with youth.

A certain amount of specialization has developed among the *madrichim.* The so-called "social *madrich*" (*madrich chevrati*) concerns himself more with after-hours activities and problems of the trainees, while the "training *madrich*" (*madrich hadracha*) is more directly concerned with the study program. Full-time tutors are primarily teachers, but to some extent also function as *madrichim.* While this partial specialization modifies the *madrich*-educator role developed in Youth Aliyah, the basic theoretical concept of the *madrich* and his functions has not changed. The goals of the technical assistance *madrich* are not ultimate absorption and integration of the trainee into Israeli society, of course, but are the more limited goals of developing know-how and new attitudes. Judging from the closeness that prevails in Israel's training courses between trainees and their *madrichim,* and the fondness with which many trainees and *madrichim* speak of each other after years of separation, these pedagogic goals seem by and large to have been achieved.

The *madrich* undoubtedly occupies a prominent place in the trainee's experience in Israel; the exact importance of his contribution cannot be determined without further research, and undoubtedly varies from case to case. It can only be said that where few and sometimes no *madrichim* were used—as in the earlier stages of Israel's long-term academic training programs—there also was a large amount of dissatisfaction among the trainees. Without giving this indirect evidence undue weight (for there are various factors involved), it is safe to say that by applying their system of youth leadership to Israel-based training programs, the Israelis have made an important contribution to the technique of training for development. Many Israeli experts and instructors abroad also have a youth movement background and have to varying degrees integrated the outlook of the *madrich* into their work and personal relations.

The human qualities and attitudes the Israelis bring to their cooperation program are, as we have seen, a combination of skill, social idealism and practicality. These characteristics also provide the basis for the mystique that has grown around the Israeli efforts, as discussed in the following chapter.

Chapter 5

Characteristics of the Programs

DEVELOPMENT means many things. It means dams and factories, roads and canals, bush-clearing, electrification, soil improvement, universities, secondary schools, primary schools, sanitation, research and a multitude of other activities and achievements. But above all, development means people.

The story of Israel's program of cooperation abroad can best be told in terms of people, not only because skilled and motivated people are the key to successful development, but also because Israel's activities are so often concerned with what the experts call the development of human resources—the preparation and activation of people in the cause of economic and social development.

The Mystique of Nationalism

The Israelis have no secret formula for success. Experience has taught them that the magic that the ideas of Zionism had at one time woven around Israel's own rebuilding and development cannot simply be transplanted to another environment. Yet implicit in much of Israel's program of cooperation—in both the activity abroad and the Israel-based training activities—is the assumption that a positive ideological orientation is essential to successful development. Acting on their own historical experience, the Israelis seek to inspire the participants in the programs with which they are associated with a certain mystique that goes much beyond the provision of technical skills or material resources. It is not based so much on a particular political or economic ideology as it is on the assumption of the regenerative and constructive powers of modern nationalism.

In a world that has but recently paid a terrible price for the excesses of nationalism, and that continues to be plagued by nationalistic jealousies and prejudices, it is easy to overlook the tremendous reserves of constructive energy and talent that can be mobilized under the banner of nation-building. Modern Israel, itself the product of precisely such energy and talent, does not overlook their potentialities, but on the contrary has made their mobilization a principal aim of its cooperation program. The fact that the Israelis can point to their own considerable achievements makes the mystique and their identification with it credible to the developing nations. This identification with the mystique of nation-building, perhaps more than anything else, explains the popularity of the Israeli program abroad, and constitutes an exceptional contribution to the art of development assistance.

The following accounts of the author's visits to Israeli projects abroad and observations of training programs in Israel reflect some of the flavor and atmosphere of the Israeli program.

The grassy field was bumpy and uneven as the Ethiopian Airlines DC-3 came to a gradual stop. On the ground near a small one-room shack, which served as terminal building and constabulary office, stood a crowd of people waiting for the arrival of this once-a-week plane from Addis Ababa. From among them emerged a smallish, stockily built, gray-haired man in his sixties to greet the arriving visitor. The host, who was an Israeli agricultural expert working in Ethiopia, asked rather apologetically if the visitor, who had come to observe the operation of an Israeli-aided project, would mind riding the 30 kilometers to the temporary camp of the training farm by tractor, the only conveyance available and the only one he knew how to operate.

Back at the camp site, on the edge of the sparsely settled Ethiopian lowlands, 30 young school dropouts were learning to farm, so that they could operate their own farms on land that the government had promised them if they would clear it and cultivate it. They told of the hardships of bush-clearing and their hopes for the day when they would have their own farmsteads and equipment. The Israeli host, 4 months on the project after a year's service in India, explained sadly that the 30 were all that remained of 350 who had been trained at a nearby agricultural station. The rest had refused to take on the rigors of this new settlement scheme, and gradually had trickled back to the city or their native villages. Would the project survive? No one could be sure. But the host's eyes sparkled with enthusiasm, nevertheless, as he showed the visitor experimental garden plots with string beans and luscious tomatoes, rough earthen dikes to collect rain water for washing and irrigation, and a row of multipurpose iron plows, which he had designed himself and made at the camp with the help of his Israeli mechanic. The plows cost next to nothing, for they were made of scrap iron discarded by the agricultural station, but they were far superior to the primitive wooden plows used in the area. Some day, he assured the visitor, the temporary camp would be replaced by a permanent one, and hundreds of landless peasants would train there before settling on new land given by the government.

A few hours away by airplane, in one of the hottest places on earth, the Israeli physician in charge of a 250-bed hospital—a gift of Czechoslovakia—nodded a friendly greeting to patients and nurses as he showed the visitor around the spotlessly clean wards. "These people are among the most appreciative I have ever encountered," he commented. Anticipating the visitor's question, he continued: "It was not always that way, however; this town and the surroundings are over 90 per cent Moslem, and when we first arrived, leaflets were distributed, warning the people against us. 'The Israelis will poison you,' the leaflets said. We went on with our work; and after a while, the propaganda stopped, for it had nothing to feed on. On the contrary, people would see us working hard, often through the night, and they were grateful. No matter how poor, they would bring little presents, a cherished ostrich egg, for example, to show their appreciation. Now even the Moslem religious leaders are our friends, and at the festive celebration ending the month of Ramadan, the Israeli physicians are invited along with other town notables." As the visitor took his leave, the youthful doctor said wistfully that in another two days he would be leaving for his weekly visit with his family, some three hours' difficult drive away from the hospital.

Half way around the globe from this hospital, we entered a large room in a ramshackle house, decorated on the outside simply with the letters "MNJ"—Movimiento Nacional de Juventudes. The house stood in a small village some one and a half hour's drive from Costa Rica's capital, San José. The room was unfurnished except for a table and two dozen rough, unpainted low stools.

"The youngsters made those themselves," explained a young volunteer youth leader, with obvious pride. She worked as a secretary during the day, but in the late afternoons and evenings was one of a small group of leaders of this fledgling youth movement. The group had been working together only a few months, but the leadership training course they had taken together and the joint responsibility of leading about 100 village teenagers had forged them into a strong team.

"Our major problems are obtaining the cooperation and understanding of the community, and finding enough money to operate a meaningful program for our young people," said the earnest director of this youth center. A man in his twenties and a teacher by profession, he headed a small cadre of leaders, all of whom had been trained in a two-and-a-half-month course conducted by three Israeli instructors.

The center was still in its infancy and materially it lacked almost everything. Yet the youngsters were coming to it in droves. It was the first time young people of the area had been given the opportunity to come together for wholesome recreation, informal education and social activities. Following the pattern of Israeli youth movements, their leaders stressed the goals of nation-building and self-help. They proudly pointed to the whitewashed walls and the carefully scrubbed floor of the meeting room—among the first achievements of the group;

with even greater pride they showed the visitor the neatly laid out basketball court nearby—the first and only one in the area.

"Until we built this court," the director explained, "the youngsters didn't know the sport existed. Now they are wild about it, and we already have championship meets with young people from other towns. But," he added somewhat sadly, "the village leaders aren't behind us yet, and it makes everything so hard."

Back in Israel, some 30 farmers from a Latin American country were gathering for one of the last sessions of a training course in rural cooperation before returning home. Most of the men had little formal education, but had been selected for their standing in their communities.

The Israeli leader, who had spent practically all his time during the last three months with the members of the group, was guiding the discussion, trying to bring out, by his questions, what they had learned from the course and how they would apply it in their own country. Joining him in posing questions for discussion were two other instructors who had also worked with the group.

"How do you organize a cooperative?"

"How do you make it work?"

"What should be its relation to other cooperatives and to the community at large?"

At first, the responses were halting, but as the hour-and-a-half session progressed, discussion became heated.

"The main thing we must do is work together, if we ever want to amount to anything," said one of the trainees.

"One thing is certain," declared another, "if we don't form our own marketing co-ops on top of producers' co-ops and eliminate those blood-sucking middlemen, we're licked."

A burly farmer in his forties had a question of his own. "Now that I have learned some accounting, I realize for the first time that for the last 12 years I have been losing money on my plot of corn. I'm wondering if I should give it up."

"Not necessarily," explained one of the instructors, "you should try to improve your productivity before you decide to chuck it."

An intense young man had two ideas for the future: the government ought to establish a series of agricultural settlements, patterned after Israel's Nahal Fighting Pioneers, to counter potential subversive movements; and, more important, his comrades should join him in urging the government to establish a National Fund, which, like Israel's Jewish National Fund, would acquire land and lease it on a long-term basis to rural cooperatives.

With the general approval of the group, the elected spokesman announced their determination to work together and help one another in the future.

As the meeting broke up, the visitor spoke to one of the Israeli instructors about the apparent earnestness and determination of these farmers. "Our chief purpose," the instructor replied, "is to show them what voluntary cooperation, combined with knowledge and serious work, can accomplish. If they get this message, we're satisfied."

Criteria for Programs

The Israelis prefer to participate in activities that, like most of those just described, have the mystique of constructive nationalism. While this may imply an emphasis on romantic pioneering ventures, the Israeli approach is in actuality sober and practical. Teaching farmers the fundamentals of cost accounting and of cooperative organization, or equipping Africans to enter the business sector—for centuries the exclusive preserve of non-African foreigners—is as much in keeping with the Israeli preference as is the creation of a new youth movement in Central America.

Nation-building projects have special appeal to Israel, for they are often high on the host government's priority list, and can therefore be expected to have adequate local support and financial participation. For Israel, whose financial resources are very limited, this is an important consideration. In addition, such projects usually have high visibility or high political importance for the host government, or both, so that they may contribute to Israel's political goal of cementing close and friendly relations. Israelis, drawing on their own recent experience in developing a modern country, seem particularly well-equipped to assist in projects of this type.

The mystique of constructive nationalism alone is, of course, no assurance of the developmental value of a project; nor are Israeli concepts necessarily fully shared and understood by others who are participating in the project. Nevertheless, at the very least, Israel's own commitment to the mystique adds a vitally needed educational dimension to its cooperation program.

Not all activities in which Israel participates, however, can have this mystique appeal. The work of Israeli medical teams in developing countries, though vitally important, is less likely to have the appeal of constructive nationalism than is the settlement of school dropouts on newly cleared agricultural land. Both activities may be necessary to the well-being of the host country, but one provides a service within the existing framework, while the other breaks new ground—literally and symbolically—in the country's social and economic development.

Despite the Israelis' skill and ingenuity in mobilizing resources, lack of money severely limits their work, and cost is an all-important consideration in the choice of projects and programs. As explained in Chapter 2, Israel seeks to overcome its financial limitations by insisting on contributions from the host governments and by seeking multilateral financial backing for its activities.[1] Emphasis on training, including, more recently, the growth in the number of lower-cost on-the-spot training programs in the developing countries themselves, is another reflection of Israel's financial pinch. Financing its technical assistance projects abroad is becoming an increasingly difficult problem for Israel, not only because of rising costs, but because, like other countries, Israel has learned that it is easier to start programs than to stop them. The need is so great that the successful conclusion of one project, instead of relieving the financial or manpower strain, only generates demands for two or three new activities. Politico-geographic considerations and manpower supply, of course, also play an important role in project selection.

Geographic and Professional Focus

Israel's effort abroad has been concentrated in Africa south of the Sahara, largely in agricultural or agriculture-related projects. Of the

[1] See Chapter 3 for a more detailed discussion of the financing of Israel's program.

TABLE 5-1 *Foreign Assignments of Israeli Experts and Number of Foreign Trainees in Israel, by Geographic Area and Year, 1958–1966*

Geographic Area	Total [a]	1958	1959	1960	1961	1962	1963	1964	1965	1966
					Assignments of Experts					
Total	3,476	40	80	163	280	395	544	698	636	640
Africa	2,485	25	51	122	211	265	424	528	453	406
Asia	345	15	25	31	44	52	43	39	44	52
Latin America	270	—	2	3	11	19	37	73	55	70
Mediterranean Area [b]	376	—	2	7	14	59	40	58	84	112
					Trainees in Israel					
Total [c]	12,627	137	213	672	1,250	1,621	2,272	2,446	2,267	1,749
Africa	6,640	59	75	291	876	899	1,231	1,363	1,032	814
Asia	2,167	71	109	309	267	197	199	224	376	415
Latin America	1,467	2	11	37	17	137	289	399	342	233
Mediterranean Area [b]	2,059	5	18	35	90	346	545	428	354	238

SOURCE: Ministry for Foreign Affairs, Department for International Cooperation, Jerusalem.

[a] The number of experts who served abroad was smaller, since many experts carried out several assignments during the period. The actual numbers of experts, by area, were: total, 1,815; Africa, 1,261; Asia, 180; Latin America, 144; Mediterranean Area, 230. The actual number of trainees who arrived in Israel was also smaller, since some long-term trainees spent more than one year in Israel. The numbers of trainees arriving, by area, were: total, 9,074; Africa, 4,482; Asia, 1,163; Latin America, 1,281; Mediterranean Area, 1,853.

[b] Includes Cyprus, Iran, Malta, Turkey and Yugoslavia.

[c] Totals include 295 trainees from other areas, not shown in annual figures by area.

TABLE 5-2 *Israeli Experts Serving Abroad and Trainees Arriving in Israel, by Field of Service or Training and Geographic Area, 1958–1966*

Field of Service or Training	Total	Africa	Asia	Latin America	Mediterranean Area[a]
			Experts		
Total	1,815	1,261	180	144	230
Agriculture	523	261	73	75	114
Youth organization	256	234	4	17	1
Engineering	64	42	10	2	10
Medicine and health	202	173	26	3	—
Education	106	102	1	3	—
Cooperation	24	21	—	3	—
Management	63	46	10	4	3
Construction and building	65	49	5	1	10
Social work	23	22	—	—	1
Miscellaneous	489	311	51	36	91
			Trainees		
Total[b]	9,074	4,482	1,163	1,281	1,853
Agriculture	2,264	805	213	553	673
Cooperation and trade unionism	1,048	664	162	138	73
Community development	712	493	124	17	27
Youth leadership	529	285	42	165	34
Health and medicine	265	211	21	6	22
Commerce, transport, finance, industry	156	37	9	1	107
Study tours and seminars	1,622	537	238	198	503
Individual academic studies	230	102	60	26	35
Miscellaneous	2,248	1,348	294	177	379

SOURCE: Ministry for Foreign Affairs, Department for International Cooperation, Jerusalem.

[a] Includes Cyprus, Iran, Malta, Turkey and Yugoslavia.

[b] Totals include 295 trainees from other areas.

more than 1,800 Israeli experts who carried out some 3,500 assignments abroad on projects sponsored by the Israeli Government between 1958 and 1966, more than two thirds worked in Africa. The rest were scattered through Asia, the Mediterranean area and Latin America. (See Tables 5-1 and 5-2.) Although Israel's program of cooperation began in Asia, many more experts have been sent to African countries than to Asian countries. Similarly, many more African than Asian or Latin American trainees have gone to Israel for training. In fact about half the trainees who went to Israel from the developing countries in the period 1958–1965 were African. Israel's program of "on-the-spot" courses, moreover, which has grown rapidly during the past few years, is largely Africa-oriented. (See Chapter 10 for an analysis of this program.)

For political reasons the largest of the Asian countries do not welcome cooperation with Israel. Others accept Israeli assistance, but with much restraint, and out of concern for Arab sensitivities they prefer that it be given little publicity. Some of the developing countries in the Mediterranean area follow a similar course. Africa was therefore the logical "next-door neighbor" to receive Israeli attention. The political taboos and restraints regarding Israel were largely absent in the new countries south of the Sahara, whose needs were acute. Latin American countries also had great needs and little prejudice against accepting Israeli cooperation, but they are far from Israel, and for a long time after the inception of the Asian and African programs, Israelis hesitated to approach Latin American governments with concrete proposals for cooperation. This picture has changed, however, and, as Table 5-1 shows, Israeli activities in Latin America have increased in recent years.

The professional focus of the Israeli program is reflected in Table 5-2, which shows the specialties of the experts who served abroad during 1958 to 1966, and the fields of study of trainees in Israel. More than a quarter of the experts were specialists in agriculture. The emphasis on agricultural projects was actually greater than this figure indicates, for many of the experts listed under "youth organization" in the table were in fact instructors or advisers on projects related to agricultural settlement. It is safe to assume therefore that well over one third of the Israeli advisers and specialists working abroad have been engaged in projects connected with agriculture. In Israel-based training programs the attention to agriculture is probably even higher, for both the youth and cooperation courses include agricultural subjects in their curricula.

Manpower Utilization

There is reason to believe that Israel has more experts working abroad in proportion to its population than many economically advanced countries. In 1964, the Israeli ratio of experts to total population (.028 per cent) was almost twice that of the OECD countries combined (.015 per cent).[2]

Some observers have suggested that Israel's program may be motivated, at least in part, by the desire to dispose of surplus manpower. Israelis, on the other hand, especially those involved in recruiting experts for foreign service, have complained of chronic difficulties in finding personnel for overseas assignment. There are probably elements of truth in both positions.

Israel enjoyed relative prosperity between 1958, when the program began, and 1965. Unemployment declined from almost 6 per cent of the labor force in 1958 to less than 4 per cent in 1963, and some branches of the economy were experiencing shortages of skilled personnel.[3] But in certain specialties—water development, farm management, agricultural extension, for example—supply at times exceeded demand, as large development projects were completed. The availability of foreign assignments therefore offered opportunities to individuals whose skills would otherwise have been insufficiently utilized. The economic slump that began to be felt in 1966 has no doubt increased the available supply of skilled manpower for work abroad. However, the effect of this development may be offset in part by the reluctance of able professionals to risk their job security by accepting foreign assignments.

Inefficient utilization of manpower has been a persistent problem in some branches of Israel's economy. The ratio of engineers to

[2] Angus Maddison, *Foreign Skills and Technical Assistance in Economic Development*, Development Centre, OECD, Paris, 1965, p. 22; *General Statistics*, OECD, Paris, September 1964, p. 31; *Statistical Abstract of Israel, 1966*, Central Bureau of Statistics, Jerusalem, p. 20; and Table 5-1, this study. (OECD figures are for 1963, the latest year available.)

[3] *Statistical Abstract of Israel, 1964*, Central Bureau of Statistics, Jerusalem, p. 250; and *Facts About Israel, 1964–65*, Information Division, Ministry for Foreign Affairs, Jerusalem, p. 118.

technicians, for example, is estimated at 1:1, against 1:3 to 1:4 in industrialized European countries, according to I. Vilentchuk, a senior Israeli water engineer. Similarly, the number of engineers is estimated at 3 per 1,000 of population in Israel, against 1.1 per 1,000 in the Netherlands. This is as much a reflection of inefficient organization, requiring excessive inputs of engineering skills, as it is of the underproduction of technicians, and thus many engineers are forced to perform technician functions, Vilentchuk claims.[4] This imbalance undoubtedly makes it possible for Israel to respond to requests from abroad for engineering skills.

At the same time, Israel has the highest proportion of doctors to population in the world—1:428, according to a 1965 survey of the Israeli Labour Ministry's Manpower Planning Authority[5]—but this relative abundance has thus far not been reflected significantly in Israel's foreign cooperation program. One reason may be that while Israel's cities have a high concentration of physicians (1:243 in Jerusalem, for example), rural areas, especially remote ones, are sparsely served.[6] Since, in general, the same type of physician is needed for service in the rural or remote sections of Israel as is needed for service abroad, the internal and external needs are in competition. Despite continuing efforts of officials, the chronic doctor shortage has forced them to keep the medical assistance program small, even while greatly expanding the rest of the foreign program. Experts in health, principally doctors, rank only third in number of specialists serving abroad. Taking a somewhat different measure, of the more than 1,800 experts and advisers who served abroad from 1958 through 1966, only about 200 were health personnel. In the

[4] *Jerusalem Post,* May 30, 1965.

[5] *Jerusalem Post,* June 11, 1965. Estimates of Israel's proportion of doctors to population vary. The U. S. Agency for International Development has estimated that the ratio is 1:400, compared with 1:740 in the United States and 1:21,200 in Africa, excluding South Africa. (*Selected Economic Data for the Less Developed Countries,* Washington, May 1964.)

[6] *Jerusalem Post,* June 11, 1965. There has been much public discussion in Israel about this "doctor shortage" and its possible relation to a steady drain of young doctors to the United States. (*Jerusalem Post,* May 26, 1965.) In fact, a 1965 bill introduced (though not passed) in Parliament, would have channeled Hebrew University medical school graduates into shortage areas, and barred them from leaving the country for three years after graduation. (*Jerusalem Post,* May 21, 1965.)

Israel-based training effort, the number of trainees in health and medicine is the smallest of the major types of professional skills offered. (See Table 5-2).

About one quarter of the Israeli experts abroad are on short-term missions, and the recruitment of these experts has not been a serious problem. However, Israel has not always been able to fill the demand for experts for long-term assignments, especially in some critical professional areas, which, in addition to health, include education and public administration. Even in fields in which Israel's manpower supply is less limited—such as agriculture, cooperatives and youth development—Israel operates only projects requiring relatively small staffs.

Thus, limitations on available manpower as well as on funds have helped to shape the character and selection of projects abroad and training programs in Israel. These limitations explain in part why the Israelis concentrate on pilot or demonstration projects or short-term training and are reluctant to undertake large-scale programs of social and economic transformation or assume direct management responsibilities.

Cooperation in Project Planning

There is another reason for this policy: Israelis do not want simply to "plug holes" with their activities, important as this might be in some situations. They feel—with some justification—that they have a special contribution to make and hence prefer to carry out programs that bear their special mark and have high visibility.

These considerations have at times led to a certain haphazardness in the choice of activities. Programs may have been launched more because of chance encounters of dignitaries or professional colleagues, political ambitions of local officials or the resourcefulness of Israeli representatives abroad than as a result of considered planning. Israel's urgent desire to please the partner government has contributed to this tendency by limiting the bargaining strength of Israeli negotiators. All technical cooperation programs have no doubt experienced similar problems, but a small country with limited manpower and financial resources and a strong political interest is particularly vulnerable.

Considering these handicaps, it is to Israel's credit that the great majority of its projects and training programs have been in key developmental sectors. Others—organizing and staging independence day celebrations, extending credits to build luxury hotels or conducting certain "catch-all" seminars, for example—had high symbolic or political value and therefore were considered important. However, Israeli officials are realizing increasingly that successful development programs and projects, carefully chosen and planned in cooperation with the partner governments, are in the long run the best kind of political advertising. In the early days of Israel's program the desire to be accepted was an overriding concern. Now that the high reputation of Israel's program has been established, the Israelis can be expected to exercise greater independence and discrimination in selecting their activities.

Chapter 6

Cooperation in Agriculture

Not even the boldest seer, at the turn of the century or even more recently, could have predicted that Israel's most sustained contribution to the developing world would be in the cultivation of land. Jews, by and large, had been landless for 2,000 years, after all, and consequently had developed primarily urban occupational traits. Although the ancient cultural and religious tradition placed considerable value upon agricultural pursuits, for the majority of Jews this part of the tradition retained only symbolic significance.

The modern Zionist movement wrought a major transformation in the attitude of many young Jews toward agriculture. No longer was agriculture to be relegated to mere symbolism. Agricultural colonization became the key to national revival in Palestine—crucial to the political struggle and essential to economic survival.

The early groups of agricultural settlers were farmers by conviction, not by training or background, and it soon became obvious that ideology alone could not produce satisfactory harvests. Scientific agriculture and specialized agricultural education became and have continued to be vital elements in the country's development process.

Today Israel has over 40 secondary agricultural schools and the Hebrew University and the Israeli Institute of Technology have faculties for advanced agricultural training.

Israel's agriculture has been transformed within a few decades from a sector with low productivity and high labor input, characteristic of developing economies, to one with high productivity and low labor input, typical of economically developed countries.

Happily, Israel's well-known capacity for quick agricultural development coincides with the priority needs of many developing countries. The high regard for Israeli technical assistance in agriculture is based not only on the extraordinary growth and efficiency of Israel's farming sector but also on the mystique appeal of Israel's agricultural cooperatives—the *kibbutz* and *moshav*. The psychological impact of these two elements, especially on the young African countries groping for national identity and rapid modernization, cannot be overestimated.

Chief G. Akin Deko, former Minister of Agriculture of Western Nigeria and currently FAO Regional Representative for Africa, commented: [1]

> During my visit to Israel I was able to make personal contact with the Israel system of agricultural development and expansion and saw how some of their modern methods of approach and organization could be adapted to set a new pattern for our rural industry where there is a need to remove the present stagnation, to attract young educated persons to the field and to substantially increase our agricultural output. I think we are on the way to finding an answer.

A similar point of view was expressed by François Tombalbaye, the President of Chad:

> I still preserve a very strong impression of my visit to Israel. There, one is inspired by the example of an entire people fully confident in their ability to effect the miracle of creating a country. The methods employed in Israel, notably those concerning agriculture, could be applied to Chad. Unfortunately our country does not have the same possibilities from the point of view of both capital and personnel. Nevertheless we are hopefully launching a campaign to mobilize the right people for this work.

[1] This and the statement of President Tombalbaye are from "Israel-Africa—A Story of Cooperation," Ministry for Foreign Affairs, Jerusalem (pamphlet, no date).

The high expectations of the representatives of African and other developing countries place an extraordinary responsibility on the planners and experts responsible for Israeli agricultural projects abroad.

Having but recently gone through the painful process of developing a modern agricultural system almost from scratch, the Israelis are acutely aware of the interdependence of human, material and scientific resources. Their agricultural activities abroad, like their training programs in Israel, therefore stress an integrated and balanced application of resources. As a result, education and training are emphasized, settlement is frequently combined with some form of cooperation in production and/or marketing and regional development programs are decidedly favored. The Israelis also stress agricultural extension, water utilization and irrigation and supervised credit.

As of 1966 Israeli advisers and experts were engaged in agricultural projects and activities in at least 10 African, 5 Asian and 8 South American countries. Israeli agricultural advisers and experts have also been making short-term surveys in several African, Asian and Latin American countries and in the Mediterranean area. The variety and scope of activities can be gauged from the brief summary of projects in operation in 1966, by geographic area, shown in Table 6-1.

In order to give a better idea of Israel's agricultural program in developing countries and provide an insight into some of its problems, four projects have been selected for closer analysis. They do not include examples of youth pioneering and paramilitary projects, some of which are included in Table 6-1. Projects of these types usually combine agricultural with educational and/or military programs and are therefore described separately in the subsequent chapter.

Cotton Cultivation in Tanzania

A pilot project for partially irrigated cultivation of cotton and other crops in the Mwanza region near Lake Victoria in Tanzania is one of the most challenging of the East African agricultural projects in which Israeli farm experts are assisting.

Cotton has been an important Tanzanian export crop for some years, and 45 per cent of it has been coming from the Mwanza area—

TABLE 6-1 *Israel-Aided Agricultural Projects, by Geographic Area, 1966* [a]

Geographic Area	Description of Project
Africa	
Cameroon	Three cooperative-type training villages are designed to train about 500 young people for permanent cooperative settlement or as *animateurs* (catalysts) in their native villages.
Central African Republic	Four cooperative villages of 70 to 80 members each have been established by the national pioneer movement. The settlements serve as focal points for neighboring villages that receive help from Israeli extension officers and assistance with mechanical equipment.
Dahomey	In two cooperative villages about 80 ex-soldiers, members of the Dahomey Pioneers, and their families are training for 18 months prior to settling on 8.4-acre units, to be given to each family by the Government.
Guinea	A training center to teach vegetable production and poultry husbandry has been established. It is hoped that the center will supply Conakry and the surrounding area with vegetables and poultry.
Ivory Coast	A training center and 5 farms of about 250 acres each have been established. Several hundred young men are being trained annually in agricultural work as part of their military training. Israeli extension advisers are also working with several native villages in the vicinity of the farms.
Tanzania	Three demonstration cooperative settlements share 1,000 acres of land, on which modern methods of cultivating cotton and food crops have been introduced. Elsewhere in the country about 400 members of the Tanzanian National Service are being trained in agricultural work each year.
Togo	At an agricultural training center 120 members of Togo's Agricultural Pioneer Youth are trained every 6 months in cooperative agriculture. The trainees are drawn from agricultural clubs established under the supervision of Israeli youth instructors. After completing their training, club members return to their own villages, where they farm cooperatively for 3 years. They are then expected to establish new cooperative villages. The first of these, consisting of 100 family units on 2,450 acres of land, has been set up.
Upper Volta	A multipurpose agricultural center, financed jointly by the UN Special Fund, Upper Volta and the Government of Israel, is operated by an international team consisting largely of Israeli agricultural experts. The center, comprising 480 acres of land, trains 45 to 50 students in 3-year courses, organizes short training courses and demonstration "field days" for farmers, sends extension experts to villages

TABLE **6-1** (*continued*)

Geographic Area	Description of Project
Africa (cont'd)	
	in the region, produces quality seed and livestock and is conducting a long-term study of the economics and practice of family farming in the country.
Congo (Kinshasa) and Uganda	Israeli poultry experts are assisting in the expansion of poultry husbandry and are introducing new methods for increasing egg production.
Asia	
Cambodia	A demonstration farm for the development of industrial crops has been established by Israeli experts working as part of the international team developing the Mekong River Delta. An irrigation system on a Prek Thnot River tributary is also being developed in conjunction with a Japanese dam construction team.
Ceylon	A team of irrigation specialists is drilling for water in two arid regions, in the hope of establishing three farms to produce citrus, industrial crops and rice.
Thailand	A new settlement is being established in conjunction with a demonstration farm. Israeli experts are also developing a comprehensive plan for the region.
Nepal	A 10,000-acre tract of state land is being developed for settlement by 1,100 families in new villages with some cooperative services. Additional development is planned later.
Iran	Several dozen peasant villages in the province of Kazvin, hard hit by an earthquake in 1962, are being rehabilitated. The work involves regional planning, reconstruction and introduction of modern methods of irrigation and cultivation.
Latin America	
Argentina-Chile-Peru	Two agricultural planning teams consisting of planners and agricultural specialists are preparing regional development plans and agricultural settlement projects.
Bolivia	A training farm has been established on which Bolivian soldiers, predominantly from rural areas, are taught modern farming methods. It is hoped that upon their return from military service they will serve as catalysts in their native villages.
Brazil	A demonstration farm in northeast Brazil produces mainly seed corn and provides training in modern agricultural methods. It is hoped that this will encourage the spread of new techniques to other parts of the region and thus

TABLE 6-1 (*continued*)

Geographic Area	Description of Project
Latin America (cont'd)	
	produce better and cheaper seeds. Israeli drillers are also drilling for water in Rio Grande do Norte.
Ecuador	A portion of an 8,000-acre estate is being developed along cooperative lines under Ecuador's land reform program. Improved methods of growing citrus, other fruits and industrial crops are also being taught.
Venezuela	A center has been established to train professional agricultural personnel, economists and engineers involved in regional planning. Several new settlement areas are being developed in accordance with Israel's regional planning methods and village rehabilitation through supervised agricultural credit is being carried out.
Colombia	Agricultural advisers are working on improving the growing of citrus and other fruits and are helping to promote agricultural cooperation.

SOURCES: Ministry for Foreign Affairs, Jerusalem; and field research and interviews.
[a] Some of the projects listed here are Nahal projects and are described in detail in Chapter 7.

7,000 square miles of almost treeless plains, broken occasionally near the eastern shores of Lake Victoria by low ridges and rocks. In 1963 the region produced some 100,000 bales of cotton, which sold for almost $8.4 million.[2] The Tanzanian Government's purpose in supporting the pilot project has been to test whether the productive capacity of the area could be raised and whether farmers of the region, many of whom eke out a bare subsistence from neglected soils, can successfully engage in cooperative agriculture, using modern methods and producing for a market economy. Six Israeli farm experts in three settlements of the Sukuma tribe in the Mwanza region have been responsible for the project. The magnitude of their task is difficult to conceive, but the environment in which they operate has been described candidly in President Nyerere's party newspaper, *The Nationalist:* [3]

[2] "Mwanza—10 Years of Progress in Mwanza Region, 1954–1964," Social Training Centre, Institute of Publicity Media, Mwanza (pamphlet, no date).

[3] Richard Kisch, "Nation Builders," October 16, 1964.

For years Sukuma peasants and farm workers have scratched a bare living from cotton, cultivated casually on their plots and *shambas* [farms]. They enjoyed a reputation for working about three hours a day, when the weather was suitable—and hoping for the best in the dry season. Existence was a hand-to-mouth affair, even if occasional attempts were made to demonstrate newer methods. Generally the practical rewards were not sufficient to impress anyone with the advantages of a cash economy over subsistence living.

The Israeli advisers have been working with 3 groups of villagers, comprising some 200 families, in 3 areas totaling 1,000 acres of land. In addition to the customary cotton culture, marketable food crops, such as onions, corn and groundnuts, have been introduced. In two of the three areas, moreover, the Israeli advisers introduced irrigation on a limited scale, to test whether the greater yields thus obtained justified the high investment required. Even where there was no irrigation, the Israelis applied modern methods of cultivation, including extensive application of machinery, fertilizer and pesticides. Introduction of a double cropping system on the irrigated portion of land was designed to show how the two to five months of the year previously spent in idleness or underemployment could be utilized productively and profitably.

The initial investment required was about $300,000. Additional investments of more than $1 million were contemplated over a five-year period.[4] Within five years the settlements were expected to be financially independent.

The three cooperative farms are managed separately, but the farm equipment is jointly owned and is allocated among the settlements according to need. In a radical departure from past local practices, the entire farming area of the settlement is treated as a single unit

[4] According to a June 1964 agreement between the government-sponsored Agricultural Development Company of Israel and the Government of Tanzania, Tanzania's cash outlay for the first full year of operation was to be $146,970, with an additional investment of $154,000 to be provided by an Israeli Government loan, for pumps, pipes and irrigation equipment. Four fifths of the salaries of Israeli experts were to be paid by the Government of Tanzania; the Government of Israel was to pay the remainder. The estimate of total outlays for the five-year period of Tanzanian Government sponsorship of the project is based on data from Tanzania's *Five-Year Plan for Economic and Social Development, 1st July, 1964–30th June, 1969,* United Republic of Tanganyika and Zanzibar (now Tanzania), Dar es Salaam, 1964, Vol. II, pp. 30, 32, 35.

for purposes of mechanized operations, such as plowing, ridging, fertilizing, harrowing and spraying; other necessary operations, however, including weeding, thinning, seeding and harvesting, are done manually for the most part and are the responsibility of individual families. Certain tasks that benefit all settlers, such as minor construction jobs, are handled on a communal basis, while recurrent chores are rotated among all members.

The farms are directed by the Israeli managers and their local counterparts, assisted by an elected committee of members. Major decisions are submitted to a general meeting of the members. Such meetings, or *barazas,* are familiar to the tribes of the area, but the social and economic organization of production introduced by the Israeli experts was totally new for the farmers. The projects have therefore become, in effect, social laboratories in which, through trial and error, it has been necessary to test the new forms of organization. The benefits of mechanization and the principles of cooperation were the first to be challenged.

"If the machine can do the clearing, plowing, ridging, fertilizing, harrowing and spraying," some of the farmers seemed to think, "why can't it do everything? Why should it still be necessary to do manual labor, and even work as many hours as before?" Communal work and careful attention to the crops at all stages of cultivation were equally strange concepts for people accustomed to subsistence farming on small, scattered *shambas.* But the new cash income that would come with the higher yields—more than any of them had earned before—offered a way out. If the farmers were allowed to hire laborers (usually in exchange only for food), absenteeism and inadequate attention to the crops might be stopped or at least eased. Cherished cooperative principles might have to be modified (as, incidentally, they had also been modified in Israel when hired labor was introduced in some collective settlements), but the crop would be saved and the project allowed to go on.

Another challenge came on questions of planning and discipline—both essential to efficient commercial agriculture. "Should valuable high-cost irrigated land be used to produce cotton for some distant market, or food for hungry stomachs right in the settlement?" "Was it fair to deduct tractor charges from cash payments due the settlers?"

"Did the settlers with political connections have the same work obligations as those without them?"

With great patience, tact and flexibility, the Israeli team managed to steer a course through the perilous rapids of social change and keep the settlements intact. Once the first high yields of cotton were in and initial suspicions had worn off, many more farmers asked to join. In 1965 there were reportedly already three applicants for every open place.

The support of the ruling party, the Tanzanian National Union (TANU), and the Victoria Federation of Cooperative Unions (VFCU), the largest cooperative organization in east Africa, has played an important role in launching and sustaining the Mwanza project. "Evidence is accumulating," wrote the TANU organ, *The Nationalist,* in a two-part series on the Mwanza projects, "that the consolidation of new production methods and the establishment of cooperative farm settlements, inspired by TANU's socialist objectives, is boosting the standard of living throughout the United Republic." [5]

The VFCU markets virtually all the cotton, sisal and rice produced in the area. Its former general manager, Paul Bomani, is Tanzania's Minister of Development, and also has long been influential in the leadership of TANU. The three settlements are organized as primary societies within the Victoria Federation and in 1963 and 1964, according to an official of the Federation, received credits totaling more than $30,000.

Average yields of cotton on the three farms in 1964 ranged from 900 to 1,600 pounds per acre, a very high output in any country, and 3 to 5 times that of the average cotton farmer in the area. Income did not rise in proportion, since the cost of production was also very much higher than formerly, but it rose substantially and probably more than doubled for the more diligent farmers.

As might be expected, the pilot project has been the subject of considerable controversy, particularly because of the novel approach of the Israelis and the relatively high capital investment required. Dr. A. J. P. Brown, a British expatriate cotton pathologist at the Ukiriguru Agricultural Research Center near Mwanza, summed up the views of the critics: "Frankly, we believe that if the farmers fol-

[5] Kisch, *op. cit.*

lowed the advice we have already given, then yields would be just as high as those claimed on the Israeli projects. We have already produced a practical recipe for success—and if our elementary rules were followed, it would be just as effective and cost far less than some of these expensive projects."[6]

Regardless of who may turn out to be right from the standpoint of the economic viability of the pilot project itself, there are indications that the project may be having a catalytic effect on other agricultural activity in the area. Agricultural stations, extension offices and the VFCU have suddenly had to face the challenge of new ideas and new approaches. Perhaps in part responding to the challenge, the VFCU adopted the intensive use of insecticides, and in 1965 airsprayed 5,000 to 6,000 acres of land periodically. In cooperation with the Ministry of Agriculture, the Federation also began to use its tractors on 200- to 300-acre tracts of land, instead of allowing uneconomical contract work on 3- or 4-acre plots, as it had formerly.

The double cropping through irrigation and intensive cultivation, introduced by the Israelis, has not been adopted elsewhere, and any significant expansion of the project may be barred by unfavorable soil conditions in the area originally considered for expansion. Moreover, despite the clamor for admission to the settlements after they started producing high yields, it is by no means clear that the outlook and work habits of the members will change sufficiently to meet the requirements of modern farming, or that after five years the settlements will be economically viable. Yet the pilot project has apparently already provided a wealth of invaluable experience and has served as a significant stimulus to socioeconomic development in the area.

Within the general framework of Israeli agricultural work abroad the Mwanza project represents a noteworthy pattern. It applies cooperative principles to both production and marketing and involves an agricultural crop in which Israel has had brief but successful experience. By using a team of experts who live for the most part right in the settlements, it has been possible to mobilize available manpower resources quickly and to maintain sustained close rapport with the local people and their leaders.

[6] *Ibid.*

State Farming in Ghana

Since the overthrow of Kwame Nkrumah in January 1966, Ghana's state farm system, comprising some 100 farms of various sizes, has been in the process of dissolution. Nevertheless, Israel's participation in the management of several of these farms at the invitation of Nkrumah's government is of more than historical interest, for it affords a unique opportunity to observe the role of the foreign adviser within a system of state-controlled agriculture in a developing country. Moreover, it is probably the only place in the world where Israeli agricultural experts have shared the scene with Soviet agricultural managers doing essentially the same job.

Of Ghana's 100 state farms scattered throughout the country, 5 were managed by foreigners—3 by Soviet experts and 2 by Israeli experts. The state farms and the Agricultural Wing of the Worker's Brigade were established in the early 1960's in a major effort to increase production of food crops, which in turn would reduce expenditure of precious foreign currency for food imports. The five state farms entrusted to foreign experts, it was hoped, would demonstrate the feasibility of state-controlled agriculture. To the Israelis, accustomed to a cooperative form of agriculture, the state farm idea was new, but they readily adapted themselves to the pattern desired by Ghana. The two Israeli-managed farms, established in 1963, included a mixed crop farm of 1,200 acres at Akatsi and a cattle ranch of 2,000 acres at Tatsube, in eastern Ghana.

In contrast to the Tanzanian pilot farms and most other agricultural projects in which Israel has participated in developing nations, the Ghana state farms had no cooperative features. The approximately 230 workers at Akatsi and the 35 at Tatsube, like other state farm workers, earned a fixed daily wage of 6/6 (approximately $0.91 at the official rate of exchange) as employees of the State Farmers Administration, a Ghanaian Government agency. This was considered an adequate wage, according to Ghanaian standards, and the Government had hoped that it would not only satisfy the farm workers but would also indirectly force improvements in conditions on private farms. Something went wrong with this calculation, however, to the sorrow of many a Ghanaian state farm manager.

With an assured cash income and protected jobs on state farms, workers flocked to these farms, swelling farm payrolls unnecessarily and leading to the neglect of private farms.

Another problem affecting the performance of the state farms was the country's acute foreign exchange shortage, which in turn caused a critical shortage of spare parts for machinery and resulted in uneconomic use of imported farm equipment. Trucks were sometimes supplied where jeeps were needed; equipment lay idle for months for lack of repair parts. In some instances, also, the Government nationalized locally owned land for state farms, but deferred compensating the previous owners. This led to widespread pilferage and stealing of crops,[7] and in 1965 on one Soviet-managed farm disaffected peasants reportedly joined in a squatters' movement in which they started cultivating land and then claiming it as their own.

Political control and influence also played an important role on the Ghanaian state farms. Administratively they were part of the state machinery, and ideologically they formed a major tenet in the socialist program of Ghana's single legal party, the Convention People's Party. Political pressure resulted in employment of favorites and, often, the hiring of more field workers than were needed. These problems, added to the others described above and to the generally low productivity of labor, created a chronic deficit in the state farm system as a whole.

Against this unpromising general background, the performance of the Israeli team appears to have been remarkably good. Despite administrative bottlenecks and acute maintenance problems with equipment, the cultivated area of the farm at Akatsi expanded steadily. Starting with only 80 acres of cleared land in the second cropping season of 1961, the farm grew to 1,200 acres of cultivated land by 1965, including 160 acres under irrigation. The main crop was maize, and yields were quite good. In 1964, for example, Akatsi produced 52 per cent of all the maize harvested on state farms, though its acreage planted in maize was only 3 per cent of the total state farm acreage devoted to maize cultivation. Yields from tobacco and from

[7] On one state farm about 60 per cent of one season's maize crop was stolen.

tomatoes, lima beans and other vegetables grown on irrigated land were satisfactory. If marketing facilities had been better, the Akatsi farm might have been at least on the way toward economic viability.

The Israeli-directed cattle ranch at Tatsube was established in the second half of 1962, but received its first shipment of 250 head of cattle much later. When Israel's then Minister of Agriculture, Moshe Dayan, visited the area in October 1964, he reported that "the land and the fences are ready, but although a mission set out for Mali six months ago to purchase cattle, they have not yet arrived." [8] After the cattle did arrive, the farm began doing very well, and continued to operate under Israeli management even after Nkrumah's overthrow. By utilizing part of the available acreage for maize cultivation, the Israeli manager was able to produce more than enough fresh fodder for the farm's needs (with some left over for marketing) and for silage to tide the animals over the difficult dry season.[9] The Tatsube farm, in fact, was not utilized to capacity, and it was generally recognized that it could easily support several times the number of cattle it was supporting.[10]

In the present transitional period from the Nkrumah era, it is still not possible to assess whether the two Israeli-directed farms are likely to have a lasting demonstration value, or whether they will be swept away, along with other vestiges of the Nkrumah regime. It is clear, however, that in the circumstances under which the Israelis operated, they could not introduce the fundamental changes needed to make the farms economically sound. The best they could hope for was to manage the projects as well as circumstances permitted and to gain Ghana's appreciation for this effort. Whether Israel might have applied more rigorous criteria to its assistance and still have retained Ghana's friendship is a question for Israeli policy makers to assess.

[8] Moshe Dayan, "West African Diary," *Jerusalem Post,* December 6, 1964.

[9] The cattle reportedly gained 50 to 60 pounds per head in a 10-month period in 1964–1965—quite a satisfactory record for the climatic conditions of the area. The amount of land needed to sustain cattle was reduced from an average of 10 acres per head to only 1 acre per head.

[10] The chief Soviet agricultural adviser to the Ghanaian Government paid a rare tribute to the Israeli experts when he told a meeting of state farm managers in February 1965: "The Israeli state farm at Tatsube is working well. It has an excellent manager, but instead of giving it 1,000 head of cattle, which it could have, it has received only 250."

Regional Planning for Rural Development in Venezuela

In Ghana Israeli experts found themselves in a predetermined and unfamiliar institutional setting. In Venezuela, on the other hand, rural development involves the more rewarding but in some ways more challenging process of adapting Israeli methods and ideology to an evolving, flexible planning system. Before analyzing this interesting experiment in greater detail, a brief description of Israeli concepts of rural development and planning is in order.

Under the impact of mass immigration in the early 1950's, Israeli ideas about settlement programs underwent a fundamental change. Instead of treating each settlement project substantially as a separate unit, the planners concluded that a comprehensive regional approach to rural development would better meet Israeli's over-all social and economic development goals. The basic purpose of regional development, according to Dr. Raanan Weitz,[11] the Israeli planner who has spearheaded the idea, is

> . . . to bridge the gap between town and country; to prevent the mass migration of the rural population to the cities, and to improve the situation of both the farmers and the industrial workers who remain in rural surroundings. Integration of industry, agriculture and services at a suitable level within the . . . settlement areas . . . requires appropriate overall planning.

Weitz also argues convincingly that regional planning constitutes the essential link between macroplanning—the allocation of factors of production to different activities on a national level—and microplanning—the structure and allocation of individual production units in order to meet the national goals. Rural development in particular, he maintains, can best be achieved through planned development of natural regions.[12]

[11] *Agriculture and Rural Development in Israel; Projection and Planning,* The National and University Institute of Agriculture, Rehovoth, 1963, Bulletin No. 68, p. 115.

[12] For further elaboration of this view, see Raanan Weitz, "Rural Development Through Regional Planning in Israel," *Journal of Farm Economics,* Summer, 1965; also papers by Weitz and Yehuda Landau in a collected volume of papers read at the "Rehovoth Conference on Comprehensive Planning of Agriculture in

Several Israeli rural developments have been built on this concept. The most advanced of these is the Lachish District in the central part of Israel, comprising 225,000 acres, 65,000 of which are now cultivated. An underpopulated, unproductive area in 1954, the Lachish District today supports a population of over 30,000 people, about half of whom live in the newly established district town of Kiryat Gat and the rest in some 60 settlements and villages.[13]

According to the Lachish concept of regional planning, four or five settlements are built around a so-called "rural center," which contains a school, cultural center, dispensary and agricultural services. These clusters are in turn grouped around a new "regional town," which has secondary schools, industries, cultural attractions and central administrative, social, health and agricultural services. Despite some growing pains and continuing problems, this concept is still the preferred pattern for rural development in Israel, and has attracted considerable attention in developing countries.

The Israeli team of agricultural planners in Venezuela was headed by one of the architects of the Lachish scheme, Yitshak Abt, who also directed all other Israel-sponsored agricultural projects in Latin America. The Israeli group went to Venezuela in 1962 at the invitation of Venezuela's central planning agency, CORDIPLAN,[14] to assist in the planning and development of Las Majaguas, a large, newly irrigated region in the central part of the country. The Israelis insisted not only that Venezuela provide qualified counterparts, but also that a joint management committee be formed, consisting of representatives of the various ministries and agencies involved in the Las Majaguas project (the Ministry of Public Works, Agriculture and Animal Breeding, Health and Social Assistance, the National Agrarian Institute and the Agricultural and Livestock Bank). Simultaneously, a number of young Venezuelan agricultural economists, agronomists, engineers and agricultural extension officers went to Israel for three-month courses, which included the philosophy of regional comprehensive planning.

Developing Countries" and published by the Jewish Agency for Israel, Jerusalem, August 1963.

[13] *Facts About Israel, 1964–65,* Ministry for Foreign Affairs, Jerusalem, p. 94.

[14] The Central Office of Coordination and Planning of the Office of the President of the Republic (Oficina Central de Coordinación y Planificación de la Presidencia de la Republica).

The Israelis and their counterparts worked on the spot at Las Majaguas and at their office in Caracas, laying out the physical and economic plans for the project.

Venezuelan officials were eager to see the principles of regional planning applied to other agricultural development projects in Venezuela's newly adopted land reform program, but a major bottleneck was trained manpower. The Israeli team was small, fluctuating from three to six people, and to send large numbers of trainees to Israel would have been expensive. The solution arrived at was the establishment in Caracas of an interdisciplinary planning and training institution, now known as the Centro de Capacitación e Investigación Aplicada en Reforma Agraria (Center for Training and Applied Investigation in Land Reform). Since its inception, several hundred young professionals involved in agricultural development have studied at the center. "We have brainwashed them," Abt told his visitor with a smile, "but at least now they all speak a common language."

For the first two years the sponsoring governmental institutions limited their allocations to the center and their participation in its activities. It was finally given semiautonomous status in 1965, under CORDIPLAN, though the sponsoring organizations retained control of the purse strings. An ingenious system of applied training and research has been developed by the center. After some theoretical and ideological indoctrination the students are put to work under supervision on concrete planning projects that have been given to the center. In addition, it has undertaken the planning and execution of several pilot projects for the provision of supervised agricultural credit, using a pattern developed in Lachish and other Israeli rural developments. Thus, in effect, the center operates as a training institution, as an agency for microplanning and regional planning of agricultural development projects and as an executing agency for experimental agricultural credit schemes.[15]

[15] This description is based in part on an unpublished memorandum prepared by the Center for Training and Applied Investigation in Land Reform, September 1965. According to the memorandum the center's work program in the fall of 1965 was: conclusion of the first and second stage of development projects for the Western zone of the state of Cojedes; conclusion of the development and settlement project "El Castillo" in the state of Aragua; conclusion of the project for integrated development for Camatagua, in the states of Guárico and Aragua; execution of the plan for supervised credit in the settlement of El Amparo, in

By all accounts the center is an example of successful institution-building, for which the Israeli team of advisers deserve high credit. But their work must also be seen on the more prosaic level of project execution. The Las Majaguas project, in which Israeli advisers have been active since 1962, provides some insights on this part of their activities.

The Las Majaguas plan is based upon an elaborate irrigation system fed by a newly constructed dam. Its total area is 12,000 acres, much of it suitable for rice, sugar and corn cultivation as well as diverse vegetables. The plan calls for settling 2,200 family units supported by 6 rural service centers—a total population of approximately 24,000 people. Each peasant family, it is hoped, will within 10 years achieve an annual income of 10,000 *bolívares* ($2,230), which is 80 per cent of the average salary of an unskilled industrial worker.

The social goals of the project are described as follows in a pamphlet issued by the joint management committee of the project: [16]

> From the beginning to the end of the Plan primary importance has been assigned to the development of the human element, the creation of aspirations being considered the basic factor of success. To this end we envisage the advancement of man and of the peasant family through the optimum use of available resources in education, sanitation, social assistance, agricultural extension, community development, home demonstration, etc. In cold economic terms, we start from the principle that, in order to make a producer efficient, you must first make him a consumer, and at the same time furnish him with sufficient means of production.
>
> We also hope to have elaborated a Plan based on democratic principles by respecting the idiosyncrasies of the individual, and by making him participate in the micro-planning of the different stages, particularly those regarding his own plot, house and community.

The visitor to Las Majaguas is struck by the enormous contrast between these goals and generous government investments, on the

the state of Cojedes; execution of the plan for supervised credit for the second year in the settlement of El Cortijo, in the state of Aragua; two-month courses in supervised credit in the states of Aragua and Cojedes and a two-week course in credit in the Las Majaguas Plan, state of Portuguesa; three-month course in physical planning; one-month course in economic evaluation of projects; participation in a course on rural education sponsored by the Inter-American Center for Rural Education in Rubio, in the state of Táchira; one-week seminar on "Techniques of Planning in Agricultural Reform."

16 "El Plan de Las Majaguas," Comité Coordinador del Sistema de Riego, Cojedes-Sarare, Región de Las Majaguas, Caracas, August 1965.

one hand, and the reaction of the *campesinos* who are being helped, on the other. By the end of 1965 the visitor could see at Las Majaguas miles and miles of concrete canals, wide all-weather roads, water and electricity lines, two schools and some 300 neat concrete houses, each with three rooms, kitchen, inside toilet and washing facilities, septic tank and a small barn. But only a handful of *campesinos* had moved in and settled, the rest preferring to stay where they were and commuting to Las Majaguas, mainly to work in the *finca escuela*—the farmer training department established to tide the settlers over the first year by giving them an assured cash income and teaching them modern farming methods. Lack of familiarity with the new surroundings and methods and latent fear of government seemed to be principally responsible for the peasants' reluctance to move into the development.

At the same time problems of coordination and cooperation were also present in Las Majaguas, as elsewhere in the country, despite the fact that at Las Majaguas all five Venezuelan Government agencies with an interest in the project work through the joint management committee. The establishment of the committee, while only a first step, was in fact regarded by local observers as an important advance in achieving better coordination between various agencies. A perhaps even more important achievement is the creation of an elected farmers' committee, which has responsibility for the project's farm machinery and has ready access to the government-appointed managers. The farmers' committee seems to offer the best promise of closing the gap between government and *campesinos*.

Unlike many other development projects in which Israelis have participated, Las Majaguas is a project conceived—strange as it may sound—in plenty. The available infrastructure, before the first homestead was even surveyed or the first potential settler identified, was formidable. The cost of settling a family unit is estimated by competent observers at $12,000. When the infrastructure is included, the cost is close to $20,000. (Settlement costs in Israel also average about $20,000 per family unit.) But as in many other instances, heavy investments provide no guarantee of ultimate success. Those concerned with Las Majaguas know that, given the relatively bountiful resources, the real test of success will be the number of *campesinos* who actually settle on the land instead of commuting, and the settlers' financial responsibility once they cease drawing fixed wages and become independent producers.

Israel's planning team in Venezuela, as indicated earlier, has not put all its eggs into the Las Majaguas basket. Through the broad-gauged work of the Center for Training and Applied Investigation in Land Reform, it has influenced many other areas and elements of Venezuela's agricultural planning and development program.

Potentially one of the most important innovations of the Israeli experts through the center was the planning and execution of an experimental supervised credit program. Using an approach applied to the Lachish scheme in Israel, the Israelis recommended a radical departure from accepted practices. Instead of extending credit in cash to selected farmers with a good credit record, they proposed extending credit to a whole village, provided a village association is established through which the credit can be channeled. To qualify for credit, the village association, with the help of *peritos* (semiprofessional government agricultural agents), prepares a production and marketing plan, based on submissions by the individual farmers. The plan is submitted to the Agricultural and Livestock Bank, which, through the village association, grants individual credits according to need, mostly in kind rather than cash. Each farmer's produce is marketed through the village association, which in turn deducts individual credits from the amount realized to pay off the loans.

In the first village in which the system was tried, the results appear to have been exceptionally good. Income is reported to have more than doubled and the repayment ratio is high. Reporting on the latter, an official of an international agency wrote: "Working with a group that was substantially more than fifty percent insolvent, the supervised credit plan instituted succeeded in gaining a recovery rate a great deal higher than could normally have been expected." According to data collected by the center, the 110 peasants of the village repaid over 90 per cent of the credits extended.[17]

When the Israelis first proposed this approach, they met much skepticism among bank and ministry officials. U. S. credit advisers, who were engaged in a multimillion-dollar agricultural credit pro-

[17] "Memoria," Centro de Capacitación e Investigación Aplicada en Reforma Agraria (Center for Training and Applied Investigation in Land Reform), Caracas, September 1965 (mimeo.), p. 23.

gram, were equally dubious. After the success with the first village, however, the approach was extended to two more villages, and at the end of 1965 plans were drawn and personnel trained to go into 20 additional villages.

The chief obstacle to extending the approach on a larger scale, according to the Israelis, is the lack of properly trained personnel, for admittedly the plan calls for more intensive and concentrated attention by credit and extension officers than is normally given in supervised credit programs. The Israeli adviser visited the pilot village twice a week, for example, and the responsible officers of the Bank and Agriculture Ministries were especially trained to carry out the program.

In comparing the Israeli-supervised program with the parallel U. S. effort, the differences between the two are clearly apparent: The U. S. program helps the "credit-worthy" individual farmer—the Israeli program seeks to raise the material level of an entire community. The U. S. program helped develop the financial umbrella institution—the Agricultural and Livestock Bank—by extending a $10-million loan and assisted in training 163 administrators and field supervisors.[18] It makes no attempt, however, to change the institutional structure and relationships of production in the villages where the program operates. The Israelis provide no capital and are utilizing the already developed financial institutions and manpower, but they have introduced a new approach and have developed institutions and operations based on cooperative principles. The U. S. program stops at the administrative and supervisory level. The Israelis go directly into the villages and provide support and reinforcement for village leaders, agricultural agents and bank representatives. Loan repayments in the Israeli program exceed 90 per cent; in the U. S. program they reportedly fluctuate between 30 and 40 per cent.

The Israeli agricultural team in Venezuela was the first and most effective work group established by Israel in Latin America. In its activities it has sought to apply Israeli patterns of regional planning and agricultural credit in an effort to bring about basic improvements in rural development. To promote its orientation, the Israeli team set up a special local training institution. No doubt the Venezuelan expe-

[18] "U. S. AID Operations in Venezuela," U. S. Agency for International Development, Caracas, November 1965, p. 2 (mimeo.).

rience has had, and will continue to have, a strong influence on Israeli teams which have since been established in South America.

Frustration and Hope in Upper Volta

If there is any link between the development problems of Venezuela, economically one of the most advanced countries of South America, and Upper Volta, one of Africa's least developed countries, it is the lack of trained manpower for the advancement of agriculture. However, Upper Volta's needs in agriculture differ radically from those of Venezuela, both qualitatively and quantitatively. Within the scope of this study there is another link between the two countries—local agricultural training and research institutions were created in both through the instrumentality of Israel.

Formally, the Matourkou Multipurpose Agricultural Center (Centre Agricole Polyvalent Matourkou) near Bobo-Dioulasso, Upper Volta's second largest town, is not an Israeli-sponsored project. It began operating in April 1963 under an agreement between the UN Special Fund and Upper Volta, signed almost a year earlier. Funds for the five-year project are provided by the Special Fund and Upper Volta; the UN Food and Agriculture Organization, acting for the Special Fund, has over-all management and operating responsibility, in consultation with the Government of Upper Volta; at the end of five years Upper Volta is to receive title to all equipment and continue the project on its own.[19]

Although Israel may not be mentioned in all the official documents, it has been closely associated with the project. In 1961 an Israeli agricultural expert proposed establishment of an agricultural training and demonstration center in Senegal, to be financed by the European Common Market Fund. In concept and design the project resembled the present center in Upper Volta.[20] The Common Market Fund, re-

[19] "Plan of Operation, United Nations Special Fund Project, Upper Volta Agricultural Training Centre, Bobo-Dioulasso," February 6, 1963 (mimeo.). (Plan of operation provided for in Article I, paragraph 2 of the Basic Agreement signed on June 26, 1962 by the Government of Upper Volta and the UN Special Fund.)

[20] Mordechai E. Kreinin, *Israel and Africa—A Study in Technical Cooperation,* Praeger, New York, 1964, p. 84.

portedly because of French opposition, turned down the proposal. A few months later an Israeli study mission visited Upper Volta and submitted a similar basic proposal, but with two important modifications: that the center be established as a regional institution serving the four countries of the Conseil d'Entente (Upper Volta, Ivory Coast, Dahomey and Niger); that it be financed 65 per cent by the UN Special Fund and 35 per cent by Israel and the four beneficiary countries.[21]

In the end the Government of Upper Volta proposed a national project, though the Special Fund staff, in its recommendation for approval, noted that "Dahomey, Ivory Coast and Niger have expressed their interest in being associated with the project." It was informally agreed that Israel's participation in the project would consist of supplying experts to staff it and grants to Upper Volta for part of its monetary contribution. The FAO, the executing agency, insisted on maintaining its international staffing principle, but 5 Israelis, including the manager and his deputy, were recruited for the 11-man international team to head the project.

As initially planned, the hub of the training activity was to be a two-year course for the preparation of middle-level agricultural extension officers and farm supervisors. The course was to emphasize practical subjects and on-the-job training in the various branches of the center. In addition, some 200 "progressive farmers" and agricultural agents were expected to attend 1- to 6-week short demonstration and refresher courses annually. "Field days" for practical demonstration of specific farm practices to the country's farmers were also to be held several times a year. For the long-term training program, students were to be sponsored by the Government of Upper Volta—80 initially, 150 to 200 once the center's ambitious building program was completed.[22]

Implementation differed from the plan, however, for when the center opened in April 1963, the Government closed another agricultural school, transferred the students to the new center and, instead of the

[21] Zvi Gat, *Projet relatif à l'établissement d'un Centre Agricole Polyvalent à Bobo-Dioulasso,* Department for International Cooperation, Ministry for Foreign Affairs, Jerusalem, December 1961.

[22] "Plan of Operation . . . Upper Volta Agricultural Training Centre . . ."

planned two-year practical curriculum, requested a three-year program, with more academic emphasis than had been contemplated. With the completion in 1965 of well-appointed school quarters, constructed and equipped by Israel, the long-term training department, with a student body of only 45, was prepared to handle 200 students. It was hoped that this level might be reached, if the Upper Volta Government substantially increased the number of students it sponsored and if neighboring countries and international organizations could be persuaded to sponsor additional students.

The short training program is not so heavily dependent on government action and support. Participants are sponsored largely by private or quasi-private French development companies, which, after some hesitation, have decided to take advantage of the center's facilities. "Field days," on the other hand, potentially very useful for their demonstration effect on the grass-roots farmer, experienced problems primarily with the supply and financing of transport needed to bring the farmers to the center.

The seed and livestock production sections and the demonstration farm have only recently become operative, but the latter is already producing enough eggs for the local demand and some high-quality seed and livestock for distribution or sale to farmers. Interesting experiments are under way on the farm in the design of inexpensive poultry runs using local materials. In another program young farmers are brought in for short courses from neighboring villages with the hope that they can help to bring improved agricultural methods to their own areas, especially better use of the plow and of draft animals. The extension division of the center is supposed to follow up after these farmers return to their villages, in order to sustain and reinforce the training they have received at the center. This plan seems well conceived, except that the extension service at present operates only within a 50-mile radius of the center, the maximum distance a foreign expert can expect to cover in a day and still return to his base. The potential grass-roots impact of the center is thus limited to the rural area in the immediate vicinity of the center.

A unique feature of the center's program is the so-called "prototype village," a section where 15 native farming families are pursuing indigenous farming methods. To call this group a "village" is a misnomer, for the 15 families consist of 3 groups drawn from 3 different regions of the country; 2 of the groups do not understand the third one, and each of the 3 groups follows different cultural traditions and economic practices. The families from the eastern region customarily live on cattle and cereals production; the families from the central region combine cultivation of cereals with industrial crops, such as cotton and peanuts; and the families from the western region grow vegetables and fruits and raise poultry in addition to the standard cereals. The center wants to determine, on the basis of the experiences of these families, the minimum investment in tools, machinery, seeds, etc., required to raise the family income from the present $120 to $300 per annum.

On arriving at the center, each family received a cleared plot of land on which to build its hut, and building materials consisting of a corrugated iron roof and some cement. The center invests $400 per prototype unit, plus a small biweekly cash allowance. In return, the farmers are expected to follow instructions of the experts regarding cultivation and cooperate with them in the collection of statistical data.

The farmers have willingly cooperated, but they have shown the effects of this sudden transformation to a new environment. The center has no doubt improved their standard of living—more cash, better medical care, etc.—but, as constituted, the center is not equipped to meet the adjustment problems which these uprooted families are facing and which will become more acute when the experiment is over and they are expected to return to their native villages.

Lack of attention to problems of adjustment has also been criticized in the center's training program for young farmers and in its village extension program. One experienced observer has pointed out that simultaneous community development activities and programs to bring some education and sanitation into the villages are essential to the success of these programs.

No doubt some of the problems of the Bobo-Dioulasso center are teething problems which in time will work themselves out, since the Israeli planners are both imaginative and practical in their approach. The real question, however, is whether Upper Volta is able to absorb such a large and varied investment in its agricultural training and experimentation.[23] Perhaps the fact that the center was proposed as a regional institution, serving and supported by all four countries of the Conseil d'Entente, but ended as a purely national project, illustrates how the desire for prestige can become a barrier to effective development in a poor country.

The project demonstrates an ingenious sponsorship pattern—the tacit partnership between a UN institution—the Special Fund—and the bilateral assistance program of a single country. With some modifications, this pattern may provide a partial answer to the problem of financing assistance programs for Israel and other small countries that lack capital resources but have the ability and desire to render technical assistance.

However financed, Israel's assistance in agricultural development has stimulated experimentation and imaginative thinking wherever it has been given. The same quality has also characterized projects in youth development and pioneering, discussed in the following chapter.

[23] The project calls for an expenditure of $2 million over 5 years, and a staff of 11 high-paid foreign experts supported by 40 African staffers and 120 African laborers.

Chapter 7

Pioneering and Nation-Building

ISRAEL'S successful struggle for independence could not have been achieved without the dedication and accomplishments of Israeli youth. Widespread recognition of this fact helps to explain the receptivity of developing countries to Israeli assistance in establishing youth and pioneering programs, and the high priority that the Israelis themselves assign to this type of activity.

The idea of publicly supported, voluntary or semivoluntary organizations of young people engaged in national tasks is deeply rooted in the story of modern Israel. By the 1920's young Jewish pioneers had established voluntary self-defense and agricultural settlement organizations, which became the nuclei of national pioneering and defense movements during the independence struggle. After independence in 1948 voluntary national service lost some of its romantic luster, but it gained in organizational effectiveness and in the resources available to it.

While many of the political parties continued to encourage elements of national service in their affiliated youth organizations, the Israeli Government, through its Ministry of Defense, set out to establish two nonpartisan youth movements dedicated exclusively to national service. Gadna (Youth Battalions), for boys and girls aged 14 to 18, offers sports, hiking, camping, crafts, group discussions and cultural activities, as well as physical work and some premilitary training. Nahal (Fighting Pioneer Youth), which takes up where Gadna leaves off, is for young men and women of military age and includes paratroop or regular military training, followed by agricultural settlement in difficult or dangerous places.

Despite many differences, Israel's Gadna and Nahal movements can be regarded as ideological precursors of the national service movements that have been established in many countries.

African and Latin American conferences on national service and volunteer programs were convened in 1965 in the Ivory Coast and in Argentina, respectively. By that time, according to the International Secretariat for Volunteer Service,[1] 31 countries already had volunteer service programs in operation or were planning to establish them.

The importance of these and other youth programs for the developing countries was emphasized at the Ivory Coast conference by M'Bahia Blé, Ivory Coast Minister of the Armed Forces, Youth and Community Services: [2]

> Despite the diversity of our conditions and of our ideological concepts, a profound solidarity unites us. . . .
>
> We have common concerns, which have the same goals: the recruitment of youth in order to prepare them for a vocation; [finding] a solution to unemployment by the judicious use of unemployed labor; development of the rural sector; improvement of housing and health conditions by basic education; and participation by students at all levels in the development of our urban and village communities. . . .
>
> Our young people . . . must have a full awareness of the responsibilities they are to assume in the vanguard of a peace army, determined to struggle courageously and energetically against underdevelopment.

[1] "General Information," January 1965 (mimeo.). The Secretariat serves as a multinational clearing house, with headquarters in Washington, and provides a channel for contacts between national service organizations of different countries.

[2] "Proceedings and Documents of the First African Conference on National Service and Volunteer Programs," International Secretariat for Volunteer Service, Washington, September 1965, Document No. 21 (mimeo.).

Nahal-Gadna Values and the Politics of Development

In seeking to support these general concepts abroad, Israel has chosen a primarily pragmatic, nonideological approach, for conditions and requirements vary greatly from country to country. The Nahal-Gadna distinctions have been largely blurred in the process. In some countries military training is an integral part of the program (as it is in Israel), while in others it is considered undesirable; some governments insist on political indoctrination—others want to avoid it; Gadna appeals to one government, Nahal to another and a few want both types of organizations. Nevertheless, most Israel-aided youth activities in developing countries emphasize a common set of values. Briefly, these are: nationhood is a positive unifying force—culturally, politically and economically; young people have a duty to render constructive service to the nation; physical labor is honorable, essential and, at least potentially, dignified and edifying; education is the key to progress.

It is Israeli policy to organize and to teach, leaving internal political, military and social questions to local authorities and staff. However, since organized youth activities supported by governments are almost by definition politically highly sensitive, Nahal-Gadna programs have often been affected by domestic political events. This was demonstrated dramatically in January 1964, when Tanzania's (then Tanganyika's) regular army disintegrated after an unsuccessful attempt at insurrection, but National Service units, led and trained by Israeli officers, reportedly remained disciplined and loyal in their camps. The fact was not lost on President Nyerere, and shortly after the event, he requested the National Service to train 1,000 men on a crash basis as a nucleus of a new national army. The task was successfully accomplished within three months, and since then Tanzania's National Service has been regarded as a ready reservoir of loyal cadre for government, army and party service.

In the Ivory Coast, on the other hand, the Israel-aided Community Service (Service Civique) is designed primarily to train young men for pioneering activities in the hinterland. For the first three years (1962–1965) of its existence, however, it was administratively a part of the country's armed forces. Recruits serving two years in the army spent the first year in military training and the second year as members of the Community Service, preparing for agricultural work, and receiving literacy and citizenship instruction.

Here too, political events intervened, when Defense Minister Jean Banny, who had jurisdiction over the Community Service, was dismissed and arrested in September 1963.[3] Some months later the cloud that hung temporarily over the Community Service was lifted, with the blessing of President Houphouet-Boigny. In January 1965 the Community Service was administratively separated from the country's armed forces, but its orientation and the status of the Israeli advisers remained unaffected.

The flexible approach of the Israelis has for the most part enabled them and their Nahal-Gadna assistance programs to survive occasional political convulsions, as these examples indicate. Their flexibility has also resulted in programs of widely different form and scope, unified only by the basic Nahal-Gadna values.

Rural Youth Programs in Africa

In 1966 Israeli advisers were working in Nahal-Gadna type programs in 17 countries: Cameroon, the Central African Republic, Chad, Dahomey, Ivory Coast, Liberia, Malawi, Niger, Senegal, Tanzania, Togo, Uganda and Zambia; Bolivia, Ecuador and Costa Rica; and Singapore.

Many of these programs, particularly those designed for older youth, stress agricultural work, as mentioned in the preceding chapter. Israelis are convinced that the drift from the countryside to the cities, where appalling poverty prevails, can be slowed by offering young people inspiration and attractive opportunities for life in a rural environment. They know that they cannot bring all the attractions of the city to the countryside, but they hope that the appeal of the idea of nation-building combined with modern conditions of work and life will be sufficiently strong to have some effect in slowing the migration of young people to the cities.

[3] *Le Monde,* September 10, 1963.

A rural youth program was started in the Central African Republic in 1963, when 50 young people from the Republic were sent to Israel for Gadna training. After the completion of their training this group became the cadre for the Republic's new youth movement—Jeunesse Pionière Nationale, JPN (National Pioneer Youth). The advisers were Israeli Gadna and Nahal officers, the former to help organize JPN youth clubs in various parts of the country, the latter to give agricultural training and to advise on the establishment of cooperative villages.

JPN activities are conducted for eight hours a week as part of elementary and secondary school programs and outside of school hours in various youth clubs. The Israeli Foreign Ministry estimates that at least 4,000 young people are involved in various JPN activities. The primary goal of the JPN is to stimulate agricultural settlement in 6 government-sponsored cooperative villages, each with an area of between 250 and 375 acres. The villages are an adaptation of the Israeli *kibbutz,* with collective production but not consumption. Moshe Dayan, Israel's former Minister of Agriculture, who visited one of the villages in 1963, described it as follows: [4]

> There are 80 men members and two women members. Most of the men are married, but then only the husbands count. They want to arrive at 100 units by bringing in 20 girls from the movement in Bangui. Their budget is 150 [West African] francs a day [$0.60]—80 for food, 50 for clothing and 20 for pocket money.
>
> The main achievement is the fact that the people desire to remain in the village and that they have self-government. The instructor does not interfere in their affairs in any way. Their own committees distribute the food.
>
> Each family has its own room, the bachelors living several to a room. They are conscientious and thorough; they keep accurate records of work put in. They also have general educational classes and sports. A Central African woman works alongside the Israeli in the nursery school; the bigger children are driven to school in town.
>
> The two fundamental differences between the village and the surrounding ones are:
>
> Cooperative structure: the work is performed not only jointly, but on a steady and continuous basis under the direction of a committee. There are fixed working hours and rest days, recognized sick leave and annual vacation, and working hour allocations for study and sports.

[4] Moshe Dayan, "West African Diary (IV)," *Jerusalem Post,* November 26, 1963.

Modern agriculture: use of mechanical equipment, crop rotation, pest control, fertilizing, etc.

The cooperative settlement has not wrought a social revolution, nor was it expected to. Personal relations, the relationship between the sexes, the belief in spirits and sorcery remain unaffected. Nor has the educational standard been fundamentally modified . . .

Despite his generally optimistic assessment, Dayan makes it clear that few JPN members are interested in or suitable for cooperative village life. Moreover, a country as poor as the Central African Republic does not have money to establish additional cooperative settlements on the scale needed. The U. S. AID program, after intervention by an enlightened U. S. ambassador, provided $250,000 worth of equipment needed for the JPN, but such instances of multinational collaboration are rare.

Basically, therefore, the impact of Nahal-type cooperative villages, such as the one described by Dayan, must be measured by their influence on surrounding areas. "Our main problem is bridging the gap between our model settlements and the development of the traditional village," is the way Dayan put it.

The Guided Village

To bridge the gap, Nahal projects in the Central African Republic and in a number of other countries make use of the so-called "guided village" (*village en tutelle*) technique of relating established villages in some way to the model settlements or the Nahal training base. In the Ivory Coast 4 such traditional villages were being serviced in 1965, and plans in the Central African Republic called for 15 to 20 in 1965.[5]

In the Ivory Coast program 10 to 20 young volunteers were recruited into the Community Service from each of the guided villages.

[5] The concept, though not its form of execution, was undoubtedly derived from Israel's own "guided *kibbutz*" and "guided *moshav*" systems, in which the Israeli Ministry of Agriculture and the Jewish Agency jointly assume responsibility for guidance and supervision of struggling young settlements. The authorities extend technical and financial assistance, and the settlers in turn must follow instructions concerning cultivation, distribution of labor and methods of work. (See *16 Years of Agricultural Settlement in Israel,* The Jewish Agency, Jerusalem, 1964, pp. 47–50.)

After six months' instruction in Community Service principles and modern farming methods at the nearby training base, they returned to their villages, where, in agreement with local chiefs, a consolidated area of land was cleared and plowed with Community Service equipment and turned over to them for cultivation. They continued under Community Service discipline and instruction for an additional six months, during which time they received improved seed, three work animals, a plow and a cart on credit. They would not receive any mechanical equipment, but as long as they followed the guidance of the Community Service they could count on mechanized assistance with plowing and harrowing. By such methods, the Israelis hope to spread the influence of their Nahal programs gradually through the countryside, in cooperation with the traditional village leadership and at much smaller cost than the generally expensive settlement projects.

Although it is too early to know whether this and similar approaches have been generally successful, initial indications are hopeful. J. Mouly of the International Labour Organisation (ILO), following a field mission to the Central African Republic in 1964, reported that in one traditional village the introduction of poultry breeding raised annual per capita income from 4,000 CFA francs ($16) to approximately 20,000 CFA francs ($81).[6] Moshe Dayan reported: "At first the farmers would not undertake to follow the instructor's directions. Later, some of them agreed, and now, in view of the success of those who did, he is widely consulted."[7]

The guided village technique represents an ingenious modification of the Nahal pattern, though it is thus far only a supplementary activity. In the Ivory Coast less than 15 per cent of the 1965 Community Service budget was allotted to guided villages, and in Tanzania the technique apparently has not been used at all.

Training Bases and Model Villages

The training base and model villages related to it are the heart of the Nahal program in most countries.

In Tanzania the principal training base of the National Service

[6] "The Young Pioneers Movement in the Central African Republic," *International Labour Review*, January 1966, p. 26.

[7] *Op. cit.*

Corps is commanded by a Tanzanian officer with the advice of Israeli Nahal officers, and provides scouting instruction, political education, leadership training, rifle instruction and military drill. At the agricultural base new army recruits and servicemen preparing for agricultural settlement receive several months' theoretical and practical training in agriculture. According to Tanzania's current development plan, ". . . some 3,300 individuals will undergo training in National Service during the Five-Year Plan (1964–1969), half of whom will be selected for the regular establishment either of the army or the police, the other half being available for village settlement schemes."[8]

The training farm and the principal base were developed with these goals in mind. By now, however, the National Service Corps is also involved in various types of vocational training and in public construction. The development plan specifies that rural settlement projects for National Service are to be financed by the Ministry for Lands, Settlement and Water Development, but the Ministry's allocations as outlined in the plan do not appear to include funds for this purpose. Apparently little actual agricultural settlement of National Service men has taken place thus far. In one case an ambitious, influential district commissioner brought in National Service men to settle on the land, but planning and funds for the project lagged badly and neighboring state projects were pressured to provide mechanical equipment needed to get the project under way. While the National Service undoubtedly performs a useful function in Tanzania, its goals and program objectives seem less clear in practice than in the development plan and its impact on youth unemployment and other youth problems is apparently limited.

The Ivory Coast Community Service concentrates more fully than its Tanzanian counterpart on the goals of agricultural training and settlement, reinforced by the nation-building concept. The separation of the Service from the army since 1965 tends to emphasize this orientation.

The heart of the Ivory Coast program is the Ecole des Cadres du Service Civique (Cadre Training School), which in 4 years of operation (1962–1966) has trained more than 1,000 young men, mostly in

[8] *Tanganyika Five-Year Plan for Economic and Social Development, 1st July, 1964–30th June, 1969,* United Republic of Tanganyika and Zanzibar (now Tanzania), Dar es Salaam, 1964, Vol. I, p. 81.

agriculture-related occupations. The students, most of whom have had less than four years of regular schooling, receive not only vocational training, but also study the history of their country and people. Instruction is divided between classroom and practical work, with emphasis on the latter.

The school is under the command of an Israeli Nahal officer, assisted by several other Israelis and local instructors. Its primary pedagogic problems have been to instill in the students concepts of nationhood and to develop individual initiative and independent thinking. These are difficult goals that cannot be attained in a five- or six-month course, but the Israelis in charge feel that through personal example and with the aid of Israeli-trained Ivory Coast officers they have made a beginning.

What counts in the long run, of course, is not so much the impression made on students during their temporary stay at the school or at another Community Service base, but the lasting effects of this experience. From this point of view, the results of the first few years were evidently somewhat disappointing. One experienced observer put it this way: "The recruits came from many different areas, spoke many different languages, and simply did not form an effective homogeneous unit. Once they left the service, they dispersed, and there was no way of following up. Most of the time they did not return to their native villages."

The program for 1965, coinciding with an administrative decision separating the Community Service from the army, reflected radical changes in the policies and goals of the Service. A new policy emphasizing the recruitment of homogeneous regional and village groups was put into effect, in order to provide better continuity and group cohesiveness for those who completed their service. In addition, as described above, the Service initiated the "guided village" plan, which brings it closer to the village level, and offers incentives to Community Service members who return to their village.

Another important change occurred with the transformation of five Community Service farms previously attached to army camps into nuclei of regional or special service centers and "modern villages" (*villages progressifs*). By 1965 two such villages with some 120 settlers had been established. They absorbed over 55 per cent of that year's Community Service budget. The villages are similar to Israel's smallholders' settlements, with cooperative purchasing and marketing, common pasture and mechanized services supplied by a regional center, but with individual family cultivation and property.

One of the two special service centers is devoted to cattle, the other to poultry. They supply animals to the settlers in the modern and guided villages, and serve as training and demonstration centers for modern cattle handling and poultry production. For the time being the primary function of these two centers is expected to be to furnish extension services and mechanical equipment to the modern and guided villages in their neighborhoods.

It is too early to determine whether these modifications in the Ivory Coast Community Service provide the conditions for achieving lasting beneficial effects, which the original program was evidently unable to do. Conceptually, certainly, the present pattern shows much imagination. The concentration of the bulk of available resources on the two "modern villages," however, has been questioned, since these villages absorb only a small part of the approximately 1,000 young men who are in the Service at any one time. Some 80 more are being absorbed in the less expensive "guided village" scheme. For the rest of the young men the Community Service experience is a constructive but brief interlude in the difficult path toward adulthood.

The assessment of J. Mouly, based on his survey of the Central African Republic's program for the ILO, has relevance for many of the Nahal-type efforts in developing countries: [9]

> . . . in terms of tangible results, the contribution made by the [Nahal] system to the country's development is, relatively speaking, small. . . . But what is perhaps one of the fundamental aspects of the system cannot be evaluated in figures: this is the rehabilitation in public esteem of manual labor and of agricultural work. . . . the pioneer villages set a certain example in the fields of economic and social development, stimulating progress in traditional methods and in social organization . . .

Nahal Training for Women

Unlike Nahal in Israel, the Nahal-type programs abroad are, with one exception, limited to men. This is not surprising, for in most of

[9] *Op. cit.*, p. 27.

the countries where these programs have been introduced, only men participate in military and other types of national service. Moreover, social and religious barriers to the emancipation of women are still formidable, and both requesting governments and Israelis have therefore given priority to training young men.

The one Israel-aided program for young women is in the Ivory Coast city of Bouaké, where in the summer of 1964 the first camp of the Ivory Coast Women's Community Service (Service Civique Féminine) was established. Initially, 400 girls between the ages of 16 and 18 were brought together from all parts of the country for a year's training. The activities of the Service were financed by a French subsidy of $160,000—another rare instance in which a developed country financed the assistance activities of a third country.

The camp is managed by a team of five Israeli officers from the Women's Corps of the Israeli Army. The team has been headed successively by two former commanders of Israel's Women's Corps. During its first year of operation the program experienced serious growing pains, but also encouraging successes.

The first problem was to impress on 400 scarcely semiliterate girls from primitive villages the meaning of discipline and personal hygiene essential to an orderly educational program in a camp atmosphere. Within 6 months the camp population dropped from 400 to 300, mostly through voluntary departures. The remaining group, however, adjusted well, and seemed eager to take part in the training program. Tribal frictions, which at the beginning created many difficulties, began to subside, giving way to a healthy group spirit. "At first we had to discourage tribal dances and songs," one of the Israeli instructors said in an interview, "for this sharpened tensions. Later however, after the girls had become friends, we encouraged such activities, and by now the girls have learned to appreciate and enjoy them."

The curriculum consists of traditional school subjects taught by volunteer teachers from the nearby town of Bouaké and skills and discipline taught by the Israeli officers.[10]

[10] The local instructors teach geography, history, civics, arithmetic and French; the Israelis teach military drill, physical education, handicrafts, sewing, embroidery, gardening, music and so-called "social training," mainly group discussions on social and behavioral problems (e.g., "why the Government enacted a law against polygamy").

From the nearly 300 girls who finished the first course, 75 were chosen for an additional 5 months of training in such subjects as teaching, midwifery, or first aid. Most of them have since gone back to native villages as teachers and *animateuses* (catalysts), but return frequently to the Bouaké base for guidance. Some 20 of the group have been retained as staff members to assist in the training of new recruits. The second group of girls was trained in 1966, but received only six months of instruction, after which they were expected to return to their villages. Apparently no systematic plans for follow-up have been made for those girls who did not receive advanced training, though it was hoped that their experience at the camp would motivate them to act as agents of change in their home environments.

It may be too soon for a clear assessment of the program, but this bold experiment in changing the status of African women at the village level has already won high praise from Ivory Coast officials. At a public ceremony held at the camp, President Houphouet-Boigny expressed his appreciation for the results achieved thus far and congratulated the Israeli lady officers for "creating the motherhood of a modern country." [11]

Building National Youth Movements

No less vital than the Women's Corps is the work of the Israeli youth leaders who are helping organize Gadna-type programs. Costa Rica's former President, Francisco J. Orlich, was not being trite when he told the first graduating class of leaders for the Israel-aided national youth movement, Movimiento Nacional de Juventudes (MNJ) in the summer of 1965: "The youth of Costa Rica . . . has an obligation to become an instrument for progress and betterment." [12] The President's concern is understandable, for Costa Rica's population is one of the youngest in the world—75 per cent 25 years of age or under—and the population growth rate is the second highest in South America.[13]

[11] "Col. Werth and the Girls from the Ivory Coast," *Jerusalem Post Weekly*, August 26, 1966.

[12] *Acción*, August 1965, p. 2.

[13] According to the U. S. Agency for International Development, Costa Rica's population increased by 3.8 per cent in 1966.

Prior to the establishment of the MNJ there was little organized youth activity in the country. The university, of course, had its political student groups, and there were a few small Boy Scout groups, 4-H clubs and religious organizations, but for the broad masses of young people there was almost nothing. Even now the MNJ, which is strictly voluntary, reaches only about 1,500 young people between the ages of 14 and 25, but on the basis of the first year's experience it can be assumed that it will expand in the years to come, provided funds are found for its support.

The MNJ began in the summer of 1965, when 2 Israeli youth advisers organized a 3-month leadership training course for 42 volunteer youth leaders. The Costa Rican Government, though interested, had no funds to sponsor the project. In the end some funds were found, including a few thousand dollars provided by the U. S. AID mission. Salaries for the Israeli advisers were paid by Israel, with some support from the Organization of American States.

The trainees were carefully selected from eight communities on the basis of a written test, a personal essay, a psychological examination and local recommendations. The young men and women who emerged at the end of the three months of intensive technical training and ideological preparation gave promise of becoming excellent and dedicated leaders, by all accounts. They were committed to a minimum of two years of service to the MNJ, which means working at youth centers in their towns or villages several afternoons and evenings during the week. In field interviews in connection with this study it was reported that leaders are not paid for their work, but do receive token remuneration—100 colones (about $15) per month, if they do not have a job, half of that if they are gainfully employed.

With the help of the first group of leaders, eight youth centers were established. In December 1965 a second group drawn from other areas was scheduled for leadership training, so that additional centers could be founded. The busy, week-long program at the centers includes study groups to enable young people to complete their education; sports, folklore and social functions; special interest clubs and hobbies; nature study and scouting; and community service.

The impact of the MNJ on the country after only a short time of operation has apparently been favorable. The initial success seems to have been largely due to the superior quality of the leadership and to the strictly nonpartisan character of the movement. Those responsible for policy direction of the MNJ, proud of the democratic reputation of their country, have insisted from the beginning on avoiding political entanglement. This has not been simple for a Latin American youth movement, especially one sponsored by the government and launched during a lively presidential election campaign. It has succeeded, however, and the leaders of the movement have been trained in a nonpartisan spirit. When the MNJ's first Secretary General resigned his position to enable him to take part in the country's election campaign, for instance, every youth leader knew that the same would be expected of him if he decided to become active in partisan politics. Few, if any, have resigned.

The two presidential candidates in the 1965 election, on the other hand, were persuaded to issue public endorsements of the MNJ,[14] which undoubtedly helped safeguard its future.

Costa Rica's National Youth Movement, by the end of its first year of activity, was afflicted with the typical "success syndrome." Conceived as a countrywide mass movement with potential appeal to hundreds of thousands of young people, it had to keep growing. But expansion required more funds, more manpower, when there were not enough even for present needs. Budget plans for 1965–66 called for $80,000 in government funds, but whether that amount would be forthcoming was uncertain. Local community support was still lagging in some places, and even where it did exist, it could not meet the financial needs. Additional professional advisers from abroad were needed, but there was no assurance that Israel could provide them, especially after the OAS withdrew its financial contribution. An idea of combining Israeli leadership talent with U. S. Peace Corps talent produced affirmative nods among the people concerned, but little eagerness to give it a try. Thus, despite evident success and desperate need, there was a real possibility that a promising movement might stagnate.

In the Ivory Coast, where the literacy rate is 20 per cent (in contrast to Costa Rica's 88 per cent), the problem of a national youth movement is not so much stagnation as quality of local manpower and basic orientation.

[14] *La Nación,* September 19 and 22, 1965.

The Ivory Coast organization is known as Jeunesse et Travail, JET (Youth and Work), and its activities and concept are quite different from the Community Service (Service Civique), described earlier in this chapter. It was established in 1963 after four Israeli Gadna officers had trained some 50 instructors in a 2-month leadership course.[15] Previously a few young people had gone to Israel for Gadna training, but they had not been selected as leaders for the new movement. A visiting Israeli journalist observed, in fact, that the former Gadna trainees "are working in all kinds of administrative fields in the Ivory Coast, administering everything except what they are trained for."[16]

Unlike their colleagues in Costa Rica, the Israeli Gadna advisers in the Ivory Coast did not start from scratch. When they arrived, they found a few clubs in existence, administered by the Ministry of Education and designed primarily to help school dropouts obtain their elementary school graduation certificates. With the help of the Israeli team, the clubs were enlarged in scope and number and were unified into a national organization. By 1965 the movement reportedly had 35 clubs with about 5,000 members and some 120 instructors, who had been trained locally in courses of 4 to 8 weeks. Young people 12 to 18 years of age of both sexes are eligible for membership in JET. Its official program is very similar to that outlined for Costa Rica's MNJ, except that in theory it places greater emphasis on teaching the value of manual labor. Field interviews and observations revealed that in actual practice the character of the two organizations is quite different.

The educational approach and institutional structure in existence prior to the Israelis' arrival in the Ivory Coast continue to exert a major influence on JET, which consequently still has many characteristics of a supplementary educational program for school dropouts.

In theory JET is under the jurisdiction of the Ministry of Armed Forces, Youth and Community Service, which also supervises the

[15] Gadna leadership training normally includes physical education and judo, campcraft, "know your country," pedagogy, planning of excursions and hikes, topography, fieldcraft and field games, rifle and marksmanship, administration, drill, first aid and youth leadership techniques.

[16] Erso Konen, "Africa Has Its Own Realities," *Jerusalem Post,* October 18, 1963.

Nahal-type program, Service Civique, described earlier in this chapter. In actuality the Ministry of Education retains much influence over the content of the JET program, for the Ministry's 11 district inspectors share responsibility with the Israeli advisers for program planning and supervision of personnel. Many of the clubs are known as *centres de rattrapage* (retrieval centers), and in fact have a full-time program of instruction in elementary school subjects, to which Gadna-type activities are added in the afternoons and on Sundays. JET leaders—many of them instructors held over from the earlier program—are government employees with salaries at the bottom of the civil service scale (about $73 per month).

The importance of helping thousands of school dropouts pass their elementary school examinations is not debatable. JET's present proportion of 1 leader to 125 members leaves some doubt, however, as to its ability to succeed in this undertaking. A projected proportion of 1 leader to 250 members would certainly dim the chances of success even more. Moreover, it is hard to see how the nation-building goals of Gadna-type programs, including skill training and development of pioneering attitudes, can be adequately achieved in the time allotted to this part of the JET curriculum. At the same time it is understandable that those responsible for the policy of the organization are reluctant to give up its academic emphasis, which seems the only way to involve these thousands of illiterate or semiliterate young people in an essential educational process.

The Israeli advisers to JET appear to have made valiant efforts to reconcile the dual aspects of its program. However, there does not seem to be enough time, manpower and money to do both jobs well within the same institutional structure. For instance, the "work" aspects of "Youth and Work," though prominent in the official program, are virtually nonexistent in the actual program.

A clear definition of priorities and goals might result in a narrower effort, but would enable JET leadership to concentrate fully on those aspects which are of the greatest immediate importance to the nation.

The Chain Reaction Effect

Perhaps one of the most interesting aspects of the Nahal-Gadna programs is that they have spread to countries where there are no

Israelis to advise on their operations. The two following examples illustrate this process.

Peru's army in 1966 began an agricultural training and colonization program jointly with Oficina Nacional de Reforma Agraria, the Peruvian national land reform agency. The army has long been involved in so-called "civic action" programs, but this was its first attempt at agricultural settlement. The basic ideology of the new program—agricultural training of soldiers for later permanent settlement within a cooperative framework—is clearly of Israeli origin.

Leading officials responsible for planning the program reported that they had made a thorough study of Israel's Nahal establishment in developing their own pattern. Moreover, 10 Peruvian army officers were sent to Israel for a Nahal training course.

In another instance an African country wanted to establish some form of national service, and sought foreign advice and assistance. Israel offered to help, but for political reasons the offer was refused. Instead, two experts from another African country were brought in. One of them had received his own training in Israel, and proceeded to apply what he had learned there. Field interviews in connection with this study indicated that local officials had nothing but praise for his efforts.

While the chain reaction of national voluntary services for youth cannot be precisely traced, it is doubtless extensive. Particularly suggestive of this reaction is Israel's recent experimentation with a new type of volunteer for service abroad, who combines some of the characteristics of the U. S. Peace Corps volunteer, the Nahal recruit and the Israeli foreign expert. In this experiment Israeli youth, known as the "B'nai Hamoshavim" (Sons of the Villages), volunteer for agricultural service abroad on terms similar to those of U. S. Peace Corps volunteers, but perform their assignments on Israel-aided projects under the supervision of professional Israeli experts. They receive a small monetary allowance and a trip to Europe at the end of their assignment. It is an attempt to combine the pioneering spirit of the Peace Corps and Nahal with the professionalism of the expert. Out of it may come yet another form of Israeli cooperation with developing countries.

Chapter 8

Partnership for Social Development

THE PROGRAM abroad is designed to respond to a great variety of needs in the emerging countries. While agricultural and youth development are Israel's specialties, projects to aid in immediate improvement of the human condition also have high priority. Israel's policy makers are well aware that the program cannot satisfy every requirement of developing countries, but they contend that to the extent possible, Israel should be a "supermarket of skills, ideas and attitudes" for those countries that can use them.

Lighten Mine Eyes

Israel has carried out medical assistance projects in at least 10 African countries, but its most dramatic contribution undoubtedly has been the special program in the treatment of eye diseases and the education of the blind. Again Israel's own history and experience provided the background for its activity abroad.

When Israel declared its independence in 1948 there were 400 blind people in the population. Seven years later, largely as a result of the mass immigration of impoverished Jews from Iraq, Libya, Yemen and Aden, there were 4,000. From 1956 to 1963, with the arrival of Jewish immigrants from Egypt and Algeria, the number rose to 6,000. A government report in 1957 indicated that less than half of the blind had had any kind of education, less than a fifth were literate and less than a third were gainfully employed.[1]

Israel's response to the problem was an intensified program of treatment and education for the blind. The principal treatment center is the Ophthalmology Department of the Hadassah–Hebrew University Hospital in Jerusalem, headed by Professor Isaac Michaelson.

Because of the success of the program in Israel, Professor Michaelson was invited in 1959 to survey Liberia's needs for treatment and educational facilities for the blind. Out of his recommendations grew Israel's first international cooperation project for the blind. First, several Liberian nurses were given 6 months' special training at the Hadassah Hospital in Israel and a Liberian physician started several years' training in Israel under Professor Michaelson's guidance. Then, in 1960, a 30-bed hospital was established in Monrovia, staffed by a team of two Israeli ophthalmologists and the Israel-trained Liberian nurses. Additional local nurses were trained at the hospital. After the Liberian physician completed his ophthalmology studies in Israel, he joined the hospital staff. It is hoped that eventually he will take charge of the hospital and that Israel's participation will no longer be needed.

During the first two years of the operation of the hospital the Israeli physicians performed some 1,000 operations and saw 12,000 patients in the out-patient clinic. Patients reportedly came from all over Liberia and from neighboring West African countries.[2]

Following the successful experience in Liberia, a similar program was developed for Tanzania, and by 1966 plans were under discussion for initiating programs in Ethiopia and Rwanda.

These programs have been of importance not only to the African countries but to Israel itself. Since the inception of the Liberian project, Professor Michaelson's department has grown in scope, experi-

[1] "Lighten Mine Eyes," a pamphlet published by *Shalom,* alumni bulletin of Israel-trained students, Jerusalem, July 1963.

[2] *Ibid.*

ence and reputation. The department's research activities have benefited greatly from the research carried on by the teams operating abroad. To fulfill his foreign commitments, Professor Michaelson introduced a new service concept, according to which every physician accepted for training in his department commits himself to two years of service in a "hardship area." Initially the term "hardship area" applied only to service abroad, but recently it has been broadened to include understaffed hospitals in the least desirable parts of Israel.

When the program began, there was some concern that private donors in the United States who support the Hadassah Hospital might regard the foreign projects of the Ophthalmology Department as dubious diversion of resources; however, the opposite has actually happened, and supporters of the hospital take pride in its accomplishments abroad.

In related projects Israeli advisers and instructors have planned and assisted in campaigns for the eradication of trachoma and the education of blind children in Ethiopia. The significance of these activities is clear in view of the estimated 30 to 90 per cent incidence of active trachoma among school children in various districts of Ethiopia. An Israeli physician working for the Ethiopian Ministry of Health planned and organized a countrywide drive in which teachers were taught to administer the curative tetracycline ointment to afflicted students. The same physician conducted one-month training sessions in trachoma detection and treatment for health officers and nurses from all over the country.

Israeli specialists were also responsible for a new approach to education of the blind children in Ethiopia. They recommended that instead of being permanently separated from society, the blind be integrated into normal society as much as possible. In line with their recommendations, at a school near Addis Ababa some 120 blind children, ranging from 6 to 14 years of age, are taught academic subjects and trades, which include not only the handicrafts traditionally associated with the work of the blind, but also carpentry, toolmaking, bicycle repair and the production of umbrellas and lamp shades. As children get older, they are gradually placed in regular schools.

While the school's work is very valuable, its capacity is infinitesimal compared to the need. Officials of the school therefore hope to turn it into a training center, with short in-service courses on the education and treatment of blind children, not only for Ethiopian teachers but for teachers from other African countries. The school has no Israeli advisers, but most of the staff, including its director, was trained in Israel, and curriculum and plans for the future were worked out in consultation with Israeli specialists.

Israel's work with African countries on treatment of blindness and related problems is an example of cooperation at its best. It demonstrates the usefulness and potential of a limited, specialized program in which one country transmits to another particular knowledge and skills and, in turn, benefits from the effort. The potentialities of this process in international assistance activities have thus far not been fully realized.

A School for Social Workers

One of Israel's earliest projects in eastern Africa was a training school for rural social workers in Kenya, started in 1961. At that time Israel was just beginning to establish itself as a country capable of rendering assistance in development.

After an international women's meeting in Addis Ababa, an Israeli welfare expert was invited to visit Kenya, then still under British rule. The expert recommended establishment of an Israel-aided community development training institution, and the Kenya authorities were agreeable. When the Israeli director—a social worker by profession—arrived on the scene, she proposed instead a training program for rural social workers. Again the Kenyan authorities agreed, and in October 1962 the School for Rural Social Workers at Machakos opened its doors. The project was initially staffed and financed wholly by Israel, except for a small student fee of £3 ($8.40) per month.

The school offers a two-year program of studies to 25 young women 22 to 35 years of age, who must have at least 8 years of education plus a year's experience in teaching, community development or related work. The two-year course is divided into theoretical and practical studies—two and one half months of practical work during the first year in and around Nairobi and six months of practical work at the conclusion of the second year in the student's home town or village. The curriculum combines regular social work subjects with theoretical and practical preparation for work in general community development.

Despite the undoubted need for trained welfare workers in Kenya's rural areas, the graduates of the school have had a difficult time finding employment. The social work concept is new to village officials, and many of the villages lack not only funds to pay social workers but also a social welfare structure in which they can function. The central government, which participated in setting the educational policy for the school, also has found it difficult to absorb the graduates.

In tacit recognition of these problems, "rural" was dropped from the name of the Machakos school in 1964, indicating that it was hoped that some of the graduates might be absorbed by urban rather than rural communities. In 1965 the school became a Kenyan Government institution, although Israel continues to contribute to its support and provides the five-man professional staff. At the same time the school planned to expand its facilities and to put more emphasis on community development by offering in-service courses for community development workers. With its new orientation the Machakos school may yet fill an important gap in Kenya's educational system. However, its experiences of the first few years demonstrate the need for careful advanced planning before projects are launched.

Trade Union Cooperative and Advisory Service

In another sector of Kenya's economy, Histadrut, Israel's powerful labor movement, has made advisory service available to the Kenyan Federation of Labour. In doing so, Histadrut is following its policy of cultivating foreign contacts, which, as we have seen in Chapter 2, served as the starting point for the Israeli cooperation program abroad. As an influential labor organization that has successfully combined economic and cooperative enterprises with urban and rural trade union activities, Histadrut is admired by labor leaders from many of the developing countries. However, some of the advisory and related activities that Histadrut has undertaken abroad demonstrate that success in one environment is no guarantee of success in another.

In Kenya, for instance, the Federation of Labour, influenced by its then General Secretary, Tom Mboya, in 1963 announced the formation of an Economic Division based on the Histadrut pattern. Plans called for establishing a consumer cooperative chain of stores, a wholesale supply organization and a construction company, to be aided by a Histadrut loan and Histadrut advisers.[3] Most of these plans were stillborn, however. Only the plan for cooperative stores was actually carried out, with the establishment of two supermarkets in Nairobi. They were to be the first of a countrywide chain, managed by the Labour Federation's newly established cooperative wholesale society. In fact, numerous difficulties were encountered in attempting to establish local stores, reportedly because of poorly trained local personnel and the weakness of the parent labor organization. The Kenyan Federation of Labour, beset by internal problems and by competition from a growing state marketing system, was in no position to give the cooperative chain the support it needed to survive and expand. At last reports, Histadrut participation had ceased.

In Ghana, where the Histadrut model at first seemed most attractive and welcome, the attempt to adopt the Israeli pattern became hopelessly entangled in the country's internal political quarrels.

John Tettegah, Secretary General of Ghana's Trade Union Congress (TUC), after a visit to Israel in 1957, requested that Histadrut advisers be sent to Ghana to assist him, and Histadrut was happy to oblige. At that time the Congress was a loose federation of many small, often ineffective, unions. Tettegah wanted to transform it into a strong organization, capable of playing a central role in the social and economic development of the country.

Aided by his Histadrut advisers, Tettegah proceeded with plans for strengthening the TUC structure, and for broadening its base by organizing cooperatives, economic enterprises, women's organizations and youth groups.

Some of the internal organizational reforms of the TUC were acceptable to the country's leadership, but the major thrust of Tettegah's policy was not. Dr. Kwame Nkrumah, intent on unifying the country under his personal leadership, wanted no new foci of influence that might conceivably contest his power. In April 1961 the TUC and other public organizations were formally integrated into and subordinated

[3] A. J. Hughes, *East Africa: The Search for Unity*, Penguin African Library, Penguin Books, Harmondsworth, Middlesex, 1963, pp. 45–46.

to the dominant Convention People's Party.[4] The attempts to organize economic enterprises and cooperatives immediately ran into management problems and into powerful opposition from government circles and from competing organizations, such as the National Cooperative Council. By the end of 1962, Tettegah was out of office. Cordial relations between Ghana's TUC and Histadrut continued, despite these convulsions (and despite the earlier break between the TUC and the International Confederation of Free Trade Unions, of which Histadrut is a prominent affiliate), but the dream of a Ghanaian version of Histadrut was clearly dead.

Two apparently promising undertakings, patterned after Israeli labor enterprises—one in Peru and the other in Ethiopia—were narrow in scope and involved a minimum of ideological content. Both were limited to the establishment and operation of efficient bus transportation, based on the experience of Egged, Israel's Histadrut-affiliated, nationwide bus cooperative.

In Peru, an Egged expert on temporary assignment helped organize a bus cooperative in the summer of 1965. His work showed promise and it was hoped that he could remain long enough to organize additional transport cooperatives in the country, with help from Peru's Cooperative Institute, INCOP.

While Egged's work in Peru is too recent to evaluate, its earlier work in Ethiopia has already borne fruitful results. In 1961–1964 Egged supplied the general manager and the technical manager to the General Ethiopian Transport Share Company, the country's major bus company. During this period the operations of the company were thoroughly modernized and reorganized. Near bankruptcy in 1960, the company was able to report in 1964 net profits before taxes of almost 550,000 Ethiopian dollars (about $220,000) and an expected dividend of 12 per cent on paid-up capital shares.[5] Bus service in Addis Ababa as well as on interurban routes evidently improved significantly during the period of Israeli assistance. In 1964 the company carried an estimated 22 million passengers in Addis Ababa, compared with 12 million in 1961, but interurban service was still lagging badly.

[4] Ronald Segal, *African Profiles,* Penguin African Library, Penguin Books, Harmondsworth, Middlesex, 1963, p. 265.

[5] General Ethiopian Transport Share Company, *Report for the Year Ended 5th Pagumen, 1956* [*1964*], Addis Ababa, pp. 14–15.

However, the number of passengers carried on interurban lines rose from 250,000 in 1961 to 600,000 in 1964.

During their work in Ethiopia the Israeli managers instituted in-service training courses for local personnel, sent several department heads to Israel for special training with Egged, raised salaries and introduced differential fares favoring low-income areas.[6] Even after the departure of the two Israeli managers in 1964, the company retained an Israeli adviser.

In terms of its organization and operation, the company follows closely the Egged model, with one important exception—it is not a cooperative. The Imperial Court holds a controlling 35 per cent interest through the powerful Haile Selassie I Foundation, but the company operates much like any other private enterprise.

Attempts to copy Histadrut's broad social, economic and political structure have apparently not succeeded, although some limited, concrete projects have shown considerable promise. In this respect the Histadrut experience parallels somewhat the experience with youth and agricultural programs, in which imitation of the Israeli model proved unwise or impossible, but creative adaptation was often successful.

Scientific and Educational Cooperation

Probably the least controversial programs promoted on a significant scale by Israelis in developing countries have been those involving university education and scientific collaboration. Israel's place in the world of science and learning is, of course, well established. But its capacity to utilize its reservoir of knowledge for the benefit of other countries is severely limited by the demand for first-rate personnel in its own institutions. Israel reportedly has twice as many requests for assistance to academic institutions in developing countries as it is able to fill. It is therefore very selective in supplying academic and scientific personnel through its cooperation program.

In Israel's oldest academic and scientific assistance program, which has been in operation at the Kumasi University of Science and Tech-

[6] "Egged Experts Helped Ethiopia Modernize Buses," *Jerusalem Post* (Zambia Independence Supplement), October 24, 1964, p. xvi.

nology (formerly Kwame Nkrumah University) in Ghana since 1958, an Israeli professor was until 1965 Pro-Vice-Chancellor and Dean of the Engineering Faculty. Several Israeli instructors have been working in other departments there and at the University of Ghana.

After a survey of Ghana's medical education needs by the Dean of the Hadassah–Hebrew University Medical School in 1964, close relations were established between the research staffs of the Hadassah Medical School and Ghana's National Institute of Health. Several Israeli medical scientists have since worked at the Ghanaian institution. By their own testimony, they have perhaps gained as much as they have given, for their work in Ghana has offered them opportunities for research they would never have had in Israel.

Scientific collaboration between Ghana and Israel was further strengthened by an agreement between the Academies of Science of the two countries, signed in August 1965. The agreement provides for exchange of personnel, participation in scientific meetings, mutual consultation and exchange of information and literature.[7]

Numerically, the largest program of Israeli academic assistance has been in Ethiopia. Since 1959, when a professor from the Haifa Technion became Dean of the College of Engineering at Haile Selassie I University, many Israeli professors and instructors have taught at the university. In 1963 there were 14 Israelis on the faculty, including the Deans of the Faculties of Science, Engineering, and Social Sciences. However, the number has been declining recently, as Ethiopians, with strong encouragement from the Israelis, have begun to take over. According to present plans, which Israelis in policy positions at the university helped to formulate, instruction at the undergraduate level in many of the departments will be entirely in local hands by 1970. Arrangements have been made for Tel Aviv University to supply an instructor in Semitic languages in exchange for an instructor in Amharic from Haile Selassie I University. The Israeli orientation toward encouraging and developing the talent of the host country is well known in academic and government circles, and evidently has contributed greatly to the esteem in which the Israelis are held.

A much smaller, but in some ways quite important, program of

[7] *Jerusalem Post Weekly,* September 17, 1965.

academic cooperation has developed during the past few years between Turkey's Middle East Technical University (METU) and Israel's National and University Institute of Agriculture. This exchange is particularly interesting, for it involves the first conscious attempt to explain Israel's theories and experience in comprehensive regional development in another academic climate and expose them systematically to the scrutiny of students and faculty in another developing country.[8]

The program at METU is sponsored in part by the OECD, and calls for the development over a three-year period of a Department of Regional Planning in the university's Faculty of Architecture and Design. The department, initially headed by an Israeli, offers a two-year Master's course in regional planning. It also participates in research programs of related departments of the university and is expected to conduct its own research projects in collaboration with the Turkish Government, particularly the Ministries of Reconstruction and Settlement and of Rural (Village) Affairs. While the newly created department goes through its initial trial period, three promising young Turks are being trained in Israel, Japan and Western Europe as replacements for the Israelis and others assigned temporarily to the department.

As a general rule, Israel invests its academic manpower abroad carefully, but in a concentrated fashion. In Ethiopia, Ghana and Turkey, Israeli academicians have served in key positions in which they were able to fashion new policies or programs, train local replacements and foster the development of mutually beneficial relations with Israeli institutions.

[8] For further discussion of the theory of comprehensive regional development, see Chapter 6.

Chapter 9

Capital Assistance and Joint Ventures

"ISRAEL IS far too small and poor to extend financial and technical aid on the scale which great industrial countries can afford," reads the opening passage to a description of Israel's program in a Foreign Ministry publication.[1] The effects of the shortage of funds in limiting Israel primarily to technical assistance and in shaping the character of the program in other ways have been discussed in Chapters 2 and 3. However, Israel does make some grants and loans and also uses an ingenious combination of investment and technical assistance in so-called "joint ventures."

Loans and Grants

Strictly speaking, Israel does not have a loan and grant program analogous to the programs of the United States, Great Britain and other large donor countries. Yet some $20 million to $25 million in

1 "Sharing—Cooperation Between Developing Countries, Israel's Programme," Jerusalem (no date), p. 6 (pamphlet).

loans have been extended or pledged since Israel signed its first credit agreement with Ghana in July 1958, and several million dollars worth of commodities have been dispensed as grants.[2] Israel's loans and grants are usually extended in support either of projects to which Israel has assigned technicians and experts or of companies owned jointly by Israel and cooperating developing countries. A few examples illustrate the types of projects that have received capital assistance.

Malawi, in recognition of its independence in July 1964, received hospital equipment, medical staff and a two- to three-year nurses' training program in Israel. Kenya was given equipment and staff for a rural social workers' school, discussed in Chapter 8. In Gambia Israel equipped a dental clinic and sent a dentist to operate it. Equipment was donated to Tanzania's National Service, in which Nahal officers have been active (described in Chapter 7). One of the largest grants, reportedly $250,000, went to Upper Volta toward the equipment and construction of facilities for the Multipurpose Agricultural Center near Bobo-Dioulasso, discussed in Chapter 6. Many Israel-supported agricultural projects receive free seeds and some have received tractors and other equipment.

Loans have been extended to Ghana, Ivory Coast, Liberia, Nigeria, Sierra Leone and Tanzania—all countries in which Israel has relatively large technical assistance programs. The capital made available has been invariably for development activities (except in Ghana, where a small portion was earmarked for trade credits). The terms have understandably been more stringent than capital assistance terms of many of the developed countries. The biggest single loan agreement—for £3 million ($8.4 million) over seven years—was negotiated with Nigeria in 1960, and carried an interest rate of about 6 per cent. (See Table 9-1.)

Two thirds of the loan was for the Eastern Region: £1 million for construction of two hotels by the Eastern Nigerian Construction and Furniture Co., a joint venture between Israel's Solel Boneh Construction organization and the government of the Eastern Region,

[2] These estimates do not include contributions of $300,000 to $400,000 annually to multilateral technical assistance programs in recent years. The Israeli Government has published no statistical information on its loan and grant activities.

TABLE **9-1** *Israeli Loans to Developing Countries, 1958–1966*

Country	Loan	Terms	Date
Sierra Leone	£400,000 ($1.1 million)	0.5% above Bank of England rates; repayment over 5 years beginning 1 year after signature of promissory notes	8/16/60
Nigeria	£3 million ($8.4 million)	0.5% above Bank of England rates; repayment in 14 semiannual installments, beginning with issuance of promissory notes	7/13/60
Ghana	£3.75 million ($10.5 million) (£1.1 million—$3.08 million—drawn as of June 1965)	Trade and Development Credits. 50% credit over 5 to 6½ years on Trading Account (up to £200,000—$560,000) and Development Account (up to £7.5 million—$21 million)	7/4/58
Liberia	$3 million	[a]	[a]
Ivory Coast	[a]	[a]	[a]
Tanzania	£504,198 ($1.4 million)	1% above Bank of England rates, but no less than 5% per annum. (14 semi-annual payments to begin 6 months after signature)	Aug. 1963
	£55,000 ($154,000)	Same as above, repayable in 6 installments	Aug. 1963
	£600,000 [b] ($1.68 million)	[a]	1965
Inter-American Development Bank	$3 million [c]	Short-term bonds at 5 to 5¼% maturing in 1 to 5 years	April 1966

SOURCES: Israeli Ministry of Finance, except as noted.
[a] Not available.
[b] *Jerusalem Post,* May 10, 1965.
[c] Inter-American Development Bank, *Proceedings—Seventh Meeting of the Board of Governors,* Mexico City, April 1966, pp. 41–42; and *IDB Newsletter,* Washington, July 1966, p. 3.

£500,000 in cash and £500,000 for purchase of Israeli goods. The remaining £1 million was for the central Nigerian Government, which in turn lent 50 per cent to the Western Region to help finance projects of two other Israel-sponsored "joint ventures," Nigersol Construction Co., Ltd., and Nigerian Water Resources Development Co.,

Ltd. Disbursements on this portion were half in cash and half for purchase of Israeli goods.

In 1966 Israel also became a contributor to multilateral development financing through an international lending institution. It subscribed $3 million to a short-term $65 million bond issue of the Inter-American Development Bank (IDB)—one of only two non-American countries to subscribe.[3]

This step supplemented greatly increased technical assistance activities in South America and was part of an Israeli effort to enlarge its contacts and broaden its cooperation with Latin American countries.

Loan activity from 1958 to 1966 is summarized in Table 9-1.

The terms of Israel's loans have generally been similar, as the table indicates. Two interesting characteristics of the terms (not shown in the table) are that no strict distinction seems to have been made between program loans, which support activities within a broad framework, and project loans, which are restricted to a particular project; and that provisions for procurement have been relatively liberal, allowing large portions of the loans to be used for local costs or procurement from third countries. This liberality in part compensates for the relatively high rate of interest and short repayment terms. It also reflects recognition of the fact that in many branches of industry Israel's capacity as a supplier of goods and services is limited. The table shows not only the modest proportions of Israel's lending activities but the declining use of loans in its cooperation effort. Considering Israel's own increasing problems in obtaining external financing, this trend is not surprising.

The Concept of Joint Ventures

More important perhaps than loans have been the temporary transfers of capital and know-how from Israel to developing nations through "joint ventures." Joint ventures between foreign and domestic companies in developing countries, or between foreign interests and the governments of developing countries, are of course not new. Sometimes these enterprises are established to meet legal require-

[3] Inter-American Development Bank, *Proceedings—Seventh Meeting of the Board of Governors,* Mexico City, April 1966, pp. 41–42.

ments, to tap local capital resources or to conciliate local nationalistic sentiments. None of these considerations apply in any appreciable measure to the joint ventures that the Israeli Government has supported. These enterprises, the Israelis maintain, are set up to "create national instruments for economic development, incorporated in the developing countries and subject to the control of the relevant countries." [4] Mordechai E. Kreinin, in his study of Israel's assistance program in Africa, presents a more comprehensive description of the concept underlying the joint ventures: [5]

> The joint ventures embody important elements of technical assistance. They are potentially self-liquidating. And their objective is to leave behind a viable indigenous organization, supplying essential services and engaged in basic developmental activities. To that end each project calls for the training of local personnel at both the intermediate and university levels who will gradually, under supervision, assume central positions within the organization.

Accordingly, joint ventures represent a combination of capital investment and management and training functions. The joint companies have usually been capitalized at $300,000 to $500,000, with the Israeli partner holding between 40 and 49 per cent of the shares and the host government the rest. A majority of the members of the board of directors is from the host government as is the board chairman. The partnership normally is for five years, at the end of which the Israeli partner is supposed to withdraw and sell his shares to the host government. In the interim the Israeli partner supplies key managerial personnel, and is obliged to carry on a training program designed to prepare local personnel to replace the Israeli staff. For this service the Israeli partner receives a management fee, ranging from 10 to 16 per cent of profits.[6] These characteristics distinguish the Israeli-sponsored joint ventures from ordinary commercial partnerships in developing countries.

[4] Jacob Shur, "Housing and Organizing a Construction Industry in Developing Countries," paper presented at the Conference on Housing for Millions, International Confederation of Free Trade Unions and International Federation of Building and Woodworkers, Brussels, October 29, 1964, p. 6.

[5] *Israel and Africa–A Study in Technical Cooperation,* Praeger, New York, 1964, p. 137.

[6] Shur, *op. cit.*, pp. 11–13.

A further important distinction arises from the fact that the Israeli partners are not private entrepreneurs, but quasi-public corporations in which the Israeli Government has an important voice.[7] The largest of these is Solel Boneh, Israel's principal construction enterprise, which is wholly owned by the Histadrut Labor Federation, and operates abroad as the Solel Boneh Overseas and Harbour Works Co. Ltd. Others are Mekorot Water Co. Ltd., which operates abroad as Water Resources Development (International) Ltd. (WRD), owned jointly by the Israeli Government, Histadrut and the Jewish Agency; Zim Israel Navigation Co., owned jointly by the same partners; and Amiran Ltd., an Israeli Government export company. These companies function abroad in a dual capacity—as enterprises pursuing normal commercial objectives and as partners in joint ventures, designed to develop indigenous enterprises in developing countries. Only their work in the latter capacity is considered in this study.

Partners to Newborn Nationalism

Joint ventures first and foremost support the aspirations of developing countries to assume control over their own economic destiny. A recent sympathetic analysis of the African scene had the following to say on the subject of economic independence: [8]

> Two processes are considered necessary. First of all, the basic control over the national economy must pass into the hands of the country's own citizens. Secondly, this economy must be transformed, reshaped so that its old mercantile character will give place to something new. . . . The classic European, American, or Japanese "Industrial Revolutions" cannot be repeated . . . because none of the new states has a group of local entrepreneurs large and experienced enough to undertake this task. In the absence of such groups it is the political elite which must take the initiative, and it does this by using the power of the State, the machinery of which it controls.

[7] There are also partnerships between private Israeli companies, such as Mayer Bros. Ltd. and Federman Enterprises, and African governments or private interests, but these are primarily commercial ventures and are not considered in the present study.

[8] Ken Post, *The New States of West Africa*, Penguin Books Ltd., Harmondsworth, Middlesex, 1964, pp. 118–19.

In the light of this analysis, which also applies *mutatis mutandis* to non-African developing countries, it becomes clear why Israeli companies, in assisting the developing countries to achieve their objectives, invariably become allied with the governments. Such alliance is basic to the joint company concept, and it inevitably links the fate of the joint venture to the fate of the government that concludes the partnership agreement. By the same token it involves the Israeli partner deeply in internal economic policies and political affairs of the partner country, but without the power (or for that matter the desire) to influence these affairs. How this situation can affect the operation of joint enterprises is best shown by several examples.

David Hacohen, while Ambassador to Burma in 1955, had produced Israel's theoretical model for the joint company, but the Burmese Government did not form a joint construction company with Solel Boneh (which Hacohen had served as director before going to Burma) until early in 1959. A year earlier, the "honeymoon" relationship between Ghana and Israel had already resulted in the establishment of the Ghana National Construction Co.—a 49 to 51 per cent partnership between Solel Boneh and Ghana's Industrial Development Corporation; and of the Black Star Shipping Line—a 40 to 60 per cent arrangement between Zim Israel Navigation Co. and the Ghana Government.

The Ghanaian and Burmese companies apparently performed satisfactorily, yet all three partnerships were dissolved prematurely, at least a year before expiration of the five-year contracts. The reasons, evidently, were not primarily economic but political. Ghana in 1962 and Burma in 1963 made the political decision to nationalize many industries, including those in which the governments themselves shared ownership with Israeli partners. In the face of a major change in the economic policies of these countries, the joint partnership concept had to yield. The Israeli partners were understandably concerned, not only because the developmental goals of the partnerships were as yet unfulfilled, but also because the premature dissolution of the partnerships could affect their investments.

Zim, the Israeli partner in Ghana's Black Star Line, reacted gracefully and promptly, a financial settlement was reached, and Zim was retained under a management and training contract that expires in 1967. Solel Boneh, the partner in the Ghana National Construction

Co., sought similar terms, but was not given a management contract and simply left much of its Israeli staff behind under individual contracts with the nationalized Ghanaian company. It did, however, reach a satisfactory financial settlement. The Burmese experience was the least satisfactory for Israel, and in 1964 Solel Boneh lodged an official claim to recover the nearly $200,000 of invested capital and compensation for expenses.[9]

Another partnership dissolved before its time was in Tanzania, where in 1964 Amiran Ltd., the Israeli Government export company, voluntarily gave up its 20 per cent share in the government-supported cooperative marketing organization, Cossata, after two years of operation. A management contract, later scaled down to include only advisory functions, replaced the previous partnership arrangement.

In other countries where the partnerships have been established—Nepal, Ivory Coast, Sierra Leone, Niger and Nigeria—they remain in effect.

In their quest to establish themselves as "national instruments for economic development" the joint companies have often required considerable support from the governments of the developing countries, sometimes in face of competition from established foreign companies fearful of losing their markets.

Government support has usually come in the form of guaranteed government contracts or of a monopoly over certain key imports, as the Cossata marketing organization of Tanzania was given. Not surprisingly, established competing interests have protested and pressed for the elimination of the upstarts.

In 1963 in Western Nigeria, for example, when the Nigersol Construction Co. and Nigerian Water Resources Development Ltd. (NWRD) began operating on a fairly large scale, a campaign, reportedly promoted by competitors, was launched against the two companies. Although both companies had been established for the explicit purpose of developing a Nigerian capability in fields heretofore dominated by foreign firms, they did not escape criticism for receiving "preferential treatment" and the accusation of being Israel-dominated.[10]

[9] *Jerusalem Post,* February 4, 1964.

[10] *Nigerian Tribune,* Ibadan, January 28, 1963.

These charges, even if self-serving, illustrate a crucial problem encountered by the joint ventures. What forms should such partnerships take? How much preferential treatment should they receive and for how long? Can they be Israel-managed without becoming, in the public view, "Israel-dominated"?

The importance of these questions and their political and economic implications were demonstrated further when the two joint companies operating in Western Nigeria became deeply embroiled in the political convulsions that rocked this part of Nigeria in May 1962, with the downfall of Chief Obafemi Awolowo, leader of the powerful Action Group Party. For almost a year Nigersol and NWRD operations were paralyzed, with millions of dollars worth of equipment going unused, for both companies were considered instruments of Chief Awolowo and his faction. For six months of 1962 a federal commission, headed by Justice G. B. A. Coker, of the Lagos High Court, investigated the operations and particularly the financial affairs of a number of Western Nigerian public corporations, including Nigersol and NWRD. The commission concluded: [11]

> We are satisfied that . . . the Israeli partners have done their best to promote the business of the two companies . . . and indeed we have no strictures to make with respect to the activities of the two companies except with respect to the ways in which the companies have been used by the persons to whom we have referred [the Nigerian Chairman of the Board and certain Nigerian officials] for the achievement of their selfish and maybe criminal purposes.

In addition to these political problems joint companies have sometimes had difficulties financing and efficiently managing their enterprises.

It had been assumed by the Israelis that the partner governments, as the majority shareholders and promoters of the joint ventures, would finance or at least procure financing for the projects of the companies. However, this assumption has not always been realized, for governments of developing countries are generally short of funds and development funds from external sources are often tied to the procurement of goods and services from the donor countries. Fre-

[11] *Report of Coker Commission of Inquiry into the affairs of certain statutory corporations in Western Nigeria*, Federal Ministry of Information, Lagos, 1962, Vol. IV, pp. 38 and 40.

quently, therefore, joint company contracts have had to be contractor-financed, that is, financed on credits procured by the Israeli managers from Israeli or other sources. Contractor financing has not only added to the cost of projects and the burdens of the Israeli managers, but it has also often imposed an unexpected financing requirement on the Israeli parent company.

In other instances joint ventures have at times perhaps been used as instruments of government policy, without much economic justification. "Opening this last branch made absolutely no sense," a competent observer told the author in discussing a joint company in an African country. "The company had neither the capital nor the trained local personnel to staff it. But the Israeli managers were under orders, and did as they were told."

As the foregoing discussion suggests, partnership to newborn nationalism, envisaged in the joint ventures, is not without its complications and risks. Because of this fact, perhaps, Israel seems to be approaching new joint ventures very cautiously and with more reserve than in the past, though it continues officially to support the concept.

The chief Israeli delegate to the 1965 Congress of the International Chamber of Commerce, representing private industry, even proposed that the Israeli joint venture model be expanded to encompass short-term partnerships between private groups of the developed and the developing countries.[12]

Mutual Benefits

Israelis familiar with the joint ventures believe that despite the complications they offer valuable benefits to both partners. Unlike the ordinary commercial expatriate company, the joint venture company "leaves behind something of value"—an indigenously controlled industry or service, managed by a well-trained staff. The successful joint enterprise can at the same time offer both partners a fair return on invested capital, and can provide Israel opportunities for new commercial contacts abroad.

In Ghana, despite the premature dissolution of the partnership,

[12] *Jerusalem Post*, February 13, 1965.

both sides evidently benefited from the arrangement. The Ghana National Construction Co., while under Israeli management, gave a satisfactory return on investment to both partners. A number of Ghanaian employees of the company were also trained either in Israel or on the job. On dissolution of the partnership in February 1962, the Ghanaian Government officially expressed its appreciation "for the excellent services performed by Solel Boneh . . . reflected in the handsome profits that have accrued to the company," and voiced hope that "the training the various grades of Ghanaian staff have had under your tutelage will stand them in very good stead."[13]

As pointed out earlier in this chapter, the Zim Navigation Co., unlike Solel Boneh, retained management, training and overseas representation contracts with Ghana's Black Star Line upon dissolution of the partnership contract. Under the new arrangement Israelis continued in key management and advisory positions and Ghanaian employees continued to go to Haifa and Zim's overseas offices in Antwerp, London and New York for advanced training. The Israelis welcomed this arrangement and Black Star also profited from it. As of 1965 the Black Star Line had the almost unique distinction among Ghana's state enterprises of being in the black.

The policy of mutual benefit has not always been easy to implement, for the key officials of a joint venture have an extraordinarily complex task. They have two bosses—the government of the developing country and the parent company in Israel—with sometimes divergent responsibilities, mores and operating standards. They also have two major, not always fully reconcilable, goals—to make money and to prepare the company for takeover by nationals of the developing country. It is not surprising that managers and supervisors have at times found it difficult to work toward both goals at the same time; nor is it hard to comprehend that protecting the viability of the company has sometimes received higher priority than the goal of training indigenous personnel to replace the Israeli managers.[14]

The joint ventures have been of direct benefit to the Israelis in

[13] Shur, *op. cit.*, Annex B.

[14] See Kreinin, *op. cit.*, p. 143, who said in this connection: ". . . with a few exceptions the joint companies do not do enough toward equipping indigenous personnel to fill key posts . . . and are reluctant to entrust them with positions of responsibility."

various ways. Many young Israeli engineers, technicians and experts have gained invaluable experience by working for them. To some the higher foreign salaries have offered a welcome change from Israel's egalitarian wage structure. In certain branches, such as water development and construction, foreign activities have helped take up slacks that have inevitably followed the completion of major development projects.[15]

Finally, joint ventures have enabled Israeli companies to enter new markets with relatively small capital investment and under the benevolent protection of the governments of developing countries. Since in many of these countries domestic markets are closely guarded by long-established foreign or expatriate firms, the Israeli firms might have found it difficult to establish themselves without the partnerships.

To the governments of the developing countries the greatest attraction of the joint ventures is undoubtedly the opportunity to gain the services of experienced management and training for their own people, enabling them to establish indigenously controlled industry with a relatively small investment of capital and skilled manpower. The enterprises also serve as checks on pricing and marketing policies of other—often foreign-controlled—companies. Most important, governments know that this particular foreign partner is only a temporary tenant, prepared to leave the scene after a limited time.

To cite just a few examples of concrete accomplishments: companies in which Solel Boneh is or was a partner have built, among other projects, Parliament buildings in Sierra Leone and Eastern Nigeria, the international airport in Accra, luxury hotels in Eastern Nigeria, university buildings and 800 miles of roads in Western Nigeria, and military installations in the Ivory Coast.[16]

Despite the accomplishments of the joint ventures and the mutual benefits that both sides can derive from them, problems of control

[15] In 1964, for example, Mekorot, the parent company of Water Resources Development (International) Ltd., completed the complex $80-million Jordan-Negev project. (*Water Resources Development [International] Ltd.—The Company and Its Activities,* Tel Aviv.) This meant that dozens of specialists and hundreds of pieces of heavy equipment became available for other jobs. Their relocation was no doubt aided by the existence abroad of four joint companies, four branches and two subsidiaries.

[16] Shur, *op. cit.,* pp. 7–8.

and financing seem to be inherent in this organizational pattern, as the foregoing discussion shows. It has been suggested that comprehensive management and training contracts might accomplish the main goals of the joint ventures, while avoiding some of these difficulties. Under such an arrangement the share of paid-in capital heretofore provided by the Israeli partner might be supplied on loan by an international financial institution. Officials of the local company would assume responsibility for policy and would have control—so that there would be no question of foreign domination—but they would also have the benefit of expert management advice and a competent training program. The Israeli parent company holding the management contract would still have the opportunity to enter a new market and give its personnel foreign experience. Zim's experience in Ghana suggests that such a pattern might be acceptable, but whether it will replace the joint venture in Israel's program remains to be seen.

A noteworthy element of virtually all the development activities described in this and earlier chapters has been the preparation and training of local personnel to replace the Israeli experts. Much of this training has been informal and on-the-job, related directly to particular projects.

Parallel and supplementary to this type of training the Israelis have placed great emphasis on organized training activities within and outside of Israel. These programs, discussed in the next chapter, are the vital backbone of Israel's cooperation program.

Chapter 10

The Short Training Programs

MODERN Israelis share the longing of the developing countries for quick progress. "We cannot wait," Israel's former Foreign Minister, Golda Meir, told the United Nations. "We must develop quickly. As a friend from Kenya who visited Israel said, 'Must I walk in an age of jet planes, because those that now have jets were walking generations ago?' "[1]

Because they are convinced that time is a crucial political, psychological and economic factor in development, Israel's policy makers have emphasized short-term training in Israel's program of cooperation with developing countries. The two broad types of these short programs conducted in Israel are: conferences and seminars, organized to exchange views, ideas and information; and training courses, designed primarily to transmit Israeli attitudes and know-how. Abroad, a comprehensive system of training—the "on-the-spot" program—has been developed to supplement the work in Israel.

[1] As quoted in "The Rehovoth Declaration, 1960," International Conference on Science in the Advancement of New States, American Committee for the Weizmann Institute of Science, New York, p. 17 (pamphlet).

Conferences and Seminars

While the resources invested in conferences and seminars do not compare with investment in Israel-based training courses and in the on-the-spot programs, the conferences and seminars are regarded as important components of Israel's program of technical cooperation. More visible than the training courses, they promote Israel's public image as an international center associated with and serving the interests of the developing world.

The Rehovoth Conferences

The most significant of the international conferences held in Israel on problems of the developing world have been the "Rehovoth Conferences on Science in the Advancement of New States," sponsored by the Israeli Government and the Weizmann Institute of Science.

The so-called "Rehovoth Movement" started in 1960, when some 120 distinguished participants from 40 countries gathered in Rehovoth, home of the Weizmann Institute of Science, in an effort to "build a bridge" between the advances in science and the aspirations of emerging countries. Abba Eban, then President of the Institute, summed up the results of that first conference as ". . . an exhortation to new states to link their future to the scientific age . . . an effort to galvanize the scientific conscience into a deeper preoccupation with the problems of new struggling societies . . . the first statement ever fashioned through the joint spiritual interaction of two human groups —the leaders of new nations and eminent exponents of scientific disciplines."[2]

The delegates, many of them distinguished men of science and politics, engaged in 12 days of serious, often stirring discussion of the needs of the developing countries and the blessings that scientific progress can bring to the suffering masses of the world. The meeting was a forerunner of the UN Conference on the Application of Science and Technology for the Benefit of the Less Developed Areas, held in 1963.

[2] *Ibid.*, p. 7.

The same year a second Rehovoth Conference was held, devoted this time to the more restricted subject of "Comprehensive Planning of Agriculture in Developing Countries." It was attended by some 90 delegates from 38 countries, including ministers, planning officials, economists, sociologists and agronomists. A principal feature of the conference was Israel's interdisciplinary approach to agricultural development. Discussion sessions were followed by field trips to agricultural settlements and regional development areas.

Unlike the first meeting, the second Rehovoth Conference passed no official resolutions and issued no ringing declarations. One suggestion that seemed to have general approval, however, called for the establishment of a new international body "to coordinate and disseminate research and education based on this new (comprehensive) approach to agricultural planning." [3] In this connection Gunnar Myrdal, the distinguished Swedish economist, proposed that a center for regional planning and development be established in Israel, a suggestion enthusiastically received by the conference and accepted by Israel. The Settlement Study Center in Rehovoth, which conducts research and courses on problems of regional development, was founded in 1965 in response to this proposal. (See Chapter 11 for a discussion of the teaching program at the Center.)

The most recent Rehovoth Conference, held in 1965, was to have focused on the monetary and fiscal problems plaguing developing countries. It was attended by 81 delegates from 41 countries and, as in the past, was characterized by lively, even heated, discussion. Among the papers presented were: proposals for international monetary reform, by the former French Premier, Pierre Mendes-France; a new classification of countries according to types of underdevelopment, by J. Kenneth Galbraith, American economist and former Ambassador to India; a proposed massive transfer of capital to the developing countries, based on contributions of 2 per cent of GNP by the developed countries, presented by Israel's leading financial expert and Governor of the Bank of Israel, David Horowitz.

This time, too, there were no resolutions and not even proposals

[3] "The Rehovoth Conference on Comprehensive Planning of Agriculture in Developing Countries," Interim Report, Continuation Committee of the Rehovoth Conference on Science in the Advancement of New States, Rehovoth, p. 2 (pamphlet).

for new organizational or institutional arrangements. The main emphasis was on stimulating a meaningful dialogue between the two types of participants—the political or operating officials and the academicians and theoreticians. The difficulty of achieving this goal was indicated by Dr. Yadav Prasad Pant of Nepal's Finance Ministry, who commented, "there is a gap between the theories elaborated by the economists and the thorny practical problems encountered by the men of affairs."

Small workshop meetings on specific topics seemed to be more successful in promoting the desired dialogue than the lengthy plenary sessions and generalized speechmaking. But without the latter it might have been harder to attract prominent personalities from abroad, and to project the proper image of the conferences in Israel and abroad. Thus, besides dealing with monetary and fiscal problems—the purported themes of the conference—discussions ran the gamut of economic and social problems confronting developing countries. If there was any central theme, it was that there is no prototype or pat formula for the emerging countries to follow. Professor Dan Patinkin of the Hebrew University, one of the organizers of the conference, expressed this theme in these words: "From the very beginning of this conference we have been walking humbly. Different countries in different periods have found different ways to economic progress. The developing countries must take care to select as examples those patterns which are most appropriate to their own experiences."[4]

Short Seminars

The planners of the many seminars held in Israel on problems of development, sometimes under Israel's own auspices and sometimes under international sponsorship, face the perennial dilemmas of what subjects and field visits to include in the short time available and how to take account of the varied backgrounds and interests of the participants. The broader the attendance and the less time available, the harder the task of the planners.

For example, one seminar in 1964, on "Social and Cultural Integration in Urban Areas," had 49 participants from 32 countries of Asia,

[4] *Jerusalem Post Weekly*, August 20, 1965.

Africa and South America and in two and a half weeks was supposed to deal with problems of urban integration in Israel, regional planning and development in Israel, migration and health, education and integration, physical and social development in urban communities, problems of children and youth in urban areas, problems of integration in urban society and reports by seminar participants on their own countries. The program also included numerous field trips and a two-day tour to see holy shrines and visit a *kibbutz.*

So many weighty problems could not possibly have been handled adequately in the time available, especially in light of the many cultural, linguistic and educational disparities among the participants. It is therefore not surprising that the general "Recommendations and Proposals" that emerged from the seminar were uninspired. The participants undoubtedly did gain personally by their firsthand exposure to the Israeli approach to the problems discussed. These broadly conceived seminars should thus perhaps be judged largely in terms of intangible personal impressions and attitudes they stimulate among the delegates rather than on the basis of professional results. Seminars devoted to more narrowly defined problems and comprising more homogeneous groups of participants, on the other hand, have apparently been successful from a professional point of view.

One such specialized seminar was conducted by the Productivity Institute in 1965 for directors of the Latin American Productivity Institute. It brought together officials at the highest professional level, primarily for the purpose of exchanging ideas and information. Participants from Chile, Mexico, Venezuela and other countries made valuable contributions, although Israel's own experience and practice inevitably predominated, because of the volume of material available and the opportunity to see programs in action. While Israel took the initiative and, with the Organization of American States, sponsored the seminar, it also derived practical insights for its own development from the proceedings. This seminar thus represents an important landmark in Israel's avowed efforts to promote mutuality in its technical cooperation with developing countries.

Most of the seminars conducted in Israel, while related to Israel's training program, are not a part of it. Clearly, rigorous standards and specific achievements should not be expected from these activities and yet they form a valuable link in Israel's foreign cooperation program, providing opportunities for exchange of ideas, exposure to Israeli attitudes and on-the-spot inspection of Israeli achievements for many individuals from developing countries who would not be reached through Israel's formal training program.

Training Programs in Israel

Studying in Israel was a breathless, highly concentrated experience in learning new attitudes and skills to most of the more than 9,000 trainees who went to Israel from the developing countries between 1958 and 1966, but it meant different things to different students. To some it meant a glorious joy ride of little lasting significance; to others it was a profound, life-changing discovery of the twentieth century.

Of the short-term programs conducted in Israel, the training courses involve by far the greatest expenditure of time, money and facilities. Most of these last three or four months, and many are much shorter. Only a few hundred students have spent more than a year in Israel.

The Israeli courses are generally not designed for novices, but for experienced middle-level personnel. Thus, the emphasis has been on exposure of trainees to new attitudes and ways of applying skills rather than on teaching basic skills. While few if any basic skills can be taught in three months, new ideas and attitudes can be successfully transmitted in that time. When this is achieved, the hope is that trainees will return home inspired and ready to build on the foundations laid in Israel.

There are other, largely pragmatic, reasons why Israelis favor short-term training. The first is that because of the scarcity of trained manpower in developing countries, middle-level personnel cannot be spared from their jobs for long periods. If the training courses lasted longer than three or four months, which employers and families will usually tolerate, it might not be possible for people at this level to come at all.

The Israelis have also learned that trainees brought to Israel for short periods of highly intensive, controlled exposure usually carry away with them a more favorable image than those who stay for longer periods. The short courses, packed with organized activity from morning to night, leave little time for the inevitable loneliness, homesickness and linguistic and social frustrations of foreign students in a strange environment—problems that have hindered the effectiveness of long-term courses for foreign students in Israel, as discussed in the following chapter. Since the exposure to Israel is selective, the trainees encounter the most attractive aspects of Israeli life and society. Moreover, financial considerations favor the short-term approach. Since funds and resources are limited, the Israelis have had to choose between training in depth for the few or more superficial training for the many. In light of all the circumstances, the preference for short-term training is both logical and sound from Israel's point of view.

It is an open question, however, whether "education in a hurry" is sound from the point of view of the trainees, who are expected to absorb an enormous amount of information and many new impressions and attitudes in a few short weeks. Many of the participants in short courses interviewed in connection with this study indicated that they felt overwhelmed by the work load and the intensity of the schedule. This reaction was also borne out by a survey conducted by *Shalom,* the magazine for alumni of Israeli training courses. Almost two thirds of some 200 ex-students responding indicated that their courses had been too short. "Most of those critical of the length of the courses regretted that they had had time only to skim the surface of subjects which they had hoped to explore more thoroughly," commented an Israeli Foreign Ministry official.[5] (Other reactions to the short-term training courses are discussed later in this chapter in the section on "Impact and Follow-up.")

Selection and Preparation of Trainees

Considering the demands made on participants in short courses, selection and orientation of trainees are very important. Yet, as in programs of other countries, these seem to be the aspects of the short training programs that are the most difficult to carry out successfully, primarily because of the distance of the prospective trainees from Israel and the inability of officials abroad, sometimes only vaguely

[5] Yaacov Yannay, "Technical Cooperation Between Israel and the Developing World," *International Development Review,* September 1964, pp. 13–14.

informed and often overworked, to convey the flavor of the unique experience awaiting trainees in Israel. Ill-chosen participants, such as the foreign military officer who objected to working alongside enlisted men, the trainees who rebelled against doing physical labor and the lawyers who didn't know enough mathematics to understand lectures on economic planning, are examples of the kinds of problems created by faulty selection and inadequate orientation.

The directors and instructors of training establishments in Israel say that differences in the caliber, education and expectations of their students are among their most serious challenges. In an effort to improve the situation, they have sought to obtain greater control over the selection process itself.

The Afro-Asian Institute for Labour Studies and Cooperation, for example, suggests to the Foreign Ministry the national composition of the trainees in its courses. Candidates are recommended by their trade union and cooperative organizations and by their governments, and are often interviewed by Israeli diplomats serving in their countries. Whenever possible, Institute staff members traveling abroad and alumni of the Institute meet candidates and submit their recommendations. A selection committee in Israel makes the final selection.

The numerous courses conducted in Israel for trainees from a single country are more homogeneous than the multinational courses. For both types of courses Israel must rely heavily on the cooperation and competence of the officials of sending countries. These officials must recommend candidates to Israel and intercede with employers of prospective trainees to secure leaves of absence. Often they must approve the funds needed for international travel. The Israelis have learned that in order to assure minimum educational standards and a certain amount of homogeneity, the recommendations of these officials should be balanced by advice from professionals in the specialties being offered who have a thorough understanding of the Israeli philosophy of training. For this reason, active participation of Israeli training specialists in the selection of trainees has recently become accepted practice for most of the short training programs. The joint Israeli–Organization of American States (OAS) training program was one of the first in which this pattern was developed. Initiated early in 1963, it is one of Israel's most successful training efforts.

After consultation and discussion between OAS and Israeli officials, the following pretraining procedures were established: Israeli embassies and OAS field offices are supplied with periodic information on current and proposed courses. Courses are generally planned for groups of trainees from only a few countries at a time. Israeli and OAS officials in Latin America screen applicants from the countries whose nationals are to be included in a particular course. The candidates who pass this screening are then interviewed by a two-man team, consisting of an Israeli educator associated with the training program and an OAS representative. Based on these interviews, the OAS recommends participants in the training courses, and Israeli training officials make the final selection.

Careful selection procedures add to the cost, of course, but they also assure smoother course operations and better educational achievements. In a short-term program that emphasizes development of attitudes rather than of skill, suitability of the trainee is all-important.

Courses in Labor and Cooperatives

Formally, Israel's training program began in 1958 with a course on cooperative enterprise, held in the lecture rooms of the Histadrut Workers' College in Tel Aviv. Labor-related courses are still a major component of the training program.

Many of these courses and programs are administered by the Afro-Asian Institute for Labour Studies and Cooperation. The Institute was established in 1960 by Histadrut, with assistance from the American, British, Swiss and Scandinavian labor movements.[6] Physically, the Institute is probably Israel's best-equipped training center for foreigners. Located in a pleasant residential quarter of Tel Aviv, it has comfortable accommodations for up to 60 students, a well-equipped library, classrooms, social rooms and a permanent professional staff of 12, including the Director and 6 tutors.

[6] The Institute's orientation and sponsorship were perhaps natural in light of the fact that Histadrut has occupied and continues to hold a paramount place in Israel's own development. Maurice Samuel, an astute chronicler of modern Israel, writes of Histadrut: "There is nothing like it anywhere in the world, simply because nowhere else was a labour organization created under such conditions, and with such a purpose. It is at once a colonizing agency, an instrument of industrialization and a moulder of social forms." (*Harvest in the Desert*, Knopf, New York, 1944, p. 313.)

The goals of the Institute, according to its official description, are: [7]

> To train manpower for the Labour and Cooperative Movements in Africa and Asia in order to enable each movement to integrate more effectively in the general process of social programs and development of its own country. The study program is designed for trade unionists and cooperators, as well as for government officials dealing with development, labour and cooperation. It combines the study of basic ideas and theory with practical experiences and personal training in trade union work, and in cooperative enterprises and settlements.

The concept and operational pattern of Histadrut, with its combination of cooperative, trade union and management activities, pervades the training program at the Afro-Asian Institute. Whether this orientation is applicable to conditions elsewhere is debatable. What is not debatable is that most of the trainees at the Institute come from countries where there is little, if any, connection between trade unions and the cooperative movement. Their past experience has been as trade unionists, as cooperators or as government officials dealing with one or the other. To expect that after three and a half months in Israel they may want or be able to strike out in a new direction and combine cooperation and unionism along the lines of what they affectionately call "the big H" would be unrealistic.

Akiva Eger, the Institute's able director, has no such exaggerated expectations, but he holds fast to the basic orientation of the Institute. "Only a united effort between the workers' movement and rural development . . . can bring about social and economic progress," he says. "It is the mission of the labor movement to integrate the whole of a developing nation into a cooperative way of life." [8]

Nowhere else in the developing world has the labor movement been able to assume this integrating function. Sporadic attempts, such as those of John Tettegah of Ghana to model his country's Trade Union Congress after the Histadrut and of Tom Mboya's Kenya Federation of Labor to establish marketing outlets patterned after the Histadrut's *Hamashbir Hamerkazi* (Cooperative Wholesale Society), ended in failure. (See Chapter 8.)

[7] "The Afro-Asian Institute for Labour Studies and Cooperation," Tel Aviv (pamphlet).

[8] As quoted by Adam Ben-Horin, "Israel's Afro-Asian Institute" (unpublished paper).

Moreover, by combining trade unionism and coopera single curriculum, and drawing its students from both backg the Institute has inevitably increased the heterogeneity of its stu body and diluted the focus of its curriculum.

A 1962 study of Israel's assistance program touched on this problem, and also suggested greater emphasis on practical as against theoretical training.[9] Comparison of the curriculum of a 1965 course with that of a 1962 course (described in the 1962 study) reveals that this has been partly accomplished. The standard Institute course on labor and cooperation in 1965 allotted almost half the time to work in cooperative settlements, excursions or specialized observations, and placed considerable emphasis on group discussions of problems confronting the trainees' own trade union or cooperative movements.[10]

The Institute, like most other foreign training institutions in Israel, has a small full-time staff, and relies heavily on outside lecturers. This causes some qualitative unevenness and overlapping of instructional material, but Institute officials believe lecturers who are also practitioners have a certain freshness of approach which comes from being in daily touch with real life and its problems. Moreover, even in a polyglot country like Israel, it would undoubtedly be difficult and expensive to recruit a permanent staff with the breadth of knowledge and language facility required for the Institute program.

The Center for Cooperative and Labour Studies in Tel Aviv is closely related to the Afro-Asian Institute and yet different from it in important respects. The Center parallels the Institute, but works largely with trainees from Latin America. Supported mainly by the Foreign Ministry, with some contribution from Histadrut, its staff,

[9] Mordechai E. Kreinin, *Israel and Africa–A Study in Technical Cooperation,* Praeger, New York, 1964, pp. 126–32.

[10] Kreinin, *op. cit.,* pp. 127, 200. See also Afro-Asian Institute, Tel Aviv: *Program of Studies, Tenth International Course,* 1965; and *List of Study Material,* January 1964, p. 7.

In addition to two courses per year on labor and cooperation the Afro-Asian Institute also conducts special courses or seminars tailored more closely to specific needs of participants. Illustrative of this type of activity are courses on trade unionism for Tanzanian union officials and Kenyan printing workers and seminars on cooperation cosponsored by the International Labour Organisation in 1963. (Israeli Ministry for Foreign Affairs, *Pe'ulot Hamachlaka Leshituf Beynle'umi, 1962 U-Hatchalat 1963* (Activities of the Department for International Cooperation, 1962 and Beginning of 1963), Jerusalem, pp. 73 ff.)

, is drawn principally from the ranks of ……es not have its own quarters and uses the …… Workers' College. The Center's curriculum …nstitute's and is geared closely to the back- …… Occasionally the Center runs three-week …can trade unionists sponsored by the Amer- …bor Development (AIFLD), but these are …t superficial impressions. The Center also …, such as one in 1965 for Venezuelan rural leaders. Its most important regular activity are periodic courses in rural cooperation for Latin American government officials and leaders of cooperative movements held under the Israel-OAS training program.

Cooperative Agriculture Courses

Although Israel's cooperative agricultural sector accounts for only a small fraction of the population and total production, it occupies a key place in the political, economic and social life of modern Israel.[11] Israel's policy makers believe that in this sphere Israel has much to offer to developing countries, though they agree that the advanced form of collectivism represented by the *kibbutz* (communal settlement) is not exportable.

Training in cooperative agriculture is offered to Latin American trainees by the Center for Cooperative and Labour Studies. The heart of the three- or four-month courses on the subject given by the Center during the early years of its functioning were lectures and practical work related to the *kibbutz* or the *moshav* (cooperative village). In order to make these studies meaningful and useful, the Center arranged for the trainees to have firsthand experience in seeing and facing the problems of the settlers at a *kibbutz* or a *moshav*. But it was not always easy to find hosts in the settlements who had

[11] In 1964/65 the 8 per cent of the population living in collective and cooperative settlements held 20 per cent of the seats in Israel's *Knesset* (Parliament), and supplied two thirds of the value of the country's agricultural production. (*Statistical Abstract of Israel, 1964,* Central Bureau of Statistics, Jerusalem, p. 21; and Asher Zidon, *Beit Hanivharim* [The House of Deputies], Achi Assaf, Tel Aviv, 1964/65, p. 384.)

the knowledge, personality and language facility to give adequate attention to the trainees. There was, moreover, doubt as to whether the study of the *kibbutz* was the most efficient use of time for the trainees. In 1964 the Center shifted the emphasis, and gave its Latin American trainees a choice of practical work assignments organizing agricultural services (marketing, supply, etc.), planning the agricultural production unit or working at a *moshav*. Omission of the *kibbutz* from the period of practical work indicated a realistic assessment that this form of cooperation, despite its contribution and accomplishment in Israel, had little practical value for trainees from Latin America.

Courses in agricultural cooperation for trainees from other parts of the world are conducted by the Foreign Training Department of Israel's Agricultural Extension Service. They are generally shorter than those conducted by the Center, and are mainly for groups from a single country. These so-called "national" courses are an interesting Israeli innovation, which utilizes Israel's rich linguistic resources. The courses can accommodate trainees who, because of language difficulties, would otherwise be barred from foreign training. Because of the common nationality, there are also usually fewer cultural and educational disparities than in multinational courses. These courses resemble the Center's courses in general content, but there are differences worth noting.

The Foreign Training Department, as discussed in the following section, considers practical work and attitude-changing of overriding importance. A typical six-week course in rural cooperatives allows about three weeks for travel and observation, one of which is in a *moshav*. In addition, students are called upon to prepare independent exercises and discuss practical problems of the places they visit. Except for a visit of a half day, the *kibbutz* is omitted from the practical program, although it is covered in the lectures. The Foreign Training Department makes no pretense at being able to teach the trainees a great deal in terms of skills or methods of cooperation during so short a period.

The ideology and techniques employed by the Department can be seen better in the somewhat longer courses on agricultural extension and related specialties, which constitute the bulk of the Department's activity.

Ideology of Agricultural Training

The Foreign Training Department of the Agricultural Extension Service conducts courses in agricultural extension, cooperation, poultry husbandry, irrigation, agricultural planning, arid zone agriculture, fisheries and fertilizers; it also arranges and supervises dozens of individual training programs on specialized agricultural subjects. Since the establishment of the Department in 1960, courses and individual programs have multiplied.

"The basic orientation of our courses," explained Yehiel Admoni, a former director of the Agricultural Extension Service, in an interview in connection with this study, "is to reach down to the grass roots, getting officials and others to work directly with the farmer, and getting the farmer himself to participate in decision-making. Another goal is to convince the trainee that, given the right attitude and organization, he can achieve good results in his own country."

Gershon Fradkin, director of the Foreign Training Department, adds another dimension to these goals: [12]

> The course . . . can influence the attitudes of the trainees . . . One way of doing this is to try to inculcate in the trainee a sense of mission about his future task. He can be helped to see that by increasing production and preventing waste he is not merely improving agriculture but also keeping human beings alive and healthy, giving new hope to depressed people and areas, and helping his country to assume its place among the free nations of the world. We try to help him realize that it is his leadership and initiative which will prove most important in effecting changes, and that he must not wait for or rely upon government grants (which may never come) in order to effect changes.

The tasks that these Israeli officials have undertaken are by all counts among the most challenging of the current efforts to aid in the modernization of the developing countries. They involve not just changing long-established habits and beliefs, which is difficult enough, but actually opposing a tradition of alienation of the educated elite from the people and of avoidance by this elite of occupa-

[12] "The Objectives of Training Courses Provided for Students from Developing Countries," paper presented to the Ad Hoc Working Party of Selected Administrators of Agricultural Training Programs Intended for Trainees from Developing Countries, FAO, Rome, May 1965, p. 4.

tions most vitally required for economic progress of the developing countries.[13] Fradkin's description of the attitudes of many of the students attests to the difficulties involved: [14]

> Many of our students come with the idea that manual labor in itself is demeaning and that one of the objectives of obtaining an education is to place oneself in such a position that manual labor can be avoided.
>
> There have been cases of trainees who asked that all mention of physical work or practical training be eliminated from documents concerning them, including their certificates. . . .
>
> The majority . . . had previously learned only by rote. It was therefore a completely new and sometimes difficult experience for them to become accustomed to thinking things out for themselves and expressing their own opinion. . . . Many trainees prefer to be told what to do [and are] disinclined to take personal responsibility for implementing a job or making even minor policy decisions.

In response to these problems, the Training Department has evolved a dual approach. Classroom studies, discussions and observation tours seek to pierce the barriers of established attitudes and beliefs on the intellectual level. At the same time, trainees are put to work with highly motivated Israelis in collective settlements or villages, in the hope that the new environment, reinforced by intellectual preparation, will help to change the trainees' attitudes. Fradkin describes the process: [15]

> After working all day alongside a member, stacking manure or cleaning chicken houses, he is invited to spend an evening in his host's room or house. There, invariably, he discovers shelves of books, a radio and a record player, art of a high standard and conversation which is informed and intelligent. His conception of manual labor as demeaning and unfit for educated people begins to be shaken, and a new image of what a working man can be like begins to emerge. . . .

[13] In *Tropical Africa,* George Kimble quotes a report on the attitudes of the new African intelligentsia, prepared by one of his collaborators, A. T. de B. Wilmot: "Students freely admit that their main interest is to secure the employment which is at once the most lucrative and the least arduous or uncomfortable . . . Where materialistic considerations are dominant . . . ambitions toward any particular vocation show little rigidity. . . . In west Africa there is often some contempt for the illiterate peasant and no marked enthusiasm for rural occupations which would throw the educated man among such people . . . There is no widespread pity or sympathy for the illiterate." (The Twentieth Century Fund, New York, 1960, Vol. 2, p. 366.)

[14] *Op. cit.,* pp. 5–6.

[15] *Ibid.,* pp. 7–8.

> To uproot the fear of making mistakes . . . trainees are given small tasks to perform on their own responsibility. . . . [they are] gradually given more and more responsibility and thus afforded the opportunity to develop self-confidence. . . .

The extent to which a few weeks of this type of experience can change deeply ingrained habits and attitudes is hard to measure. It seems indisputable, however, that it is a first vital step in the process of transforming attitudes, and the Israelis responsible deserve great credit for having developed this approach. But in order to have lasting effect, this first "shock treatment" must be reinforced by other steps after the trainees return home. All signs, as indicated later in this chapter, point to the need for systematic, effective follow-up if the developing countries are to reap the fruits of an imaginative, dedicated training effort.

Community Development

Israel's community development training programs, primarily for women, were organized in response to suggestions made at an international seminar on "The Role of Women in a Developing Society," held in Israel in 1961. A year later the Mount Carmel International Training Center for Community Services was established in Haifa.

The objective of the Center is to "help women in developing countries acquire knowledge and skills which will enable them to contribute to the up-building of their country."[16] The Center's courses emphasize health and nutrition or, increasingly since 1965, adult education and literacy. The various organizational and educational skills associated with promoting community development in these areas are taught as much as possible from the point of view of the developing countries, with emphasis on improvisation and using to best advantage whatever human and material resources may be available in the trainees' own countries. In this connection, Israel's experience in organizing intensive language and literacy courses is utilized when applicable. Trainees are asked to report on projects they have undertaken or intend to undertake in their homelands.

[16] *The International Training Centre for Community Services* (Mount Carmel, Haifa), Department for International Cooperation, Jerusalem, and the municipality of Haifa, January 1963, p. 2.

An additional goal of the courses is development of informed, constructive national pride, blended with internationalism. To help achieve this orientation, the curriculum includes two weeks of lectures, discussions and lessons on the themes "Know Your Own Country" and "The World Around Us" and a shorter series of lectures and discussions on the "Aims, Functions and Institutions of the United Nations." Also, guest lecturers, preferably from countries represented in the course, are brought in to provide another perspective. The trainees may be asked to help prepare traditional meals of their countries, organize folklore evenings or prepare exhibitions of national arts and crafts, using materials from their own countries which they had been requested to bring with them to Israel.

Like the Afro-Asian Institute, the Mount Carmel Center runs a number of special activities in addition to its regular courses.[17]

The Center also offers short seminars of the type described earlier in this chapter. These activities probably take up at least as much staff time and effort as the training courses in community development. The Center thus fulfills the dual function of a facility for seminars and a training institution providing competent instruction in various phases of community development to women from developing nations.

Youth Development and Pioneering

The training programs devoted to youth and pioneering are both unique and exciting. Youth and pioneering movements occupy an honored place in the history of modern Israel and even now they carry out vital jobs in the defense of the country and the settlement of new areas.

When Israel began its program of cooperation with developing countries, the Defense Ministry, through its Gadna (Youth Battalions) and Nahal (Fighting Pioneer Youth) departments, which had been responsible for the Government's youth program, took charge of all

[17] One course in 1963 on handicrafts for home industries and cooperative marketing sought to combine Israel's cooperative orientation with the development of home industry skills. Another, conducted in 1965 under UNESCO-FAO auspices, linked technical training in nutrition and dietetics with study of community development concepts and techniques. (*Shalom*, December 1963, pp. 44–46; March 1966, pp. 37–40.)

foreign activities related to youth. The Ministry was equipped to do so, for it had especially designed agricultural and military training facilities, an experienced staff, and a ready organizational and administrative structure. (See Chapter 7 for a more detailed discussion of the Nahal-Gadna movements.)

The idea of mobilizing young people and soldiers for constructive nation-building tasks has always been of great interest to developing countries with which Israel has established contact. In August 1954 a Burmese military mission made an extensive tour of Nahal installations in Israel; in 1959 two groups, over 100 Burmese ex-soldiers and officers with their families, lived and worked in Israeli agricultural settlements for about a year. Formal youth training courses for developing countries began in 1960, with a group of 57 participants from both French- and English-speaking Africa. Since then over 500 young men and women have taken part in more than a dozen courses which have emphasized the Gadna or Nahal aspects of training.[18]

In 1962 the Israeli Foreign Ministry and the Ministry of Defense announced that a permanent youth leadership training center under the command of the Gadna Department of the Defense Ministry would be established,[19] but this has not materialized. The Defense Ministry operates an eclectic program, both as to content and frequency of courses, with the virtues as well as the defects of such an approach. Its chief virtue is considerable flexibility in accommodating different needs and backgrounds, but on the other hand there seems to be little continuity of staff, and consequently, some fluctuation in quality of instruction.

Two types of courses are generally offered: "Youth Leadership," which emphasizes Gadna; and "Youth Pioneers," with an emphasis on Nahal. Both types of courses include Gadna and Nahal-type instruction and visits to institutions or settlements of both organizations, but they vary somewhat in the proportions of time and attention devoted to agricultural training and to youth movement and

[18] *Israel's Programme of International Cooperation,* Ministry for Foreign Affairs, Jerusalem, July 1966, p. 89.

[19] "Youth Leadership Training Centre," Department for International Cooperation, Ministry for Foreign Affairs, and Gadna (Youth Battalions) H. Q., Ministry of Defense (leaflet).

scouting activities. The Nahal and Gadna courses for foreigners do not include military training as such, although students wear military uniforms and receive instruction in marching, topography and obstacle courses. Like Israel's other training programs, Nahal-Gadna training places much emphasis on practical and visual instruction. A Panamanian participant in a course for Latin American youth leaders noted that 60 per cent of what they had learned had entered through their eyes.[20]

A course of four and a half months on youth leadership and youth movements with a Gadna emphasis normally includes: study of world youth movements, including Gadna; educational problems of youth; pioneering and Nahal; lectures and discussions on Israel; visits to institutions, historical sites, settlements and towns in all parts of the country; discussions and workshops on problems of young people; organization of governmental youth institutions and youth movements; advantages of informal education; causes of juvenile delinquency and establishment of national service centers; social gatherings, sports and cultural events; some elementary Hebrew; handicrafts; parlor games.[21]

Like the Gadna courses, courses with a Nahal slant are sporadic, although Israel seems eager to promote them. Since 1964, Nahal training has been emphasized for countries wishing to stress agricultural modernization and pioneering. Nahal courses have been held the last few years for youth from West Africa, Latin America, Tanzania and the Central African Republic.

The course for young people from Tanzania is a good example of an "integrated project," in which training in Israel is combined with the work of Israeli advisers abroad. The participants were selected from a group of 90 members of Tanzania's National Service who had passed a noncommissioned officers' course under the supervision of Israeli advisers. Their 10-week course, totaling 528 hours of instruction, included the following: Nahal, public administration, agriculture, engineering, tours, Israel and elementary Hebrew. Public administration and engineering were novel features in this training

[20] *Shalom* (Spanish ed.), December 1964, p. 66.

[21] *Curso Para Dirigentes Juveniles de America Latina* (Course for Latin American Youth Leaders), Ministry for Foreign Affairs and Defense Ministry (leaflet, no date).

course, and the latter was included at the request of the sending country. Public administration—actually a euphemism for an assortment of "general background" subjects—was found to be a useful addition to the Nahal program, and apparently will be a standard feature of Nahal training for foreigners.

There is little doubt that Israel's experience in educating and mobilizing young people for productive national service has much to offer to developing countries. It may seem surprising therefore that Nahal-Gadna training does not occupy a more important place in Israel's total training program. The reason is apparently not lack of enthusiasm on the part of Israel's Foreign Ministry, which attaches great importance to its youth training programs and has expended much effort to promote them abroad, but more likely the close association of the Nahal-Gadna training with Israel's Ministry of Defense. While some developing countries do not mind the army connection with youth training and some actually welcome it, others object to it. In at least one instance, a series of training programs of the Nahal-Gadna type probably would have been organized had it not been for the military tie. Even more important is the fact that the army apparently does not assign sufficiently high priority to the youth training programs to assure them continuity in staffing and planning and excellence in instruction and teaching materials.

Military and Police Training

Israel's youth and pioneering training programs are recognized as legitimate technical assistance activities, but Israel's policy of exporting military and police know-how has sometimes been questioned. Military-type activities, it is said, are highly sensitive, and may embroil Israel in the internal or external conflicts of recipient countries. Advocates maintain, on the other hand, that internal and external security are no less important to developing countries than are new settlements and improvements in education. Israel's official position seems to be that it responds only to requests, and is not entitled to tell other countries what they may or may not require for their security. Because of their sensitive nature, few details of military and police training programs have come into the open. It is known, however, that military training has been given to nationals of a number of Asian and African countries, starting with Burma and Ghana in the early years. Among the more recent activities that have been publicly revealed, is the training of officers and men for Sierra Leone, of paratroopers for the Congo (Léopoldville), Tanzania and Nepal, of police officers for Ethiopia and of pilots for Kenya and Uganda.

An outstanding example of Israel's capacity in this sphere of activity was the organization and training of a paratroop corps for the Congolese Army. First, early in 1963, Israeli officers were dispatched to the Congo, while in Israel preparations were made to receive the Congolese soldiers. In August 1963 and again in November, Congolese units totaling about 250 men came to Israel. The first group was joined by the then Army Commander, General Joseph Mobutu (now President of the Congo), who, along with his soldiers, won his parachute wings in Israel. At the end of their course, 45 of the soldiers stayed on for advanced training as instructors, parachute-folders and arms maintenance specialists.[22]

A similar type of program was organized in 1964 for some 120 Tanzanian policemen. The Tanzanians and their Israeli instructors take pride in the fact that their unit reportedly is the first police paratroop unit anywhere in the world. In a newspaper interview [23] the Inspector-General of the Tanzanian police, Mr. Elangwa Shaidi, explained why his country needed policemen with this type of training:

> Our roads are poor, and sometimes an area is flooded and cut off from the rest of the country. Now, if such an isolated area needs police help, we can drop our officers to them from the air. And then . . . we have the problem of cattle raids by one tribe on another in the interior, where road transport is painfully slow. Now we will be able to follow the tracks of a stolen herd by air and drop policemen to arrest the thieves.

Besides the paratroop policemen, a small group of Tanzanian police officers and specialists have trained with the Israeli Navy to become Tanzania's first marine police unit. The main task of the unit was expected to be coastal patrol along Tanzania's 500-mile coastline.[24]

[22] "Congo and Israel," *Shalom,* July 1964, p. 22.

[23] *Jerusalem Post,* December 23, 1964.

[24] *Jerusalem Post,* January 19, 1965.

Conventional police training has been given in Israel to small groups of police officers from French-speaking Africa, and in 1962 the International Society of Criminology, Hebrew University and the Israeli Government, jointly sponsored a course on "The Cause and Prevention of Crime in Developing Countries." The course brought together noted criminologists and government officials from 36 countries, and its character was more that of a seminar than of training.[25]

While it is difficult to assess the scope and quality of military and police-type training in Israel, it is clear that the Israelis attach considerable importance to it. In turn, those countries that have taken advantage of Israel's competence may also have profited by obtaining assistance in a sensitive area from a country that is outside the structure of world power blocs.

Public Administration and Management

Unlike its military and police training programs, Israel's assistance in public administration is very much in the open. While training courses in public administration and management began in Israel as early as 1961, few have been held over the years, since working administrative officials are the hardest to spare in developing countries, even for short periods, and Israel's capacity for training in this sphere of activity is somewhat limited.

In recognition of these facts, the Israeli Productivity Institute, which is responsible for technical assistance activities of this type, has emphasized primarily training courses conducted abroad, some of which are described later in this chapter. On the other hand, the Institute has encouraged the inclusion of instruction in management and administration in training courses on other subjects conducted in Israel. As indicated earlier in this chapter, this idea has been accepted by the Ministry of Defense in its Nahal-Gadna training courses.

In a 10-week Nahal course for members of Tanzania's National Service lecturers of the Institute were given 4 weeks to introduce the students to such general subjects as psychology, sociology, economics and political science, as well as to the principles and practices

[25] "The International Course in Criminology," *Shalom* (French ed.), March 1963, pp. 24–29.

of good administration and management. The program was imaginative and included case studies, group discussions and assignments, workshops, student reports and "role playing" in simulated real-life situations.[26] This approach makes heavy demands on students, however. For many of the Tanzanian trainees, some of whom had had only eight years of schooling, the demands were in fact excessive. Furthermore, Israel's own continuing managerial and administrative problems suggest that it may be wise to provide only a modest training program in this specialty.

Ad Hoc Courses

One of the virtues of Israel's program of cooperation with developing countries has been a great flexibility in responding to particular needs. This flexibility is reflected nowhere more clearly than in the large number of *ad hoc* training courses Israel has organized outside its regular programs.

Prominent among the *ad hoc* courses have been medical programs, including various types of short training courses for nurses. Quite interesting and potentially significant politically were two courses for medical orderlies from the Portuguese colonies of Angola and Mozambique. These courses, held in 1963 and 1964, brought together several dozen male nurses of the Angolan and Mozambique Liberation Movements for four months of training at Israeli hospitals and other medical institutions. The courses were the first to be conducted in Portuguese, and involved considerable additional work and expense, since many texts had to be translated. Most of the participants had had previous nursing experience, but lacked training for work under the difficult conditions in which the liberation movements operate. The participants seemed gratified by the combination of theoretical and practical instruction received in the courses, and upon their return to Africa prepared for their movements simplified manuals on first aid and anatomy. *Shalom* called the training of Angolans an expression of Israel's "sympathy" with their cause.[27]

[26] *Prospectus of Course in Public Administration for Officers in the Tanzanian National Service Corps,* Ministry for Foreign Affairs and the Israeli Productivity Institute, Tel Aviv, June 1965.

[27] "Congo and Israel," *Shalom,* July 1964, p. 16.

Another *ad hoc* program was a series of short courses for training some 100 Tanzanian school inspectors. The program, which filled an important gap in Tanzania's development plan, was initiated after a visit of Tanzania's Education Minister, S. N. Elinfoo, to Israel in February 1962. Two Israeli educators who subsequently surveyed Tanzania's educational situation recommended the training of school inspectors. By November 1962–9 months after the Minister's visit—the first course got under way, with 22 students in attendance. The five three-month courses under the program were held at Gesher Haziv, a well-established *kibbutz* in Western Galilee, many of whose immigrant members from Anglo-Saxon countries speak English. The trainees were senior teachers or inspectors of private schools, and the course was therefore conducted at a fairly high level. In addition to lectures, tours and observation visits at educational institutions, the trainees accompanied Israeli school inspectors on their rounds.

The Tanzanian educators responded to their Israeli experience by recommending that Tanzanian schools instill students "with love and respect for agricultural work in general and for manual labor specifically," and that kindergartens in ethnically heterogeneous areas be established, so that from their earliest years children may find it "completely natural to respect one another as future citizens of a single nation." [28]

Other *ad hoc* courses have been conducted for construction foremen, tourist officials, merchant marine officers, telephone linemen, high school science teachers, radio writers and others. Study missions, often lasting only a week or two, have been organized on afforestation, banking, veterinary services, housing and other subjects.

On-the-Spot Training

By 1962 the officials responsible for Israel's cooperation program faced a serious dilemma. Training facilities in Israel were almost filled to capacity, personnel was short and, most important, funds for expanding training in Israel and projects abroad were insufficient. It

[28] "Knowledge Is the Key," *Shalom,* July 1964, pp. 52–53.

had also become obvious to Israeli policy officials that a large number of potential candidates for Israeli training were not being reached. Often those who could have profited most from Israel's brief, intensive courses were either key personnel, too busy and important to be spared, or personnel at too low a level, so that expenditures for high-cost travel to distant Israel could not be justified.

The Israelis responded to the need by the creation of a system of "on-the-spot" training. A few scattered training programs for construction workers and foremen had already been tried in Liberia, Sierra Leone and Nigeria by construction companies partially financed by Israel. Moreover, Israelis remembered that only a few years earlier they too had benefited from some refresher and training programs organized by foreign technical assistance personnel in Israel. But the on-the-spot training system which Israel has evolved is more than an occasional course here and there. It has become a significant part of Israel's program of cooperation.

The rapid increase in the popularity of this program may be seen by comparing it with the program of training for developing countries conducted in Israel. In 1963, 39 courses of more than one month's duration were held in Israel, compared to only 7 on-the-spot courses held abroad. In 1966, 59 courses and seminars were held in Israel and 17 on-the-spot courses were conducted abroad. In 1965, about 2,800 trainees attended 38 on-the-spot courses—substantially more than attended Israel-based training programs in any one year. Because of the inclusion of 9 first-aid courses in Niger, which attracted 2,000 participants, it was a peak year for on-the-spot participation. Table 10-1 shows the types of programs, number of participants, and areas covered by on-the-spot courses in 1965 and 1966.

There are similarities as well as marked differences between on-the-spot training and training offered in Israel. While some on-the-spot courses, such as agricultural extension, cooperation and public administration, are on the same subjects as courses offered in Israel, many of the courses given abroad are technical and cover subjects not specifically offered in Israel. Moreover, Israel-based courses are designed by and large for middle-level professionals or government officials. Training programs abroad, on the other hand, include courses suitable for all levels—from beginning technicians and artisans to executives.

TABLE 10-1 *Participants in "On-the-Spot" Courses, by Number of Courses, Subject and Area, 1965 and 1966*

Area and Year	Total	Subject				Number of Courses
		Agric. and Co-operation	Admin. and Finance [c]	Local Govern-ment	Construc-tion	
Total						
1965	2,784 [a]	286 [b]	177 [c]	250	71	38
1966	564	285	147	82	50	17
Africa						
1965	2,615 [a]	117	177 [c]	250	71	32
1966	315	50	133	82	50	[d]
Asia						
1965	28	28 [b]	–	–	–	1
1966	14	–	14	–	–	[d]
Latin America						
1965	141	141	–	–	–	5
1966	235	235	–	–	–	[d]

SOURCE: Ministry for Foreign Affairs, Jerusalem.
[a] Includes 2,000 participants in 9 first-aid courses in Niger, not shown separately.
[b] Includes 28 participants in a home industry course in Nepal.
[c] Includes 57 participants in 3 hospital management courses in Malagasy.
[d] Not available.

These courses began in Africa, but today they are used wherever Israelis are active–in Africa, Latin America and Asia. In Chile, for example, an on-the-spot course preceded other forms of technical assistance activities.

The first on-the-spot courses–for construction workers and foremen–lasted only one or two weeks. It was quickly realized, however, that for most subjects this period was too short. Courses now include from three to six weeks of intensive instruction, with additional follow-up.

Israeli officials have found that the on-the-spot training has a number of advantages over training in Israel. The most important of these are: participants study in their own countries under the same conditions in which they will work; local officials can help to see that maximum benefits are obtained; since courses are short, key personnel selected for study spend only a short time away from their regular tasks, with no time wasted on travel abroad; governments and other bodies involved do not have to spend money for student travel; after a course is finished, it is easier to follow up on the progress of the graduates and provide them periodically with additional information useful in the practice of their trades or professions.[29]

Frederick Harbison and Charles A. Myers, in a recent study,[30] pointed out the critical need for this type of in-service training in the developing countries. Upgrading of semiskilled manpower, they maintain, is more important than establishing high-cost vocational and technical schools, and should be a prime responsibility of employing organizations and local governments. On-the-spot training, using foreign experts on short-term assignment in combination with local resources, can be regarded as a logical extension and adaptation of this concept.

In the last few years Israel has experimented with various types of arrangements for the on-the-spot courses. The typical pattern that has evolved is for teams of three to five specialists to be sent to an area for varying periods up to three months. Schedules are drawn and instructors distributed in such a way as to reach the maximum number of trainees during their periods of assignment. A four-man team of agricultural extension instructors who worked in Uganda in the summer of 1965, for example, conducted 3 courses in 10 weeks. In the fall of the same year a 3-man team in Peru taught 3 courses in cooperative principles and practices during a 2-month period to almost 100 trainees. The system adopted in Peru is a good example of the economical use of time and manpower characteristic of the on-the-spot program.

Each course was divided into three weeks of intensive instruction, a six-week practical exercise without direct supervision and four or five days of recapitulation with the instructors. In order for the team members to conduct three such courses in two months, their schedules were staggered, and local instructors—preferably alumni of other Israeli-sponsored courses—were also utilized. A more concentrated and sparing use of available resources is hard to imagine.

[29] "On-the-Spot Courses," Ministry for Foreign Affairs, Jerusalem (pamphlet, no date).

[30] *Education, Manpower and Economic Growth: Strategies of Human Resource Development,* McGraw-Hill, New York, 1964, pp. 64–65 and 90–92.

Quality of Instruction

The quality of the instructor teams under such conditions is obviously crucial. The Israelis place a great deal of emphasis on the importance of close human relations between instructor and trainees, as discussed in Chapter 4. This is particularly important in on-the-spot training, since instructors are apt to spend most of their time in the company of the trainees, sharing their food, free time and, often, their living accommodations.

Frequently instructors take with them texts and instructional material prepared in Israel, including case studies drawn from the country where the course is being held.[31] This helps to make the instruction more meaningful to the trainees.

Normally, the training courses abroad begin a few days after a training team arrives in the country, leaving little time for the instructors to become familiar with conditions in the country. Unless they have previously worked there, this may limit their effectiveness. Lengthening the time the team has to get acquainted after it arrives might help, but it would also increase the cost of the program or necessitate a reduction in the number of trainees who can be reached. If the on-the-spot program continues to expand and if it develops a cadre of experienced instructors, this problem may diminish. Individual instructors or entire teams will then be going to the same countries repeatedly, and will have less need for briefings or get-acquainted periods.

Questions of Suitability

The rapid expansion of the on-the-spot program gives testimony to its popularity with Israel and other governments. Some officials of developing countries favor this training in their own countries as a way of avoiding "been-to-ism"—the adjustment difficulties often encountered by trainees from developing countries who have trained in economically advanced countries. An official of Liberia's Ministry of Public Works said in this connection that on-the-spot training "sweeps

[31] *Jerusalem Post,* October 24, 1965, reported that an on-the-spot training team on productivity, which went to Tanzania in 1965, went "equipped with more than half a ton of written material and audiovisual aids."

away the ever-present difficulty of students, on their return, struggling to adapt themselves and the knowledge they have gained to local conditions."[32]

Another reason for the popularity of the courses seems to be that they provide frequent opportunities for public exposure. Every time a course is inaugurated or concluded, there are official functions and interviews, usually well reported in the local press. Three short courses in two to three months can therefore generate more favorable publicity, and at less cost to all concerned, than if the courses were conducted in Israel. Local authorities, eager to demonstrate their own dedication to economic and social progress, are no less mindful of this opportunity for a good press than are the Israelis.

Despite these and other attractive features of on-the-spot training, there is some question as to whether it can upgrade the skills of participants sufficiently to warrant the effort; whether the itinerant teams function effectively in strange and constantly changing training situations; and whether this type of training can have a lasting effect on the attitudes and skills of the participants.

To Padre Martinez, the young Jesuit priest who attended an on-the-spot course on cooperation in Peru in 1964 after working for a year organizing cooperatives in northern Peru, the experience was entirely satisfactory. The course gave him badly needed background in administration and fired him with new enthusiasm for the ideas of cooperation. He also profited from the six-week practical exercise, for as the local representative of Peru's Cooperative Institute, he used the opportunity to work out a plan for expanded cooperative activity in his region. Others who attended the same course or a similar one a year later evidently gained less from the opportunity. The six-week practical exercise, especially, presented difficulties, for the students were expected to complete the exercise in addition to performing their regular jobs. Many of them lacked both the guidance and the time to do so.

In other courses on cooperation in both Peru and Chile some participants felt that while the quality of instruction was high, the three-week intensive training schedule was too demanding, especially for students with limited education.

[32] "On the Spot," *Shalom*, May 1965, p. 52.

These comments indicate not only the need for strong motivation on the part of the students, but also the difficulties of conveying ideological and emotional content—the prime ingredients of so much of Israel's training—outside the Israeli environment. Because of these difficulties, technical skill courses, such as road construction and first aid, probably have a better chance of succeeding in the on-the-spot framework than courses with a strong ideological base, such as agriculture and cooperation.

Former Agriculture Minister Moshe Dayan reportedly held this view, insisting that in agricultural training, at least, firsthand acquaintance with the Israeli scene was vital. One of Dayan's former assistants told the author, "It is essential to show trainees [in agriculture] the actual experience of Israel. The only justification for on-the-spot courses is shortage of money and the fact that some instruction is better than none."

Some Israelis with a great deal of agricultural training experience abroad have expressed a more positive view in discussions with the author. However, they too admit the limitations of on-the-spot training, and have recently suggested a modified approach. According to their suggestion, on-the-spot training in agriculture would be only the first stage of the training cycle, after which superior students would be sent for additional instruction to Israel. Nevertheless, Israel's official position is still that both skills and attitudes can be taught well in on-the-spot courses.

Impact and Follow-up

It is one of the perplexities of most technical assistance training activities—and Israel's program is no exception—that the long-term impact on trainees, which is the measure of ultimate success, is also the most difficult one to evaluate.

The Israeli course directors and responsible Foreign Ministry officials are naturally concerned about the long-term effect of their work, but because of the many vital operating tasks that occupy them, they have given this question only limited attention. Their usual approach is to hold evaluation sessions at the end of each training course, with instructors and trainees meeting both separately and jointly. Sometimes questionnaires are distributed to students. Useful suggestions for improving curricula and operating procedures often come out of the discussions and replies to the questionnaires, but their value in gauging the effect of the programs on trainees is probably minimal. In most of the short courses held in Israel, for example, the evaluation sessions come in the trainees' last days in Israel, which are crammed with farewell parties and departure preparations—not ideal conditions under which to ascertain students' true reactions and plans for using their training in their homelands.

Meaningful evaluation and follow-up with graduates of Israel-based training can begin only after the graduates return home, but the effectiveness of these activities is hampered by communications problems. On-the-spot course trainees may in theory be easier to reach, because they are in geographically more compact groups. To maintain systematic contacts with both types of trainees, however, Israel requires more staff and machinery than the Israeli Foreign Ministry or the sending governments have been able or willing to provide.

Some of the training centers and the alumni magazine *Shalom* have attempted sporadically to assess the effectiveness of the training program. The Mount Carmel Training Center, for example, surveyed its alumni in Kenya early in 1966 and found that 65 per cent of those interviewed were active in the field they had studied and were applying what they had learned in Israel.[33] In 1963 and 1965 *Shalom* conducted some limited mail surveys of alumni of Israel-based training courses. The replies indicated a high level of satisfaction with the Israeli experience.[34] None of the surveys, however, have provided systematic, objective data on which to base a general assessment of the training program.

Thus two vital elements in Israel's training program—assessing effectiveness and providing follow-up—are left somewhat to chance. Fortunately, some ex-trainees have spoken or written publicly about their experiences, because sending governments or international organizations require reports and assessments by returning trainees.

[33] "Israel's Programme of International Cooperation," Ministry for Foreign Affairs, Jerusalem, 1966, pp. 88–89 (mimeo.).

[34] *Shalom,* December 1963 and March 1966.

For example, a group of women who attended a Community Development course in Israel reported to the Tanzanian Government: [35]

> We can assure that the course has been very useful and very important to all of us. We learned some of the things we thought would not be applicable in teaching adults in the village, such as teaching geography, arithmetic as part of literacy. . . . After attending this course we feel that if we were given the chance of importing the knowledge we gained, it could help improve methods in teaching literacy. . . . All of us who have attended this course are prepared to prepare some reading materials to begin with, to suit the adults according to the methods we learned . . .

A Mexican water engineer who attended an OAS-sponsored course of "Water Utilization in Arid Zones" wrote: [36]

> As far as the utilization of water, soil and vegetation are concerned, which were my interests, this small state has much to teach the foreigner. These resources are used with great economy, which is incomprehensible for countries in which such resources are abundant. . . . Israel is a country of technical, social and economic achievements which elsewhere create controversy, polemics and fears, and for this reason we believe that anyone involved in developing agricultural production should make an effort to visit it. Countries which must face these problems should also endeavor to send technicians and technical missions, preferably specialist teams concerned with agriculture, in order to study the achievements there.

As might be expected, the flaws and uncertainties of the process of selecting trainees, discussed earlier in this chapter, are reflected in an unevenness in the effectiveness of the short-term training. For example, the wife of an African party official, after three months in Israel studying home economics, went back to her domestic duties, upon returning home, and made no attempt to share her experience with anyone. In contrast, Joseph A. Taiwo, a young poultry extension officer from western Nigeria, was so enthusiastic and successful in transmitting what he had learned, that he was invited back as a staff member in a later course.[37]

Even harder to assess than the knowledge and skills acquired in the training courses is their effectiveness in instilling constructive atti-

[35] "Report on Community Development . . . Held from 15th June to 30th September, 1964." Report to the Commissioner for Community Development, Dar es Salaam, 1964, unpublished.

[36] Report (unpublished) of engineer A. A. Brondo, Mexico City, October 1965.

[37] *Shalom*, May 1965, p. 67; and field interview.

tudes toward development and nation-building, which are considered crucial elements in Israel's training programs.

The Chilean participant in a Gadna course who after returning home decided to devote her life to land reform and cooperative development, or the trainee from the Iranian Agricultural Bank who told his fellow employees that "from now on I am prepared to go to every out-of-the-way and difficult place in order to serve . . ." no doubt represent the optimum impact that could be expected. More representative, perhaps, is the following dialogue between two Argentine agronomists, several years after they had returned from Israel:

> Trainee A: "The subjects we studied had no application to Latin America. The *kibbutz* for example is located on what for practical purposes is state land, and the Jewish Agency is a peculiarly Israel institution. None of this has any meaning to our work here or anywhere in Argentina."
>
> Trainee B: "Israel showed us how to stimulate colonization efforts in a new direction and along new lines, instead of the antiquated ones we were following."
>
> Trainee A: "Nothing we studied is immediately applicable here. Many other trainees also discussed this problem and felt the same way."
>
> Trainee B: "The most important thing to learn was a new attitude toward the solution of the problems of our countries."

It may be more than a coincidence that trainee "A" is a man in his fifties, settled and established in his ways, while trainee "B" is considerably younger and exudes enthusiasm for his work. Yet, despite their differences of opinion, both men spoke warmly of their stay in the country.

The personal attitudes toward Israel that the trainees who have been there carry back to their homelands are, of course, of particular concern to Israeli officials. One way of retaining and strengthening the bonds between Israel and the alumni has been through sporadic correspondence of Israeli training institutions or instructors with their alumni. Some presumably permanent contacts have developed in this way, and training directors complain that they cannot keep up with the volume of correspondence. Normally, however, this type of contact tapers off with the passage of time, especially since the initiative depends on the alumni and not on their Israeli correspondents.

Israel's own principal means of maintaining contacts with trainees has been the lively, well-illustrated magazine *Shalom* (which is a greeting, meaning literally "peace"), distributed free to all alumni of Israel's training programs. *Shalom* began publication in February 1962 as a means of ". . . keeping abreast of daily life in Israel, new courses, progress attained, new methods of instruction, receiving news from fellow-trainees, sharing the ex-trainees' experiences . . . information and ideas."[38]

The magazine is published in English and French (6,500 and 2,600 copies, respectively), and in July 1964 a Spanish edition (2,000 copies) with somewhat different text was added. But *Shalom's* ambitious and promising goals have been only partly fulfilled. Although the public relations aspects—new courses, achievements of Israel's technical assistance abroad, accomplishments of alumni—are well represented in its columns, it has not become a serious organ for the exchange of information and experience. Even as a kind of house organ, however, *Shalom's* role is limited by lack of staff and budget, and it appears only twice a year.

Despite these limitations, the magazine has played an important part in keeping alive the personal bonds between trainees and Israel. Its issue of March 1966, for instance, acknowledged receipt of more than 200 letters, and published excerpts from the most interesting among them. In addition, *Shalom* has two special projects to its credit: it has encouraged the establishment of alumni clubs in various foreign countries, and in 1963 it promoted the previously mentioned alumni survey, which yielded almost 200 replies and resulted in useful improvements in the training program, including the utilization of alumni as staff members in new courses.[39]

The first of the alumni associations, known in some countries as "Shalom clubs," was organized in the Central African Republic in 1962, under the patronage of the former President of the Republic, M. David Dacko. Others have been established elsewhere in Africa and in Latin America and Asia, with varying degrees of success. But while they may have strengthened the bonds with Israel, they have also at times been sources of irritation. In some countries (Ghana under Nkrumah, for example) attempts to organize such groups were

[38] *Shalom,* February 1962, p. 1.

[39] "Inquiry Concerning Studies in Israel," *Shalom,* December 1963, pp. 33–41.

regarded by the government with deep suspicion, while in at least one country the association became a special interest lobby and a financial burden on the Israeli Embassy. Nevertheless, the associations continue to have Israel's qualified blessing, as a logical and relatively inexpensive means of retaining the friendship of ex-trainees and of maintaining even a limited follow-up on the effectiveness of their Israeli training.

Judging by the voluminous but admittedly scattered evidence collected in the course of this study, the short training programs, both in Israel and abroad, have had a dual impact: they have changed the attitudes of many trainees and imparted new insights or techniques; at another level, they have made many friends for Israel and greatly enhanced its reputation.

Chapter 11

Academic and Vocational Programs

ISRAEL'S long-term academic and vocational training program is on a much smaller scale than its short programs. During 1964 there were some 420 students in Israel pursuing long-term studies, in contrast to about 2,000 participants in short programs. An estimated two thirds of the long-term students were attending institutions of higher learning, while the rest were receiving vocational training or pursuing individual courses of study. While less than 300 academic students from developing countries may seem to be a small number, it compares fairly well with the number of students from the developing countries studying in some of the smaller Western European countries.[1] Moreover, because of the higher cost per student, total cost to Israel of

[1] Angus Maddison, in an OECD study, gave the following figures for students from developing countries at higher educational institutions under official bilateral technical assistance grants in 1962: Belgium, 1,329; Denmark, 34; Netherlands, 105; Norway, 20; Portugal, 389 (plus 650 in secondary schools); Sweden, 40; and Switzerland, 156. These figures, some of which are estimated, are not exactly comparable with figures given above for Israel, but they provide a rough basis for comparison. *Foreign Skills and Technical Assistance in Economic Development,* Paris, October 1965, p. 55.

these long-term programs in 1964 was probably no less than that of the short programs.

Although individuals from developing countries have been pursuing long-term studies in Israel since the late 1950's, organized programs began only in 1961, the year that also saw the greatest expansion in short programs. Israel's long-term training courses for students from developing countries strike a middle ground between the entirely separate institutions established in some countries (Moscow's Lumumba University, for example) and the practice in the majority of countries, which make no special provisions and expect these students to adapt to regular programs of their institutions of higher learning.

Long-Term Courses

The predominant pattern in Israel has been to provide special programs in English or French, but to offer them in established educational institutions. Five special curricula have been developed, including medicine, nursing, agricultural engineering, comprehensive rural planning and vocational education. Most long-term students from developing countries have been enrolled in one of these courses, although some "individual trainees" have worked on their own under the guidance of advisers or have overcome the language barrier and pursued regular courses of study conducted in Hebrew.

Medical Training

The Hebrew University–Hadassah Medical School in Jerusalem was founded a year after Israel's achievement of its independence in 1949. It has graduated more than 800 doctors, who have completed a 6-year course of instruction plus 1 year of internship.

The course for students from developing countries, cosponsored by the World Health Organization (WHO) and the Israeli Government, was inaugurated in 1961 with 15 students from 8 countries. By 1965 it had approximately 70 students from more than 18 countries. The program offered is identical to that offered to Israeli students at the medical school, except that instruction during the first four years of preclinical training is largely in English.[2] During this period students are expected to learn enough Hebrew (in special courses provided by the university) to enable them to take part in clinical training, involving frequent patient and staff contact, which of necessity requires a knowledge of Hebrew. Despite the efforts of the administration and many of the students, the language problem has been a major difficulty, and has contributed to the adjustment problems of the students.

On the other hand, the university, unlike many of the short-term training institutions, has not been beset by problems of uneven educational backgrounds. Admission requirements are standardized and carefully observed. Candidates are interviewed by joint committees representing the candidate's own government, the Israeli Government and WHO; final selection is by the medical school itself. The procedure seems to have worked well, and the caliber of the student body is high.

While the quality of instruction in the course is by all accounts also very good, the regular Israeli medical training—preparing doctors to work in Israel, with its advanced system of medical care and high health standards—cannot equip young African doctors fully for many of the challenges they will face at home, where the climate is tropical, health standards low and resources few.[3] Those responsible for the course are well aware of this problem, which students from developing countries generally encounter in medical training in more advanced countries. The Israelis hope to facilitate the later adjustment of the medical students to their home environments by arranging for rotating internships in the seventh year at approved institutions in their own countries. This would give students, after an absence of

[2] During the first 5 trimesters (a trimester is a third of the academic year, or 10 to 12 weeks) instruction is entirely in English; after that some Hebrew is introduced, but practical work continues to be in English and examinations and tests are in English.

[3] Israel has a doctor to population ratio of about 1:400, the highest in the world. It has all but eliminated the major epidemic diseases from the country, and infant mortality among the Jewish population has fallen to 22.7 per 1,000 live births, one of the lowest rates in the world. (*Israel Government Yearbook 5725* [1964/65], Central Office of Information, Jerusalem; and 1965 Medical Course prospectus of the Hebrew University–Hadassah Medical School, Jerusalem.)

six years, a year in which to adjust both professionally and psychologically to conditions at home.

The Israeli Government has attached considerable importance to the medical training course, not only for its unquestionable contribution to a vital need of the developing countries, but also because it has enhanced Israel's prestige as an international center of learning. Yet after five years of operation the Foreign Ministry evidently concluded that the returns had not justified the high expense of running the program. Therefore no new students are being admitted to the special program, although scholarships from the Israeli Government and WHO are still available for a small number of new medical students from developing countries who are prepared to enroll in the regular courses at the Hebrew University–Hadassah Medical School.

Nursing Training

Israel's training efforts in health have included some short courses in various nursing specialties, as indicated in the preceding chapter. In addition, Israel has sponsored long-term (three-year) nursing courses leading to an R.N. degree for African students. Since 1961 three such courses have been conducted for some 35 student nurses from the Congo (Brazzaville), Malawi and Liberia. The language problem for these students has been more serious than for the medical students, because, while the lectures for student nurses have been in French or English, practical training has required patient and staff contact from the very beginning. Knowledge of Hebrew has therefore been an immediate and urgent necessity. Some of the students, however, have been shocked to learn after arrival in Israel that they would be required to enroll in classes for intensive Hebrew instruction before and during their training. This reaction indicates that their predeparture orientation has been inadequate.

The curriculum prepared for the African nursing students paralleled that for Israeli students at the same institution, except for the addition of special subjects particularly needed by nurses in Africa. These included midwifery and tropical medicine. Although the African nursing students appear to have received very good training, some evidently had gaps in their educational background, and many of them encountered language and adjustment problems. In view of the difficulties and the growth of nursing education facilities in Africa, Israel is shifting its emphasis in nursing training to shorter, specialized courses at an advanced level. One of these, initiated in 1966, provides nine months of training for registered nurses in ward administration and operating room procedures.

Agricultural Engineering

A different specialty, for which training facilities are not yet so readily available in the developing countries, is agricultural engineering. A special English-language program in this subject for students from developing countries has been under way at the Israeli Institute for Technology, known as the "Technion," since 1962. The course, leading to a B.S. degree, is open to about 30 new students a year. It graduated its first class, of 24 students, in 1966.

The students follow the regular curriculum for their specialty, and in addition receive instruction in tropical agriculture. In the third year they specialize in such subjects as soil and water conservation, farm construction or agricultural machinery. Language is less of a problem for these students than for the medical and nursing students, since their work does not require frequent contact with the Hebrew-speaking public. While there have been some difficulties with the educational background of the students, the program is considered a success. In 1965 the Technion also initiated a course in food technology for students from developing countries, and in 1966 it added a year of postgraduate studies to the agricultural engineering program.

Comprehensive Rural Planning

One of Israel's most promising new ventures in academic training for the developing world is a program in comprehensive rural planning, initiated in the fall of 1965.[4] The program is given at the Settlement Study Center in Rehovoth and is based on Israel's experience in regional development of rural areas over the last decade.

[4] A more ambitious project was first suggested by Gunnar Myrdal at the Second Rehovoth Conference in 1963. (See Chapter 10.)

Its orientation is stated in the draft prospectus of the course:

> The process of development and change must begin with the rural areas, as the vast majority of the people concerned live in these areas, and are engaged in agriculture. Economic and social progress depend largely on the modernization of agriculture . . .
>
> Rural development deals not only with economic and technical problems, but also with social, institutional and organizational changes . . .
>
> The essential problem of rural development is that of reducing the gap between the urban and rural living standards, and of providing additional employment opportunities . . . so that those who have acquired education and knowledge and are able to serve as the activating and guiding elements, are attracted to remain there. To achieve that aim, integration of agriculture, services and industry within the rural area is essential.

The course, accordingly, follows an interdisciplinary approach and is offered in English to students with a bachelor's degree in the social sciences, or in agriculture, agricultural engineering, architecture, town planning or geography. Although designed primarily for students from developing countries, some Israelis have also been admitted. Academic supervision is by the Hebrew University, in cooperation with the Ministries of Foreign Affairs and Agriculture and the Land Settlement Department of the Jewish Agency.

Initially, Israel had some difficulty recruiting qualified foreign students for the course, partly because of its novel character and partly, no doubt, because graduate students from developing countries tend to prefer "name" institutions in Europe and the United States. Nevertheless, the first class included some 20 students from Turkey, Iran, Kenya, Venezuela and Mexico, plus a few Israelis.

It is too early to assess the progress of this program, but there is little doubt that students from developing countries and from Israel itself, for that matter, have much to gain from a systematic study of the principles and practices of rural development, as applied in Israel and elsewhere.

Vocational Education

Israel's program for educating students from developing countries at the secondary level began in March 1961 with a course for 71 students from English- and French-speaking Africa. The program was entrusted to the Organization for Rehabilitation and Training (ORT), which, since 1880, has operated a large network of vocational schools and centers in various countries.[5] The program was organized at the seaside town of Natanya, in Israel, on the campus of one of ORT's largest and best-equipped vocational high schools. Competent English- or French-speaking staff was available from the existing school or recruited elsewhere, and funding was adequate. All objective conditions seemed to favor success of the project, yet it was plagued by difficulties almost from the start.

As planned, in the first year of the course basic training was to be given in mechanics, electricity or carpentry. Two thirds of the students were to receive an additional two years of training as instructors in mechanics, electromechanics, agromechanics or carpentry. The option of one year or three years in the curriculum and an extremely flexible admission system were an invitation to trouble. Pressure to admit students who did not have the necessary educational background resulted in even greater unevenness of achievement level than would normally have been the case. The process of, in effect, "weeding out" a third of the students after the first year had an unsettling effect and caused anxiety and dissatisfaction among the students. As Mordechai E. Kreinin has pointed out, it was an inefficient and expensive approach, since a year's study is insufficient to achieve even semiskilled status.[6]

The original plan had to be abandoned, and the course was then programmed as two years of "instructor training." Admission requirements were gradually tightened, and while some of the "growing pains" disappeared, a legacy of problems remained. The problems arose not only from the adjustment and attitudes of the students toward their Israeli environment, discussed later in this chapter, but, perhaps more important, from the basic concept of the course.

No one who observed the program questioned that the students were getting excellent instruction, comparable to that which they

[5] At the present time ORT provides vocational training in 29 countries through 633 schools and training units. (*Programme of Studies 1964–65, Israel Technical Centre for Students from Developing Countries* [at Natanya], Department for International Cooperation, Ministry for Foreign Affairs, in cooperation with ORT, Jerusalem.)

[6] *Israel and Africa—A Study in Technical Cooperation,* Praeger, New York, 1964, p. 115.

would have received at a good vocational school anywhere. A staff of 18 instructors and 11 *madrichim* (group leaders) for 111 students, as the program had in 1965, would in fact be the envy of many a vocational school. What many foreigners and some Israelis questioned, however, was whether two years of vocational training on top of an often thin layer of education and experience was sufficient to produce vocational education instructors. ORT and the Foreign Ministry itself recognized the difficulty: first the school tightened its entrance requirements; then it revised the curriculum, allowing additional time for instruction in pedagogy, methodology and educational psychology. Israelis experienced in instructor training contended that the program was sound.

Nevertheless, at least one African country, which had a large group of students at the school, refused at first to recognize the school's diploma, and even after reluctantly agreeing to recognize it, was unwilling to employ the graduates as full-fledged instructors. In turn, some of the students considered it beneath their dignity to accept employment that they considered of a lower rank than that for which they had been trained, and preferred to remain idle after they returned to their own countries. The program had obviously been launched and operated without adequate consultation with the governments of the sending countries, and had been based too closely on Israel's experience in training its own vocational instructors. The recognition of these defects and the adjustment difficulties experienced by the students led to a decision in 1966 to discontinue the program.

Individual Training

A small number of trainees from developing countries pursue individual courses of study in Israel. This group consists of students who enroll in regular courses at the Hebrew University or other Israeli institutions and trainees whose needs are such that individual curricula must be developed for them. Two thirds of these individual trainees who were in Israel in 1965 had been studying there for over a year. The Foreign Affairs Ministry's "Program for Training Opportunities" for 1964–65 lists more than 50 subjects in which such training has been given in the past.

The various training institutions offering short-term courses are also responsible for designing and supervising specialized programs of varying lengths, as these are needed. The Foreign Training Department of the Agricultural Extension Service, for example, has developed a pattern for individual training that includes supervised field work and study tours. The program is planned in close cooperation with the trainee and his supervisor, and trainees must submit monthly reports on their studies and field work. These reports not only help in assessing the trainees' progress, but they may also suggest desirable modifications in the programs. Toward the end of the program, each trainee prepares a major report on a topic related to his training program. A sampling of these reports indicates that the students learn a great deal but that more could be done to relate their studies to the needs and problems of their homelands.

The individual trainees pursuing academic programs, usually on Israeli Government scholarships, are pretty much on their own. While the institutions are glad to receive such students, they do not make special provisions for them. Their programs do not differ conceptually from programs offered by other countries. Yet in certain areas of learning, notably agricultural sciences and Middle Eastern studies, Israel has a great deal to offer to students from developing countries capable of independent work.

The Stranger Within the Gates

As with the short-term programs, there have been problems in connection with the long-term programs, but they have not generally been associated with deficiencies in the procedures for selecting trainees. Most of the long-term students attend academic courses at the Hebrew University in Jerusalem or the Haifa Institute of Technology, both of which have fairly high entrance requirements. Arrangements are sometimes made to enable foreign students to make up for educational deficiencies, but usually selection is based strictly on educational achievement. The established academic institutions have a reputation to promote and to protect, and therefore have insisted on full authority over admissions.

Though the selection problems are fewer for the long-term courses than for the short ones, the task of caring for students is far more difficult in the long-term courses.

The three or four months that the participants in the short-term courses spend in Israel are crammed with planned activity. Their accommodations are normally in pleasant, moderate-priced hotels or guest houses or, if they are at the Afro-Asian Institute or the Mount Carmel Training Center, in modest but comfortable living quarters comparable to university dormitories. Transportation and entertainment are ample. Except for occasional complaints that the food is not appealing to particular foreign tastes, there have been few problems in regard to living conditions. More troublesome has been the question of pocket money. Few participants have much money of their own, and some have complained that the weekly allowance of up to $8.33 is inadequate, though Israel officials say that incidental expenses in short courses are minimal.

Trainees who stay for short periods have few contacts with the Israeli public. On the rare occasions when they are on their own, they receive the same hospitable, courteous treatment that tourists would receive. Some time during their stay, arrangements are made for trainees to visit with Israelis in their homes and in collective settlements, and many have taken away from these visits warm memories and even lasting friendships. A typical letter, from an Iranian veterinarian, reads in part: "Before seeing your beautiful and active country, I would never dream to get into such a warm atmosphere and see such wonderful people. During my stay in Israel I was able to find many good friends . . ."[7]

Students and trainees who stay in Israel for longer periods face an altogether different situation. Unlike their colleagues in short courses, they must find their own way in the mainstream of Israeli society. In the process, some of them may run into problems of bureaucracy, indifference and what sensitive African students interpret as discrimination.

Such experiences, whether due to misunderstandings and bureaucratic shortcomings, as they often seem to be, or to a deep clash of culture and custom, frequently result in resentment and a feeling of

[7] "Our Graduates Write . . . ," Ministry for Foreign Affairs, Ministry of Agriculture and Jewish Agency Extension Service, Foreign Training Department, Tel Aviv, June 1963, p. 5 (pamphlet).

isolation. One long-term African student described his reaction as follows: [8]

> Israeli [Jewish] society is closed for non-Jews, and to break the barrier is difficult. Israeli friendship on the whole is of very short duration . . . This leaves students to depend mostly on their predecessors for friendship who, in most cases, have met with the same disappointments . . . Africans in most cases feel this [discrimination] because he [sic] can never be mistaken because of his color. And he wonders how his host, having suffered in the Diaspora, can encourage this in his own land.

It seems strange that in a country that has sacrificed its lifeblood and untold substance to receive newcomers, the "stranger within the gate" should feel unaccepted, but competent observers agree that this is the case, particularly in Jerusalem, where many foreign students live. Contrary to the beliefs of some of the African students, however, race seems to have little to do with the situation, for some Jewish students from abroad, studying in Israel, have expressed similar feelings.[9]

A Hebrew University instructor has described the attitude of Israeli students toward their foreign colleagues as "neither hospitality, nor hostility . . . [but] apathy and indifference." [10]

Students and trainees from developing countries grumble about other things in Israel, including the occasionally heard expression "Kushi," which means "black man" but in normal usage has no pejorative meaning. Some students have objected to learning Hebrew for advanced work at the Medical School and for other studies.

Aside from the social problems, the question of allowances seems to disturb long-term students the most. As of 1966, according to the Foreign Ministry, students and trainees responsible for their own room and board received 520 Israeli pounds ($173.33) a month, plus

[8] M. E. O. Cotyya, "Israel and Her Foreign Students," *The African Student,* Jerusalem, December 1964, pp. 40–41.

[9] An American Jewish girl studying at the Hebrew University in 1963 said: "The Sabra [Israel-born] students are exclusive and cliquey. It is almost impossible to get to know them . . . The Sabras all have trouble with their English, but I don't think that this is the fundamental difficulty. I think they just are not interested in getting to know, as close friends, people from other countries. They feel that they are sufficient unto themselves . . ." (Philip Gillon, "The Stranger Within the Gates," *Jerusalem Post,* July 5, 1963.)

[10] *Ibid.*

a one-time allowance of up to 200 Israeli pounds ($66.66) upon arrival, and an annual book allowance of up to 300 Israeli pounds ($100). The basic subsistence allowance approximates salaries of Israeli lawyers, doctors, engineers and other professionals in junior positions, and is more generous than scholarship support given to Israelis. Yet African students have contended that it is insufficient, that they cannot live as cheaply as Israelis and cannot save anything to send home.[11]

It is hard to see how Israeli officials could accept this type of argument, in view of the very stringent conditions under which most Israeli students live. To raise the level of living of the foreign students further above that of their Israeli colleagues could easily turn the present apparent indifference of the latter into active hostility.

The situation has caused Israeli officials serious concern on political grounds. When some anonymous, scurrilously anti-African leaflets made their appearance in January 1966, Prime Minister Eshkol personally took to the radio to condemn this "criminal act" and to ask that "our African guests" treat the matter "with the same contempt that we do."[12]

The Foreign Ministry and other institutions concerned with the foreign students have tried, if not always successfully, to remove some of their grievances. Full-time adult advisers and Israeli student *madrichim* have been working with African students at the Hebrew University, the Haifa Technical Institute and the ORT Vocational School, the three institutions where most of the long-term students have been studying. The National Union of Israeli Students has appointed an Overseas Student Coordinator at its Hebrew University branch to help in arranging social events, invitations to homes, trips and other activities. In 1964 the Union turned over to the African Students' Association a room for its own use in the Hebrew University Student Center. At the ORT Vocational School, where most of the complaints were about food, foreign trainees were better fed than the Israeli students, and were served restaurant style, while the Israelis were served cafeteria style. Following the example of inter-

[11] According to African custom, the students say, contributing to the education of younger brothers and sisters is not only their moral obligation but is insurance against their having to support the younger ones in later years.

[12] *Jerusalem Post Weekly*, January 7, 1966.

national organizations, Israel pays for a round trip home for the students from developing countries at the end of every two years of study.

The Foreign Ministry's solicitude for the students has been sincere but unsystematic. While the ministry has placated and favored the students in many ways, in certain instances it has allowed frustrations to reach the point of strikes and angry protest meetings. Some of the educational institutions have been equally inconsistent.

Israel's problems with its long-term students from developing countries are not unique, but neither can it be said that Israel has done much better than other countries in solving them. According to one Israeli who works closely with the students, their attitudes and adjustment could be plotted along a "U" curve—great enthusiasm at the beginning, followed soon by disillusionment and depression, which in turn gives way to a realistic adjustment and more positive attitudes.

Effectiveness of the Programs

Happily for Israel, long-term students respond not only to the frustrations and problems encountered, but also to expressions of goodwill and friendship, and the fine education they generally receive. The total impact of the Israeli experience—in terms of both educational achievement and attitudes—is therefore likely to be positive.

Ultimately, it is not the adjustment of the students during their stay in Israel that is the most important measure of the effectiveness of the long-term study programs, but rather whether or not the programs prepare the students to make useful contributions to the development of their own countries. In this respect the opinions of the foreign students and independent observers are highly favorable to the Israeli effort. As the academic students begin to return home in larger numbers, the effects of the programs will probably become increasingly evident.

In the meantime, as we have seen, Israeli officials have taken steps to curtail the long-term study programs in Israel. This decision seems based on the view that because of the difficulties, the high cost of these programs and the development of indigenous facilities in nursing, medicine and vocational education, greater priority should be given to intensive short-term training in Israel or abroad.

The Israeli experience suggests that countries planning to offer long-term programs to students from developing countries should determine in advance how to cope with the adjustment and educational problems that will arise, and decide whether the projected programs are the type best suited to the needs.

Chapter 12

The Balance Sheet

It is impossible to calculate the benefits of Israel's cooperation program so as to be able to judge conclusively that it has or has not "paid off." Contemporary economists have developed sophisticated ways of measuring input-output and cost-benefit ratios, but no one has yet succeeded in measuring the cost-benefit ratio of international friendship or the input-output ratio of activities contributing to a nation's morale or élan. Nevertheless, judgments of some kind must be made.

As is typical of policies and programs that evolve in the life of a country, Israel's participation in international assistance developed haltingly and somewhat haphazardly. Few would have predicted in 1954, when Burma sent its first mission to Israel to investigate the possibilities of cooperation, that a decade later Israel would have technical assistance relations with some 80 countries. Yet today co-operation with the developing world is one of the cornerstones of its foreign policy, is basic to its international reputation and increasingly important in its national life. Similarly, many developing countries in need of foreign technical assistance prize Israel's participation in their development process and are willing to expend their own limited resources to obtain it.

The evolution of Israel's program, the elements on which its reputation is founded and the problems—solved and unsolved—that have been encountered along the way are described in the foregoing chapters. It is appropriate now to consider the effects the program has had on Israel's relations with other countries and on its own people.

Politics of Friendship

"The only people who are trusted in Africa are the people of Israel," David Ben Gurion, Israel's elder statesman, said in May 1965.[1] Yet only a few months before this statement was made, 46 so-called "nonaligned" countries, including 26 from Africa, had signed a solemn declaration in Cairo demanding the "full restoration of all rights to the Arab people of Palestine to their homeland,"[2] which, in the tangled context of the Arab-Israel conflict, is tantamount to a demand for the liquidation of Israel as a state.

Some readers might be inclined to dismiss both of these statements as extreme. They reflect, however, the duality that has governed Israel's political relations with the emerging countries: cordial bilateral relations, contrasted by varying degrees of support on the part of these same countries for anti-Israel positions in international forums.

It was hostility at international forums—notably the Bandung Conference in 1955 and the New Delhi Asian Socialist Conference at the time of the Suez crisis in 1956—that made clear to Israel's leaders the danger of political isolation from the developing world. Their response was a bold and dynamic effort to demonstrate to the world Israel's worth as a member of the international community.

In the drive for international recognition Israel faced serious obstacles—Arab hostility, suspicion of motives, distrust of the white man, shortage of funds. In Israel's favor was its small size, its own history of suffering, its struggle for freedom and, most important, its demonstrated abilities and achievements in development. These factors in combination have generated much sympathy and respect for Israel in the international community. The program of technical co-

[1] *New York Times,* May 26, 1965.

[2] *New York Times,* October 13, 1964; *Economist,* October 10, 1964, p. 130.

operation has been Israel's passport to a full range of political, commercial and cultural relations with developing countries of Africa and Asia; with the older South American republics the establishment of political relations came first, but today programs of technical cooperation are also spreading. There is no doubt that the cooperation program has become a key component of Israel's bilateral relations everywhere in the developing world.

The pressures resulting from the unresolved conflict with the Arab states still dominate much of Israel's international political activity. But most of the developing countries have not permitted these pressures to hinder their bilateral relations with Israel. The President of Tanzania, Julius Nyerere, perhaps best stated the position of these countries when he said, "We are not going to let our friends determine who our enemies shall be." [3]

While Nyerere's statement, made in 1961 upon his country's achievement of its independence, was meant primarily as a rebuff to anti-Israel agitation, it also contained an implied warning to Israel not to attempt to enlist support for its position in the Israel-Arab conflict.

With varying shadings, the doctrine of neutrality governs the bilateral relations of most developing countries with Israel. More conservative countries than Tanzania have not hesitated to state a similar position, as illustrated by the remarks of the President of Chad, François Tombalbaye, during a visit to Israel: "Chad will not permit herself to be dragged into the Israel-Arab dispute. . . . We are neither for one nor the other of the disputants. . . . We will strongly oppose any attempt to embroil us in the dispute or to turn us into a tool of any country which is interested in exploiting this dispute for its own interests." [4]

Israel has apparently accepted this position with good grace,[5] and its officials have emphasized that they do not expect or seek the adherence of developing countries to pro-Israel or anti-Arab views. "Israel's assistance entails no commitments of a political nature,"

[3] As quoted in A. J. Hughes, *East Africa: The Search for Unity, Kenya, Tanganyika, Uganda, and Zanzibar,* Penguin Books, Harmondsworth, Middlesex, 1963, p. 45.

[4] *Jerusalem Post Weekly,* October 8, 1965.

[5] In the spring of 1966 Israel concluded a new technical cooperation agreement with Chad, including a credit of about $400,000.

states an article on Israel's cooperation program by a high Foreign Ministry official. "It is available to any country that is willing to accept it in a spirit of mutual comprehension and on the basis of friendly relations." [6]

Israel's adversaries have been less ready to accept a neutral orientation on the part of the developing countries, and have persistently lobbied for their commitment to the Arab side or at least a reduction in their ties with Israel. The Arab League has devoted many sessions to ways of counteracting Israeli activities, and President Nasser of Egypt has vowed to "chase out Israel from Africa." [7]

Arab policy has been directed against both Israel's bilateral relations and its position in various international forums. Efforts to disrupt bilateral relations have rarely succeeded, and in fact have sometimes badly backfired. It is common knowledge in one African country, for example, that an Arab ambassador was caught red-handed attempting to sabotage a ceremonial parachute drop by troops who had returned from training in Israel. When Arab embassies in Nigeria agitated against the visit of Israel's Foreign Minister Golda Meir in 1964, they were swiftly rebuffed by the Nigerian Ministry of External Affairs: [8]

> The Government of Nigeria . . . views with great concern and seriousness the subtle attempt being made by some friendly countries to disturb the normal relations of friendship existing between Israel and Nigeria, and particularly regards the joint memorandum submitted over the signatures of the embassies listed above as constituting undue and unwarranted intervention in the internal affairs of Nigeria.
>
> The Ministry (of External Affairs) wishes to state categorically that it will not tolerate any such interference, and very much hopes that such acts . . . will not be repeated in the future.

Arab bloc influence has been sufficiently effective to undermine the development of normal bilateral relations with Israel in only a few non-Arab countries—notably India, Pakistan, Malaysia, Indonesia, Somalia, and Mauretania. In each of these countries the existence of

[6] Yaacov Yannay, "Technical Cooperation Between Israel and the Developing World," *International Development Review,* September 1964, p. 15.

[7] *Jerusalem Post,* November 13, 1964.

[8] *Jerusalem Post,* October 30, 1964.

strong Islamic influences or Israel's external conflicts with Islamic countries tipped the balance against Israel.

India's position, which is particularly painful for Israel, is an outgrowth of a policy initiated by the late Prime Minister Nehru and his associate, Krishna Menon. Nehru's successor, the late Lal Bahadur Shastri, gave some hints of wishing to change India's stand, but died before taking any concrete action.[9]

The Indian Government's stand has been repeatedly criticized by members of India's Parliament and some Indian newspapers on the ground that India was cutting herself off from a useful source of technical assistance and cooperation. The argument has been supported also by those several hundred Indians who, despite their government's attitude, have visited Israel or gone there for training. Thus, while technical cooperation has not yet led to normal relations with India, it has become an important issue in the continuing Indian debate on the subject.

More painful, undoubtedly, than the rebuffs from India and a few other governments has been the realization in Israel that cordial bilateral relations with most of the developing countries are no guarantee of support in international forums. The thirteen-nation Arab bloc, using its voting strength to best advantage, has carried its campaign against Israel into every possible international forum. As indicated earlier, the very countries that have had strong bilateral and technical cooperation ties with Israel have often also voted for anti-Israel positions.*

During the early days of its technical cooperation program Israelis reacted strongly against such acts. When six African chiefs of state, including Kwame Nkrumah of Ghana, Modibo Kéita of Mali and Sékou Touré of Guinea, subscribed to a resolution at Casablanca in January 1961, branding Israel an "instrument for imperial-

[9] In conversation with an Israeli journalist in January 1965, Shastri reportedly spoke highly of Israel's achievements and did not rule out the possibility of Israeli-Indian technical cooperation in agricultural development. (*Jerusalem Post Weekly*, January 14, 1966.)

* This fact was again demonstrated in the UN General Assembly debate on the latest Israeli-Arab war in June 1967, when Tanzania, Uganda, Congo (Kinshasa) and Nigeria voted in favor of the so-called "nonaligned" resolution, which demanded Israel's unconditional withdrawal from territories it occupied during the six days of hostilities.

ism and neocolonialism," Israelis were shocked. Israel's ambassadors requested special audiences with Nkrumah and Touré, and a special envoy was sent to Mali to intervene with President Kéita. The Israeli Foreign Ministry leaked the view that "in the long run, closer cooperation will develop with those countries with which there are no political differences." None of these interventions, however, were of any avail, and Nkrumah even countered by issuing a statement reiterating Ghana's support for the Casablanca resolution.[10] Yet this move did not prevent Nkrumah's participation, a short time later, in the opening of an Israeli exhibition in Accra.

It became clear in time, however, that the reputation Israel was developing at the bilateral level was beginning to work to its advantage even on the international scene. At three major Organization of African Unity conferences—at Addis Ababa in 1963, at Cairo in 1964 and at Accra in 1965—the Arab nations refrained from pressing anti-Israel resolutions. At the UN General Assembly in 1961, 1962 and 1963 Israel mobilized its friends to support a resolution calling for direct negotiations between Israel and the Arab states to solve their conflict. The list of 19 sponsors in 1963 included 10 African, 5 Latin American and 4 European countries—a total of 15 from the developing world.[11] While this was a respectable showing, the resolution lacked majority support and therefore did not come to a vote. Some of Israel's principal cooperation partners, among them Tanzania, Ghana and Ethiopia, failed to join the group of sponsors.*

A significant international confrontation involving developing countries, Israel and the Arab bloc took place at the 1964 UN Conference on Trade and Development (UNCTAD) in Geneva, where a bloc of 75 (later 77) countries was formed in an effort to unify the developing world on major economic policies affecting them. Israel wanted to be a part of this group and vigorously argued its right

[10] *Jerusalem Post,* January 8, 1961; January 27, 1961.

[11] *Yearbook of the United Nations, 1963,* Department of Public Information, UN, New York, p. 61.

* In June 1967, 42 developing countries, including Ghana and Ethiopia, voted at the UN General Assembly in support of a resolution which would have linked Israeli withdrawal of its troops from occupied Arab territories with Arab abandonment of the state of belligerency with Israel.

to be identified with the countries of the emerging world.[12] Arab bloc delegates opposed Israel's inclusion with equal vigor, stressing among other arguments that this would undermine the unity of the emerging-nation bloc, and that the character of Israel's economy (high per capita income, predominance of industry) was not compatible with the concept of a developing country.[13] It seemed that developing countries, the majority of whom had active technical cooperation arrangements with Israel, would have to choose. To this writing, however, they have evaded a definitive decision.[14] In effect, therefore, Arab pressure has thus far succeeded in keeping Israel out of active participation in the bloc of developing countries.

In less representative settings than the UNCTAD Conference, Arab delegates have often succeeded in getting anti-Israel positions adopted, but the practical effects of these declarations have not been very great. Typically, many of the participants in such declarations have advised Israel after the fact to disregard the resolutions. To judge from the 1966 "Solidarity Conference" in Havana, this seems to apply even to Communist-dominated events involving developing countries, despite the strong pro-Arab positions normally taken by China, the Soviet Union and other Communist governments. The so-called "First Tricontinental Solidarity Conference of the Peoples of Africa, Asia and Latin America" was held in Havana in January 1966, with the participation of delegates from more than 80 countries and territories. It passed one of the most sweeping anti-Israel resolutions

[12] See statement by Pinhas Sapir, head of Israel's UNCTAD delegation, at Eighth Plenary Meeting, March 26, 1964, *Proceedings,* Vol. II, *Policy Statements,* Conference on Trade and Development, UN, Geneva, pp. 235–38.

[13] Since most of this discussion took place in closed sessions, it has been impossible to secure an official statement of the Arab position. This brief summary is based on unpublished information made available to the author of the present study and on conversations with participants at the Conference.

[14] Israel's name was omitted from the "Joint Declaration of Seventy-Seven" issued at the conclusion of the UNCTAD Conference. However, Israel was invited to present its views to a nine-nation Working Group established to "study the composition and integration of the Group of Developing Countries." The Working Group, which included two Arab states, met a number of times in 1964 and 1965, rehashed the arguments made at Geneva, but was unable to reach an agreement. The question of Israel's inclusion is still unresolved.

ever presented at a non-Arab international gathering, calling for "rupture of political relations . . . an economic and cultural blockade . . . expulsion from international organizations . . . combatting Zionist infiltration and penetration . . . cancelling agreements [with Israel] . . . material and financial aid to Palestine in its fight against the Zionists . . . support [for] the Organization for the Liberation of Palestine," and warning against "so-called Israeli technical and economic aid . . . a new disguised method of imperialism and neo-colonialism of the U. S."[15] After the conference, Fidel Castro, who had hosted the gathering, hastened to relate to a group of journalists from the United Arab Republic how he had laughed off a UAR diplomat's suggestion that he comply with the call to break relations with Israel.[16]

At weightier international meetings, as we have seen, the discussions are more protracted and the nuances softer. However, the conclusion to be drawn from them is the same—that Israel's evident success in developing friendly bilateral relations with most of the emerging countries does not assure support for Israel in the international community.

Viewed in a larger context, the cooperation program has become so vital and positive an element of Israel's foreign policy that it is difficult to envisage its international posture without it. International cooperation is not only Israel's passport to the emerging world, it is a foundation upon which Israel is building a bridge to the world around it—today paradoxically to the more distant countries and tomorrow through them, perhaps, to those nearer to its borders. The respected French periodical, *Problèmes Africains*, on June 16, 1966, commented in this connection: "Africa's friendship is not only a powerful equilibrating factor that works in favor of Israel in the Afro-Asian world, but it is also perhaps the best way of bringing the Arabs to envisage the possibility of coexistence."

[15] U. S. Joint Publications Research Service, Washington, Translation No. 34350, pp. 90–91.

[16] *Al Ahram* (Cairo), January 29, 1966. According to the Israeli Communist newspaper, *Kol Haam* (February 13, 1966), the Soviet delegation also repudiated the resolution and opposed its passage at the Conference.

An Israeli Foreign Ministry official recently echoed this sentiment: [17]

> Africa's friendship has banished the spectre of Israel's isolation in the Third World. The vigorous stand taken by African leaders in advocacy of the peaceful settlement of conflicts has strengthened Israel's conviction that the States of Africa are able and willing to play a central part in bringing about permanent peace in the Middle East. President Nasser, in his "Philosophy of a Revolution," insists that the way to Africa leads through Cairo. Everything today points to the likelihood that the way to Cairo may lead through Africa.

The Tunisian weekly, *Jeune Afrique,* which cannot be accused of pro-Israel sympathies, had earlier arrived at somewhat the same conclusions, after a review of Israel's cooperation program with Africa: ". . . while at first Israel was anxious only to escape the condemnation of the 'Third World,' it seems today to be aiming at integrating itself with the new forces . . . [Israel's leaders] are certain that the road to Cairo passes through Bamako and the road to Tunis through Abidjan." [18]

Economic Relations [19]

Ambiguities in the political arena in relations between Israel and the developing countries apparently have not carried over into the economic sphere. Trade is active and growing in volume, though for various reasons, discussed below, the proportion of Israel's foreign trade accounted for by the developing countries has scarcely changed during the 1960's. In 1965 these countries accounted for about 11 per cent of Israel's exports and a little over 6 per cent of its imports—almost the same proportions as in 1960.

Prior to Ghana's independence Ghanaian trade with Israel was

[17] Moshe Leshem, "The Roots of Friendship," Ministry for Foreign Affairs, Jerusalem, August 1966 (unpublished manuscript).

[18] "Pour Israel le chemin du Caire passe par l'Afrique noire," April 10, 1966, p. 23.

[19] Unless otherwise indicated, data in this section are from the following publications of the Central Bureau of Statistics, Jerusalem: *Statistical Abstract of Israel: 1958–59,* p. 273; *1964,* pp. 214–17; and *1966,* p. 253; *Statistical Bulletin of Israel,* Part C, *Foreign Trade,* January 1966, pp. 26–28.

almost nonexistent; after independence in 1957, with the signing of a technical cooperation and trade agreement, Israeli exports to Ghana came to $183,000 and in 1958 reached $354,000; in 1965, Ghana was Israel's best customer in Africa, accounting for exports of $5.3 million, about one quarter of Israel's exports to that continent. The pattern of increase in trade has been similar for a number of other developing countries—Kenya, Ethiopia, Gabon, and to a lesser extent, Nigeria, Iran and Turkey.

While the cooperation programs themselves have by and large been free of commercial strings, commercial contacts have inevitably grown out of the contacts between Israel and partner countries. In some cases, as discussed in Chapter 9, these contacts have been reinforced through the establishment of commercially operating quasi-public joint companies, the extension of trade credits and medium-term loans partly tied to Israeli procurement. Nonetheless, trade between Israel and some of the developing countries has remained at a low level, principally because Israel's market and the markets of many of these countries do not complement each other. There is almost no demand in the developing world for Israel's two leading exports—citrus and polished diamonds; at the same time, most primary products, the characteristic exports of developing countries, cannot be absorbed by Israel's predominantly light and medium industries without prior processing elsewhere.[20]

Since 1964 Israel has imported more from developing countries than it has exported to them. In 1965, for example, its imports from African countries were $27.2 million—$5.7 million more than its exports to those countries. One reason why Israel's exports have not kept pace with its imports is that markets in many of the developing countries of Africa, and to a lesser extent of Asia, are still tied in varying degrees to the former colonial powers, through customs preferences, financial connections and tradition. Also, some Israeli industrial products are not competitive with U. S. and European products, because of higher production costs and because Israeli companies may lack comparable service and maintenance facilities.

Nevertheless, the volume of Israeli exports, particularly to Africa, has grown significantly in recent years—from $11.6 million in 1963

[20] A notable exception is crude oil, which is imported from Iran, processed in Israel and in part re-exported.

to $21.5 million in 1965. It is probably more than a coincidence that the greatest increases have been in exports to those African countries (for example, Ethiopia, Ghana, Kenya, Nigeria and Uganda) that also have an active technical cooperation program with Israel.

It seems likely that Israel's trade and economic relations with developing countries will improve still further with continuing technical cooperation. With the passage of time Israel's own production is likely to become more competitive with that of the established industrial powers. Furthermore, Israeli officials, some of whom had been averse to tying technical cooperation to trade, lest their motives become suspect, are coming around to the view that these activities can legitimately support each other, to the mutual benefit of both partners. As a first step, they believe, greater "export consciousness" among Israeli experts and training instructors will lead to greater interest in Israeli products. Some recent technical assistance contracts give preference to purchase of Israeli equipment, "if of competitive prices and quality." [21] Finally, the Israeli Government is encouraging certain foreign commercial activities of Israeli companies—including the sizable commercial operations of Solel Boneh, Mayer Brothers Ltd. and Federman Enterprises—through investment guarantees and by helping these companies train local personnel under the cooperation program.

The long-term benefits of mutually reinforcing trade and technical cooperation between two emerging countries are illustrated by the Israeli-Turkish relations. Turkey is Israel's most active trading partner among the developing countries, accounting in 1965 for more than $15 million worth of trade, or more than 15 per cent of the total trade between Israel and the developing world. Geographic proximity favors this relationship, of course, but just as important have been Turkey's rapidly advancing economy and the technical cooperation between the two countries.

In deference to Turkey's delicate political problems with the Arab countries, accentuated during the last few years by the Cyprus issue, both Israelis and Turks are circumspect in discussing their mutual ties. (Israeli-Turkish diplomatic representation is at the *chargé d'affaires*

[21] Agricultural Development Company (International) Ltd., "Agreement Between the Parliamentary Secretary to the Ministry of Agriculture on Behalf of the Government of Tanganyika and the Agricultural Development Company (International) Ltd. of Israel," Tel Aviv, June 1964, p. 3.

level only, and from time to time press reports have appeared indicating Turkish sensitivity over relations with Israel.) Nevertheless, Turkish officials, in interviews connected with the present study, expressed satisfaction over Turkey-Israel relations, terming them "very fruitful," and indicated that they hoped for their further quiet expansion. These sentiments are shared by the Israelis, who see in their relations with Turkey a model of what economic and technical cooperation between two developing countries can accomplish.

Israel's help in the development of Turkish agriculture, for instance, through training courses and other types of technical assistance, has been reciprocated by Turkish advice on the cultivation of tobacco, pistachio nuts and hazelnuts. Similarly, according to an Israeli correspondent, Israelis can profit from learning Turkish methods of road building and other construction and studying Turkish achievements in municipal planning and administration. On the other hand, Israeli assistance to Turkey in the development of tourism, in which Israel excels Turkey, could lead to increased tourist traffic between the two countries and joint planning to attract overseas tourists.[22] Other possibilities for Turkish-Israeli cooperation that have been mentioned are: Israeli technical assistance to Turkey's fishing industry, which could promote joint use of Turkey's rich fishing grounds; cooperative efforts to establish an automobile industry serving the limited markets of both countries; market-sharing for other new industries; and joint technical assistance missions to other developing countries. A Turkish official, writing in an Israeli foreign trade journal, echoed this desire for increased cooperation, with the statement that "a greater measure of economic relations could be attained between our two countries if more stress and importance were to be placed on establishing joint ventures and undertakings." [23]

Farsighted Israelis also see Israel's cooperation partners in eastern Africa—Ethiopia, Kenya, Tanzania and, possibly, the Malagasy Republic—as important future economic and trading partners. Already both Tanzania and the Malagasy Republic have sent peanuts to Israel,

[22] *Jerusalem Post,* December 15 and 16, 1964.

[23] Resat Erkman, "Trade Relations Between Israel and Turkey," *The Israel Export and Trade Journal,* August 1965.

where they have been sorted, packed and re-exported to Europe,[24] and Ethiopia has for some years been supplying meat to Israel. Active technical cooperation programs with the Ivory Coast have been followed by a new five-year trade agreement that, among other things, provides for close collaboration between the paper and pulp industries of the two countries, reinforced by Israeli technical assistance.[25] One observer, discussing the collaboration agreement, felt that developing countries should promote such pooling arrangements in order to broaden their limited markets and thus encourage trade in products and industries that might become competitive on the world market.

Even if these aspirations do not produce economic or political miracles for Israel or its partners, they have already laid the groundwork for new mutually beneficial relations.

Psychological Impact

Whether it be the urbane President Félix Houphouet-Boigny of the Ivory Coast, referring to himself as a "Black Israeli," or the dedicated Jesuit priest, Pedro Martinez in Peru, declaring that "the miracle of Israel" has been brought to arid Bajo Piura,[26] the meaning is the same—Israel has become an important symbol of progress to people in the developing world.

As this study has shown, Israel's cooperation program is not without its flaws, failures and continuing problems. In many important respects the problems are similar to those that other donor countries face. Yet by virtue of its almost charismatic appeal, Israel, the symbol, has largely remained untouched by these difficulties. The traveler in Africa or Latin America is repeatedly struck by contrasting reactions on the part of his hosts: mention the United States and it brings to the fore uneasiness, suspicion, a plea for more capital aid, a question about U. S. intervention in the Dominican Republic or the war in

[24] *Jerusalem Post,* July 23, 1965.

[25] *Jerusalem Post,* December 23, 1964; and field interviews in connection with the present study.

[26] *Shalom* (Spanish edition), May 1965, p. 19.

Vietnam; mention Israel and it evokes a cordial smile, questions about the *kibbutz,* Israel's accomplishments in a specific sphere or declarations as to how much better things would be if only the "Israeli spirit" were present. These highly impressionistic comparisons are cited not to disparage or to glorify, but because they dramatize the symbolic importance that Israel has attained in the emerging world. To Israel and to the other developing countries, the symbol is as important as the nuts and bolts of the cooperation program.

Kenya's President, Jomo Kenyatta, has written of the nation-building image that Israel evokes, in the introduction to the Hebrew translation of his book, *Facing Mount Kenya:* "You [Israelis] have built a nation with Jews coming from all the corners of the world; we want to build a unified Kenya composed of a multitude of tribes joined together through *Harambee* [working together]."[27] These sentiments go far to explain the thinking behind the symbol, for most developing countries give first priority to nation-building in the broad sense. To them Israel represents the attainable dream—a country that is small, young, still struggling, yet by the world's standards stable and successful. It does not much matter that there are flaws in the image, that this ideal, like any other, falls short of reality. In the rapidly changing economic and political landscape of more than half the world, Israel, the symbol, serves a constructive purpose that far transcends its size and material contribution.

Nor has this positive psychological impact been altogether one-sided. The cooperation program has not only "opened the world" to Israel, it has also opened Israel to the world. To be sure, modern Israel began as a country of immigrants, but few if any of these immigrants knew or cared much about that part of the developing world with which Israel has now become associated. Native-born Israelis, not generally renowned for their interest in the world, knew and cared even less. The contacts made possible through the cooperation program, however, have brought the developing world nearer to Israelis than ever before. This is reflected in the Israeli press and in many public functions. A single, six-page issue of the *Jerusalem Post,* published on an ordinary day, December 1, 1964, contained nine separate African items. When the distinguished African singer, Miriam

[27] Quoted in *Jeune Afrique,* April 10, 1966, p. 21.

Makeba, visited Israel in 1965, she drew huge crowds and generated an unprecedented outpouring of personal warmth and sympathy. As one observer remarked, "Israel has gone Africa-mad." This broadened vision of the world has brought a perceptible strengthening of national self-confidence and morale.

There is genuine popular pride in the cooperation program, which enjoys the support of Parliament, the press and all major political factions. The program has never experienced the severe domestic criticism to which the U. S. program, for example, is frequently subjected. The presumed political benefit is only part of the explanation for this broad support. Another is that the Israelis were for a long time heavily dependent on foreign assistance, and their ability now to help others has restored their self-respect. Some speak of Israel's "debt of honor" for the assistance it received. A thoughtful Hebrew University student put it this way, when interviewed in connection with the present study: "For so many years we were a beggar nation, depending for our economic survival on the generosity of others. We still have a long way to go before we become completely viable, but our ability now to aid others enables us to straighten our shoulders and look at the world with new confidence and self-esteem."

Going beyond these already apparent psychological returns, some responsible Israelis are convinced that the cooperation program can have a profound effect on Israel's character as a nation and a society. Aharon Remez, the former Director of the Department for International Cooperation and an important advocate of this viewpoint, said at a farewell reception in his honor on October 27, 1964, that the program is "as important for Israel as for the recipients," and that Israel must grasp this "new mission" lest it become "just another Levantine country."

This view is a reflection of a conviction widely held in Israel that the country's pioneering spirit and moral fiber have seriously weakened in the recent past. Independent surveys and investigations have confirmed this general impression, causing serious concern, especially with regard to the values and aspirations of the younger generation. Professor Joseph Eaton, a U. S. sociologist who recently studied Israel's youth movements, reported: [28]

[28] "The Achievement Crisis," paper published by the University of Pittsburgh, 1966, p. 6.

> Israel's youth culture was dominated by pioneer-youth movements and voluntary military youth formations. These institutions have lost impact, status, charisma since 1948. There is much concern in Israel today about the fact that only a minority of older adolescents is vitally interested in youth movements. There is much routinization in the para-military Youth Corps (Gadna). There is early emphasis on careerism. Young Israelis talk much more about personal goals than their parents recall having done at the same age. Material goods confer increasing status. Many officials . . . bemoan nostalgically the not so distant past when young people seemed to have had more sustained enthusiasm for national service programs . . . "Will Israel become just another state?" is a question many ask of each other.

The answer Remez and others give is that Israel must offer new, meaningful challenges and broader horizons, or risk losing its best people. Israel's "normalization" has been too fast, Remez said in an interview; it could disrupt the country's internal balance. He sees Israel's international cooperation programs, in their present modest form but expanding as time goes on, as Israel's "new frontier" that will stimulate Israel's own progress and pioneering spirit.

Is this a farfetched, visionary view of the future? Perhaps it is, to the *Realpolitiker*, who looks for tangible indicators and results within his grasp. But Israel's own history has repeatedly confounded the preachers of *Realpolitik*. As this century opened, Israel itself was no more than a vision in the minds of a few dozen social idealists inspired by a gifted Viennese journalist.[29]

Already some Israelis see the prestige that the *kibbutz, moshav,* Nahal and Gadna enjoy abroad as a "shot in the arm," giving new status to these institutions at home. Others are convinced that the experts and their families will increasingly bring back from abroad not only professional insights, but an appreciation of the world that will serve Israel well in the future. Israel's distinguished Foreign Minister, Abba Eban, himself a leading intellectual voice in the continuing debate on his country's role, has given eloquent support to these ideas: [30]

[29] Theodor Herzl's *Der Judenstaat* (The Jewish State) was published in 1896, and the First Zionist Congress met in Basle in 1897.

[30] "Israel in the Community of Nations," Press Bulletin, Evening Session January 5, 1965, Information Department of the World Zionist Organization, 26th Zionist Congress, Jerusalem.

> Israel will not be a great society unless it pursues great enterprises outside itself. If she is to have a national mission, Israel must have an international vocation. . . .
>
> Israel's role in the great drama of development is . . . her principal vocation in international life. . . .
>
> The international arena is peculiarly congenial to the universalist element in Israel's heritage. It offers the widest scope to our emergence from provincialism and regional isolation. . . .
>
> A small people must live its life on two levels: on the intimate level of national distinctiveness, and on the broader level of intensive international cooperation.

Even if for the majority of Israelis the vision is still somewhat remote, it is evidently not far beyond the country's conceptual horizon. Against this background it is reasonable to expect that as time goes on Israel will derive increasing psychological benefits from its cooperation program with developing countries.

It is evident that Israel's encounter with the developing world, through its cooperation program, has by and large been a felicitous adventure. As in all adventures, there are risks and pitfalls, successes and failures. Among Israel's chief attractions for other developing countries is its sincere belief in the capabilities of emerging people, its nonimperialistic background, its small size and its talent for launching short-term programs with quick impact.

Israel's success in its program of cooperation, however, also illuminates serious limitations to its present capabilities. Projects often require more time to achieve self-sustaining growth than Israel's resources permit. Yet premature withdrawal, in order to maintain the momentum of the total program, may create frictions with partner governments and jeopardize the ultimate success of a particular undertaking. Basically, Israel still has to learn to say "No" when it lacks capacity or expertise, and its partners have to learn that "easy," fast-impact projects often have limited real developmental value. Both partners must face the formidable barrier that shortage of capital imposes upon the scale and operation of their cooperation programs; they may have to face the fact that multilateral or third-country backing and longer range projects are often necessary in order to achieve optimum results.

If despite these and other limitations there is a special quality about

Israel's cooperation with developing countries, it surely springs from Israel's youth, its single-minded dedication to nation-building, and the proximity in time and experience of both partners to the modernizing process. This proximity has proved to be a most valuable asset, which has fructified these relationships far beyond the material inputs by either partner.

Part II

Cooperation Between Other Emerging Countries

Chapter 13

Multilateral Channels for Cooperation

HARDLY AN international conference or state visit involving developing countries passes without some affirmation of the need for mutual assistance. The concept is incorporated in the Charters of the Organization of African Unity, the Organization of American States, the Colombo Plan for Co-operative Economic Development in South and South-East Asia and numerous other regional and subregional groups. The "Declaration of the Seventy-Seven" at the UN Conference on Trade and Development (UNCTAD) in 1964, although intended primarily as an appeal to the industrialized nations, affirmed the need for ". . . cooperation amongst the developing nations themselves."[1]

The thesis of the present study is that as developing countries assist each other, the character of relations between them may eventually change from a one-way to a two-way flow. The traditional aid-giving countries also have an important role in this potentially reciprocal

[1] "Joint Declaration of the Seventy-Seven Developing Countries Made at the Conclusion of the United Nations Conference on Trade and Development," Geneva, E/CONF.46/L.28, Annex B, p. 2.

process. Their participation can be as "third parties," facilitating the growth of cooperative relations between emerging countries by making financial contributions and sharing administrative experience; or it can eventually be one of direct partnership. Extension of the latter form of cooperation, in particular, would help to reduce the psychologically damaging effects of the donor-recipient relationship between "rich" and "poor" countries.

At the present time multilateral organizations still provide the most effective channels for participation of both the advanced and the emerging countries in the mutual aid process. In addition, some of the advanced countries, notably the United States, have developed forms of "third-party" assistance outside established international channels.

The following examples of mutual aid that has been stimulated through various multilateral channels illustrate important patterns that have developed.

The United Nations

After twenty or more years of work in technical assistance, the various agencies and organizations of the United Nations have developed considerable experience in utilizing the talents of member countries.

The Economic and Social Council of the United Nations has been in the forefront of promoting the use of training facilities in developing countries in multilateral and bilateral assistance programs for these countries. Its reasoning was stated in a 1964 report: [2]

> The case for training in the countries themselves or within the region is based on low cost of training and the desirability of providing training under familiar environmental conditions. . . . Various bilateral and multilateral programs of technical assistance have encouraged the establishment of institutions to serve countries within regions. The programs . . . of the United Nations . . . have been instrumental in assisting such countries. . . . The main feature of training in regional institutions is the adaptability of their training programs to fill local needs, a feature which is difficult to obtain in industrially advanced countries.

[2] *Training of National Technical Personnel for Accelerated Industrialization of Developing Countries,* New York, June 3, 1964, E/3901, p. 18.

Similarly the Council has urged the various agencies of the United Nations and participating organizations to increase their use of experts from developing countries in programs involving these countries. A 1964 report of the Technical Assistance Board to the Council explained the advantages of this practice: [3]

> Their familiarity with the non-technical aspects of the environment in which they are called upon to operate tends to improve the quality of their contributions. The language barrier is also more easily overcome . . . A period of duty as an expert in another developing country will frequently benefit not only the recipient country but the expert as well, for he will broaden his experience and have a greater contribution to make to the development problems of his own country on his return.

According to this report, the number of experts from developing countries on UN assignments rose from about one fifth of all UN experts in 1956 to almost one third in 1963. Most of the experts from developing countries, particularly those from Africa, Latin America and the Middle East, were assigned within their own regions.

Table 13-1 and Appendix Table 1 show recent trends in the use of experts from developing countries and the placement of trainees in developing countries under the United Nations Expanded Program of Technical Assistance (EPTA). In recent years Africa has become the chief EPTA training location in the developing world; in 1965, 40 per cent of all EPTA trainees in developing countries were studying in Africa.

Cooperation between developing countries through the UN machinery has been stimulated principally by the regional Economic Commissions for Africa, for Asia and for Latin America and by the various UN specialized agencies. Generally the UN agencies want projects that they sponsor to become gradually independent of their support and to operate as cooperative regional ventures of the participating countries. In practice, however, because of national ambitions or political conflicts between the governments involved, many United Nations–sponsored regional projects have become national in scope when the UN has left the scene. UN agencies have often found

[3] *The Use of Experts from Developing Countries, Report of the Technical Assistance Board,* Economic and Social Council, UN, New York, April 27, 1964, E/TAC/140.Rev.1, p. 5. See also pp. 3 and 4.

TABLE 13-1 *Participation of Developing Countries, by Area, in the UN Expanded Program of Technical Assistance (EPTA), 1962–1965*

Geographic Area	Experts [a]				EPTA Fellows [a]			
	1962	1963	1964	1965	1962	1963	1964	1965
				Number				
Total, EPTA	2,381	2,817	3,292	3,130	3,831	3,099	5,109	3,657
Total, developing countries	586	711	802	964	1,134	1,052	1,912	1,291
Africa	71	81	90	115	307	417	705	515
Latin America	204	267	298	425	273	256	455	319
Asia and the Far East	215	232	254	287	323	290	552	244
Middle East	66	86	101	83	154	78	156	157
Other	30	45	59	54	77	11	44	56
Total, developed countries	1,795	2,106	2,490	2,166	2,697	2,047	3,197	2,366
				Per Cent				
Total, EPTA	100.0	100.0	100.0	100.0	100.0	100.0	100.0	100.0
Total, developing countries	24.6	25.2	24.4	30.8	29.6	33.9	37.4	35.3
Africa	3.0	2.9	2.7	3.7	8.0	13.4	13.8	14.1
Latin America	8.6	9.5	9.1	13.6	7.1	8.3	8.9	8.7
Asia and the Far East	9.0	8.2	7.7	9.2	8.5	9.3	10.8	6.7
Middle East	2.8	3.0	3.1	2.6	4.0	2.5	3.0	4.3
Other	1.2	1.6	1.8	1.7	2.0	0.4	0.9	1.5
Total, developed countries	75.4	74.8	75.6	69.2	70.4	66.1	62.6	64.7

SOURCE: Appendix Table 1.

[a] Area shown is origin of experts, destination of fellows. Placements exceed number of fellowships granted because some fellows studied in more than one country.

it expedient to allow this in order to save the projects.[4] The Upper Volta Multipurpose Agricultural Center (described in Chapter 6), for example, established with the help of the Special Fund and the Government of Israel, was originally conceived as a regional project for Upper Volta, Dahomey, Niger and Ivory Coast. When the Upper Volta site was chosen, the other countries were apparently unwilling to continue to participate. The sponsors were thus left committed to an essentially national project (with what is euphemistically called "regional interest").

These difficulties in establishing regional projects are but symptoms of some of the well-known resistances to cooperation within the UN structure. They also suggest that the UN channels are by no means the only or necessarily the best international channels through which to achieve greater mutual assistance between developing countries.

The Organization of American States

While the Latin American countries, acting through the Organization of American States (OAS), have achieved significant progress in trade and economic cooperation, they continue to depend heavily on resources outside the hemisphere for assistance.

For many years the OAS had a very small program of technical cooperation, financed almost entirely by the United States. In 1964 it established the Special Fund for Development Assistance, with an annual budget of about $7 million, financed two thirds by the United States and one third by other OAS members and by donations from countries outside the hemisphere (Israel, for example, contributed $72,000 to the Fund in 1964.) A portion of the Fund's budget is for support of independent scholarship programs at universities within the hemisphere and outside of it. The Fund also finances regional projects of the OAS itself.

One of the most important regional projects sponsored by the OAS is the Instituto Interamericano de Ciencias Agrícolas, IICA (Inter-American Institute of Agricultural Sciences), with headquarters in

[4] *Official Records: 37th Session, Interim Report on the Implementation of the 1963–64 Program,* Economic and Social Council, UN, New York, E/3871/Rev.1–E/TA/REP/265, p. 33.

Turrialba, Costa Rica, and regional branches in Guatemala, Peru and Uruguay. The IICA program includes postgraduate study, middle-level training and research, carried out both at Turrialba and at the regional centers. The Turrialba center has helped universities in Argentina, Brazil, Colombia and Peru establish graduate study programs of their own, and in 1965 convened a meeting of deans of Latin American graduate schools of agriculture to discuss common problems and stimulate closer contacts. The Turrialba facility is currently being expanded with the help of a $4.5 million UN Special Fund Project and a $2 million AID loan.[5]

The Centro Inter-Americano para Reforma Agraria (Inter-American Land Reform Center), established under IICA's tutelage in 1964, is designed to supplement the Institute's work in a vital new area of activity. It sponsors a one-year graduate course in agrarian reform at its headquarters in Bogotá, Colombia, organizes short international training courses and seminars, and carries on research and advisory activities.[6]

IICA's contribution to agricultural training and development in Latin America, through its various centers, particularly during the last few years, has been quite important. Through national and international courses, seminars and intensive short workshops almost 10,000 students, specialists and middle-level and high-level officials had participated in its various training activities by the end of 1964.[7]

Nevertheless, the IICA programs and the other technical assistance efforts of the OAS are a relatively small achievement in mutual assistance compared to the human and institutional resources of the hemisphere. This is recognized and deplored by some Latin American

[5] IICA, "Escuela para Graduados, Prospecto Año Academico 1965–1966," Turrialba, September 1965 (pamphlet). For an example of a training course at a regional center, see the announcement of a five-week course in tropical horticulture in Maracay, Venezuela, in 1965, which brought together agronomists from Bolivia, Colombia, Peru, Ecuador and Venezuela, "Curso Internacional de Producción de Hortalizas en el Tropico" (course announcement), IICA Dirección Regional para la Zona Andina, Lima, Peru, 1965.

[6] IICA, "What Is the Inter-American Land Reform Center?" San José, Costa Rica, July 1963 (leaflet).

[7] This estimate is based on figures published by IICA in a series of country pamphlets entitled *Servicios a los Países* (Services to Countries).

leaders. José A. Mora, Secretary General of the OAS, urged a new orientation when the amendment of the OAS Charter came up for discussion in Panama in 1966. "The Alliance for Progress," he said, "must be embodied in the inter-American system as a continuing obligation of mutual aid." [8]

The OAS Charter amendments adopted in February 1967 reflected this spirit to some degree. Article 36, for example, obligates member states to "extend among themselves the benefits of science and technology . . ." and Article 41 urges the member states "to give adequate priority to the preparation and carrying out of multilateral projects . . ." [9]

It is too early to assess the significance of these OAS Charter changes, and of the subsequent recommendations for multinational projects adopted at the Punta del Este Conference of 1967, but there is no doubt that they do set the stage for advances in mutual assistance within the hemisphere. Nowhere in the developing world is cooperation likely to have a better chance of success and of yielding quick benefits than in Latin America.

The Colombo Plan

Unlike the Organization of American States, the Colombo Plan for Co-operative Development in South and South-East Asia is not, strictly speaking, a regional organization. Founded in 1950 as an association of 7 British Commonwealth countries, it has since expanded greatly and includes today 23 countries, which meet annually to consult on developmental problems of the region. Through its Council for Technical Cooperation, the Colombo Plan has promoted countless bilateral assistance agreements between various members.[10]

[8] *New York Times*, February 28, 1966.

[9] *Protocol of Amendment to the Charter of the Organization of American States, "Protocol of Buenos Aires,"* signed at the Third Special Inter-American Conference, Buenos Aires, February 27, 1967, pp. 58 and 60 (mimeo.).

[10] As of 1965 the members of the Colombo Plan Consultative Committee and its Council for Technical Cooperation were (in order of accession): Australia, Canada, Ceylon, India, New Zealand, Pakistan, the United Kingdom (which together with Malaya and British Borneo comprised the original members of the

It is largely consultative and shuns involvement in political conflicts of the region.

The promotion of so-called "intraregional activities," involving the use of institutional and human resources of the developing countries within the region, has long been among the primary goals of the Colombo group. A pathbreaking study undertaken for the Colombo Plan in 1961 by H. R. Mills, of the British Council, had this to say on the subject: [11]

> There is not yet a habit of mind in the region which turns to neighbouring countries for technician or other training. . . . One of the impediments is lack of knowledge. . . . Another is the fallacy that the value of training increases with the distance travelled to get it. A third is a natural unwillingness to admit that a neighbour has better facilities than one's own . . .
>
> The principle that should guide decisions . . . is that a trainee should not be sent outside the region for any form of training if the training is available in the region. . . . The advantages of training in the region are obvious. The cost is a small fraction of what it costs to send trainees to Europe, North America or Japan. The problems and conditions of work, man-management and welfare are usually similar in neighboring countries, whereas outside the region conditions are often quite unrelated to those of the trainee's own country . . .

In line with the recommendations of the Mills Report, almost 13 per cent of the experts sent have been nationals of the region and over 9 per cent of training placements have likewise been within the region. (See Table 13-2.)

In 1964 the Colombo Plan Bureau issued its second edition of a *Handbook of Training Facilities,* which lists almost 600 regional institutions and training establishments, over half of which are prepared to accept foreign trainees. India, which has offered to accommodate foreign trainees at any Government-supported Indian institution, accounted for the bulk of the facilities listed in the catalog.[12]

Plan); Cambodia, Laos, United States, South Vietnam; Burma, Nepal; Indonesia; Japan, Philippines, Thailand; Singapore; Bhutan, South Korea; Afghanistan, Maldive Islands, Malaysia.

[11] *Report on Training Facilities at the Technician Level in South and South-East Asia* (the "Mills Report"), Colombo Plan Bureau, Colombo, Ceylon, 1961, pp. 109, 111.

[12] *Handbook of Training Facilities at the Technician Level in South and South-East Asia,* Colombo Plan Bureau, Colombo, Ceylon, September 1964.

TABLE **13-2** *Technical Cooperation in the Colombo Plan, Fiscal Years, 1950–1965* [a]

Type of Assistance	Total, 1950–1965 [a]	1950–1958 [a]	1958–1964	1964–1965
Total				
Experts supplied	7,167	1,002	4,979	1,186
Training scholarships	37,966	6,886	26,160	4,920
Expenditures [b]	$618,002,036	$31,314,836	$476,205,775	$110,481,426
Developing countries [c]				
Experts supplied	909	29	642	238
Per cent of total	12.7	2.9	12.9	20.1
Training scholarships	3,446	936	2,122	388
Per cent of total	9.1	13.6	8.1	7.9
Expenditures [b]	$5,152,067	$1,673,283	$2,755,385	$723,400
Per cent of total	0.8	5.3	0.6	0.7
Developed countries [d]				
Experts supplied	6,258	973	4,337	948
Training scholarships	34,520	5,950	24,038	4,532
Expenditures [b]	$612,849,969	$29,641,553	$473,450,390	$109,758,026

SOURCES: Training scholarships–Appendix Table 2; Experts supplied–Appendix Table 3; Expenditures–Colombo Plan Bureau, Colombo, Ceylon: *Technical Co-operation Under the Colombo Plan: Report by the Colombo Plan Council for Technical Co-operation in South and South-East Asia for the Year 1 July 1959 to 30 June 1960*, p. 86; *Report for the Year 1 July 1961 to 30 June 1962*, p. 103; *Report for the Year 1 July 1963 to 30 June 1964*, p. 69; and *Report for the Year 1 July 1964 to 30 June 1965*, pp. 99 and 100.

[a] Excludes the United States prior to 1958. It joined the Council in 1958–1959.

[b] Converted from £ Sterling, as given in source, to U. S. dollars at the rate of 1 £ = $2.80.

[c] Includes Burma, Ceylon, India, Indonesia, Malaysia, Pakistan, Philippines, Thailand, Vietnam.

[d] Includes Australia, Britain, Canada, Japan, New Zealand, United States.

The handbook also indicates that host governments within the region assume all the costs of training offered to other Colombo Plan members, including round trip international travel.[13]

In another step to promote intraregional activities, the Colombo Plan Bureau in 1964 added an "Adviser on Intra-Regional Training" (AIRT) to its staff, and countries in the region were asked to designate liaison officers to work with the new adviser. The Bureau also for the first time was given the right to screen training applications, and suggest ways of providing particular types of training within the region. In a companion move, governments requesting training out-

[13] *Ibid.*, pp. 313–327. Third-country training is not included.

side the region, even though facilities were available within the region, were asked to explain their reasons.[14]

It is too early to assess the fruits of these efforts, but the Colombo Council's report for 1964–1965 reflects a certain pessimism, when it notes that "the quantum and the rate of expansion [of training in the region] are not as spectacular as had been hoped," and that countries are not sending copies of training requests to the Bureau so that they can be screened.[15]

Published figures on intraregional activities show three important facts about the region: first, there has been no significant rise over the years in the use of training facilities; second, India is the major supplier of experts as well as of training facilities and its aid to Nepal is quite significant; [16] and third, virtually no sharing has taken place between member countries that were in conflict with each other, such as India and Pakistan, or Malaysia and Indonesia.[17] (See Table 13-2 and Appendix Tables 2 and 3.)

One aspect of cooperation between developing countries under the Colombo Plan, not reflected in the published statistics, is training financed by third countries, a system long in use by the United States. In 1963 Australia also began a small program of this type. The considerable significance of such arrangements is discussed later in this chapter.

Although the Colombo Plan has not yet achieved a real breakthrough in mobilizing the potentials for mutual aid between its developing members, it is one of the first international groups concerned with problems of development to establish a major mutual assistance policy and to back it with some action.

[14] *Technical Co-operation Under the Colombo Plan: Report by the Colombo Plan Council for Technical Co-operation in South and South-East Asia for the Year 1 July 1962 to 30 June 1963*, Colombo, Ceylon, October 1963, p. 81; and *Report of Colombo Plan Council for Technical Co-operation for 1964–1965*, p. 43.

[15] *Report of Colombo Plan Council for Technical Co-operation for 1964–1965*, pp. 5, 44.

[16] During 1963 India spent about 37 million rupees (about $7 million) on technical and financial assistance to Nepal. (*The Colombo Plan for Co-operative Economic Development in South and South-East Asia, Thirteenth Annual Report of the Consultative Committee*, London, November 1964, p. 262.)

[17] *Ibid.*, p. 94.

Near-East Technical Cooperation

Mutual assistance between Iran, Turkey and Pakistan is not comparable to the volume of activities carried out between developing countries participating in the Colombo Plan. Resources are more limited and the area of activity is smaller, but the two tools for mutual assistance developed by these countries, described below, offer useful patterns for utilizing the resources of this region.

The Multilateral Technical Cooperation Fund (MTCF)

The establishment of the Multilateral Technical Cooperation Fund (MTCF), was a kind of afterthought to the military and political structure of the Central Treaty Organization (CENTO). In 1959 its members—Turkey, Iran, Pakistan, Great Britain and the United States [18]—pledged to promote economic development in the three so-called "regional" member countries, and established the MTCF "to promote and expand facilities for the interchange of experts, technicians, technical information and ideas between the three region countries in the various fields of economic development." [19]

The Fund has spent about $1 million since its inception—not a large amount for a program of this type. Great Britain and the United States contribute two thirds of MTCF's operating costs; Turkey, Iran and Pakistan together supply the remaining third. Contributions are not made regularly, but in response to calls for funds "as needed," usually once a year. The Fund is managed by a "Working Party," consisting of delegates from each of the member countries and a representative of the CENTO Secretariat. It finances only activities carried out in the three regional countries by nationals of these countries. U. S. or British experts participating in any MTCF project are financed from other sources. The combination of developed nation financing and

[18] The United States nominally has only "observer" status, but participates in CENTO'S structure and activities.

[19] The discussion of MTCF is based on "Multilateral Technical Cooperation Fund," a pamphlet published by the CENTO Economic Division in 1963; on information from the CENTO Secretariat, Ankara; and on observations and interviews by the author of the present study.

developing nations' skills, with joint control and supervision, is a model of successful multilateral collaboration. There have, however, been problems.

The Fund uses more than two thirds of its limited resources on three projects—the Middle East Technical University (METU) and the Hacettepe Medical Center, both located in Ankara, Turkey; and the Agricultural Machinery and Soil Conservation Training Center in Karaj, Iran. Expenditures for these projects have left little money for other types of cooperation between the countries of the region.

A greater problem than limited resources, however, has been the language barrier. While English is spoken by many professionals of the region, their command of the language is often too limited for profitable exchange of ideas or training. A Pakistani participant who had attended a six-month training course at Turkey's Poplar Research Institute, for example, had only praise for the efforts of his Turkish hosts, but noted regretfully that they had had to communicate with him in "rudimentary English, by symbols, etc.," and that for the most part both he and his teachers had depended on Turkish-English dictionaries. Many middle-level people who could profit most from practical training experience are unable to participate in MTCF training because of the lack of a common language. Many others who have no language problem prefer training in the developed countries. Despite the CENTO Secretariat's assistance, moreover, the implementation of proposed projects is slow. A 1961 Iranian request for training in fish breeding, for instance, produced an offer from Pakistan in 1963, but by the end of 1964 Iran had not acted on the offer.

In part because of the problems described, the Fund is apparently not serving the three regional members equally. Turkey, in particular, despite its active interest in mutual assistance, makes disproportionately small use of the Fund, and lately has turned its attention to a new and different kind of regional grouping—the Regional Cooperation for Development (RCD).

Regional Cooperation for Development (*RCD*)

The RCD was founded at an Istanbul "little summit" meeting of heads of government of Turkey, Iran and Pakistan in July 1964. Inspired evidently by the UNCTAD meeting held earlier that year, the three countries sought to establish a broad framework for economic and cultural cooperation. All three countries were already allied through CENTO, but the new regional group was to function without the United States and Great Britain, and its primary emphasis was to be economic, rather than military and political.

Pakistan's President, Ayub Khan, who led in the creation of RCD, explained the need for it: [20]

> If we wish to protect our national integrity, it is necessary that small nations like ours should work as close together in as many fields as possible to make up for whatever weakness we may be suffering from individually. It is not enough to have military alliances and pacts . . .

The RCD has planned a broad program of economic and cultural cooperation, including an RCD chamber of commerce; joint airline, shipping conference and industrial enterprises; improved transportation and communications; and cultural institutes, cultural exchanges, etc. The Regional Planning Council, consisting of representatives of the state planning organizations of the three countries, acts as the RCD's top administrative body. At its first meeting in March 1965 it gave high priority to an RCD-operated technical assistance program.[21]

It is too early to assess the success of the RCD plans, but some of the preliminary steps already taken indicate that the participating countries are seriously interested. Turkey, for example, has prepared an impressive inventory of technical assistance facilities and capabilities, described in Chapter 14, which should prove useful not only to the RCD, but also to the MTCF, the U. S. Agency for International Development (AID) Third Country Training Program and to Turkey's own incipient bilateral cooperation program. Turkey's State Planning Organization, moreover, has offered to assist Iran and Pakistan in preparing their inventories. Member countries are apparently prepared to contribute significantly more to RCD's technical cooperation program than they contribute to the MTCF budget. It may well be that the lack of major-power involvement in the RCD has stimulated the efforts of participants for their mutual benefit.

[20] *Iran Today,* published by the Ministry of Information of the Imperial Iranian Government, Teheran, Winter 1965, p. 6.

[21] "The RCD General Agreement for Technical Cooperation . . ." (mimeo.)

The Foundation for Mutual Cooperation in Africa (FAMA)

Incipient efforts to promote the sharing of skills and resources between the developing countries of Africa began with the help of the former colonial powers.

The Foundation for Mutual Cooperation (FAMA) was established in 1959 as an adjunct to the Commission for Technical Cooperation in Africa South of the Sahara (CCTA), a loose grouping of colonial powers and representatives of African territories soon to become independent. FAMA was concerned largely with coordinating technical assistance to the area.

When FAMA was established in 1959 it had 9 members, 4 of them non-African; by 1962 it had 24 members, only 3 of them non-African; and by 1965, when FAMA became the Scientific, Technical and Research Commission of the Organization of African Unity (OAU), its membership had risen to 34 sovereign states, all African.[22]

However, the rapidly growing membership in FAMA has not been accompanied by a corresponding growth of technical cooperation between the African countries. On the contrary, the growth in FAMA has probably resulted in a net decline in cooperative activity, for when FAMA became part of the OAU structure, its European members (Belgium, France and Great Britain), who had supplied most of the funds for programs of cooperation, were automatically excluded from membership.

FAMA began its work initially along the lines of the Colombo Plan Bureau, as a channel for promoting bilateral arrangements between members. Gradually, however, its activities expanded to include training programs of its own, the promotion of permanent regional training institutions and regional joint action programs.

Typical FAMA activities have included a two-week course for veterinarians at the East African Veterinary Research Organization in Kenya; a study tour of community development programs, in which participants visited Cameroon, Eastern Nigeria, Ivory Coast and Mali

[22] This and subsequent material on FAMA are from *The Fifth Annual Report of the Foundation for Mutual Assistance in Africa,* FAMA Secretariat, Lagos, 1963; and unpublished data from the Secretariat.

under the guidance of two European experts provided by the FAO and the French Government; an intensive campaign against rinderpest (cattle plague) over a 750,000 square mile area in Cameroon, Chad, Niger and Nigeria; the establishment of three French language training centers and one English language training center; and the provision (in 1962) of 72 experts and 489 training scholarships distributed among the member countries.

The bulk of FAMA's funds, and evidently the majority of its experts, were provided by its European members, UN specialized agencies and by the United States. Before it became part of the OAU, FAMA had in fact become primarily a broker between individual African countries and the developed countries or international organizations. Although it undoubtedly also stimulated some cooperation between its African members, this purpose evidently had become subordinate to its primary activity. In light of the existence of well-established assistance channels to the UN and to major developed countries, the importance of FAMA's brokerage function had become debatable. Its future, in any event, seems uncertain, for as a Commission of the OAU it occupies a peculiar position. Its 70-man staff at the time of merger was more than twice the size of the OAU's central Secretariat staff, and through the merger it undoubtedly lost sources of financial support which had been open to it as an independent organization. It also ran the risk of losing its nonpolitical character. In sum, FAMA's approach and transformation do not suggest themselves as particularly effective patterns for promoting the growth of cooperation between African countries.

The Role of the Developed Countries

Economically advanced countries with significant programs and potentialities for assistance can play a significant role in stimulating cooperation between developing countries. Like the United Nations, they possess the funds, experience and operational structure needed to bring about meaningful cooperation. The U. S. Agency for International Development, in particular, has made a major contribution to this effort through its Third Country Training Program, which started on a small scale in the mid-1940's in Latin America. Among its early projects were a vocational education scheme for Paraguayans in Brazil and a training program for Ecuadorian and Peruvian rural leaders in Bolivia, followed by a seminar in the United States. From Latin America the program spread to Europe in the late 1940's and to other regions in the 1950's. Today, according to AID's Office of International Training in Washington, the Third Country Program accounts for more than a quarter of AID's total training effort.

Third-country training is triangular in nature, involving the trainee's home country, the host country where the training takes place and the United States, acting as the intermediary who brings trainers and trainees together. All three parties usually share the cost, though there are no firm rules governing these arrangements. The chief contribution, other than financial, of the U. S. Agency for International Development is to provide the essential administrative structure. Through its missions, located in the various developing countries, appropriate training facilities are found and arrangements for training programs are negotiated. Initially, according to a Foreign Operations Administration (FOA, a predecessor agency to AID) Manual Order,[23] the basic U. S. purpose in sponsoring this program was to provide for training needed by a developing country but which could not be obtained in the United States.

Over the years, the concept of the Third Country Training Program has been broadened considerably. The Agency for International Development now recognizes not only the technical need, but more important, the fact that third-country training can benefit all three partners by strengthening bilateral relations and cultural ties between them, broadening the available global training capability and developing greater interest in and capability for sharing among the participating countries.

European countries, in which in the past a large part of U. S. third-country training was based, have now developed their own bilateral and multilateral training programs for the developing countries. In recognition of this fact, AID sponsorship of training in Europe has steadily declined, and by 1965 had practically ceased (Table 13-3). The table also shows the twofold character of the program: training

[23] This and other FOA policy papers are available in the Office of International Training, U. S. Agency for International Development, Washington.

TABLE 13-3 *Trainees Sponsored by U. S. Agency for International Development, by Area of Training, Arrivals, Fiscal Years 1961–1966* [a]

Area of Training	1961	1962	1963	1964	1965	1966
Total	8,603	7,662	7,893	7,691	7,433	6,850
Third country	2,093	2,133	2,127	1,703	1,859	1,940
Per cent of total	24.3	27.8	26.9	22.1	25.0	28.3
Africa	10	59	89	51	55	62
Europe	575	264	362	67	12	—
Far East	542	803	701	723	715	844
Latin America	175	386	411	303	423	442
Near East and South Asia	586	621	564	559	654	592
Other	205	—	—	—	—	—
United States and third country	1,330	887	891	1,026	289	311
Per cent of total	15.5	11.6	11.3	13.3	3.9	4.5
United States	5,180	4,642	4,875	4,962	5,285	4,599
Per cent of total	60.2	60.6	61.8	64.6	71.1	67.2

SOURCE: *Report on Participant Training, Fiscal Years 1961, 1962, 1963, 1964, 1965* and *1966,* Office of International Training, U. S. Agency for International Development, Washington.

[a] Excludes training under AID contracts.

exclusively in a third country and training in the United States combined with training in a third country. The exclusively third-country training has been about 25 per cent of AID's total training effort, despite the geographic shift from Europe to, principally, the Far East and Latin America. Combined U. S. and third-country training, on the other hand, dropped sharply in 1965, evidently as a result of the decline in training activities in Europe and Japan.

The focus of AID's Third Country Training Program is now entirely on the developing countries. (See Table 13-4.) China (Taiwan), the Philippines, Thailand and Mexico accounted for over half the training conducted outside the United States in fiscal 1966.[24] No doubt

[24] Officially, the largest third-country training site has for some years been Lebanon (469 trainees in fiscal year 1966), but since the trainees are exclusively students at the American University of Beirut, which is in fact a U. S. educational institution located abroad, Lebanon has been omitted from this discussion.

TABLE 13-4 *Trainees Sponsored by the U. S. Agency for International Development in Third Countries, Arrivals, Fiscal Year 1966* [a]

Region and Country of Training	Number of Trainees	Region and Country of Training	Number of Trainees
Total	1,940	Latin America (cont'd)	
		Chile	37
Africa	62	Colombia	21
Ethiopia	9	Costa Rica	26
Kenya	19	El Salvador	2
Nigeria	10	Guatemala	30
Togo	20	Mexico	180
Uganda	4	Panama	71
		Peru	16
Far East	844	Venezuela	18
China (Taiwan)	462		
Korea	13	Near East and South Asia	592
Philippines	213	India	96
Thailand	156	Iran	19
		Jordan	7
Latin America	442	Lebanon	469
Argentina	26	Pakistan	1
Brazil	15		

SOURCE: *Report on Participant Training, Fiscal Year 1966,* Office of International Training, U. S. Agency for International Development, Washington, pp. 21–27.
[a] Excludes combination United States and third-country training.

these countries, with U. S. support, are making a significant contribution to mutual assistance between developing countries. At the same time, other developing countries which have the capacity, such as Argentina, Chile, South Korea, India and Israel (which was not utilized at all for third-country training in 1966), could be used to better advantage. Israel and India are conducting significant training programs of their own and both could accomplish a great deal more with additional financial assistance. Much of this assistance, at least to Israel, South Korea and India, could be financed with U. S.–owned local currencies.

There may be good reasons for the limited use of these and other countries as training sites by the Agency for International Development. But it is just as likely that many of the current trends in AID's Third Country Training Program are more a matter of chance—the presence or absence of dynamic, concerned local or U. S. personnel in particular countries—than of policy. AID's training program in Mexico, which grew within a few years from a few dozen to some 200 trainees annually is a case in point.

U. S.–sponsored training in Mexico began on a significant scale in 1959, with a contract concluded between AID and the Monterrey Technological Institute, providing for various study programs at the Institute for students from other Latin American countries.[25] It was followed by the establishment in the AID Mission in Mexico of a regional Third Country Training office, headed by an imaginative training officer. With the wholehearted cooperation of Mexican officials and institutions, courses of interest to other Latin American countries were organized not only at the Monterrey Institute, but also at Mexico's School of Hospital Administration, the Ministry of Hydraulic Resources, the Federal School Construction Program and elsewhere. The number of trainees sent to Mexico from other Latin American countries rose rapidly, as did Mexico's interest and willingness to share its facilities. (For a discussion of Mexico's own program, see Chapter 14.) However, attempts to repeat the Mexican experience elsewhere in the hemisphere were not very successful. Although a 300-page catalog of training opportunities and facilities in 13 Latin American countries was compiled,[26] and a bimonthly bulletin on third-country training, *En Marcha* (On the March), was published, the program fell victim to internal bureaucratic disputes. The hopes of providing a clearing house for training opportunities and promoting many regionally oriented training programs in other countries of the hemisphere were not realized.

Nevertheless the Mexican experience and activities on a smaller scale elsewhere have demonstrated the potential of this type of program, in which all the parties concerned benefit.

Third-country training, of course, is only one of the ways in which developed countries can encourage cooperation between developing countries, but it is one of the simplest and cheapest. While France and England have supported some small-scale training arrangements between their ex-colonies, at this writing only Australia has followed

[25] *En Marcha,* published by U. S. AID, Mexico, November–December 1962, p. 7.

[26] *Training Opportunities in Latin America,* U. S. AID, Mexico, May 1963, p. XI.

the U. S. lead and formally established a small third-country training program of this type.[27]

It is not possible, on the basis of our brief survey, to reach definitive conclusions regarding the success or failure of the multilateral sharing activities between developing countries. But it is clear that, despite the obstacles, these activities are receiving increased attention from the international community. It is equally clear that, for the present at least, organizational and financial participation by the economically advanced countries and international organizations is essential to the growth of mutual assistance between the developing countries.

[27] *Report of Colombo Plan Council for Technical Co-operation for 1964–1965*, p. 55.

Chapter 14

Bilateral Programs

THE MACHINERY set in motion by international agencies and the economically advanced countries, described in the previous chapter, has helped to speed the evolution of bilateral assistance programs between developing countries. The following examples of these bilateral programs serve to indicate the scope of this type of sharing between countries of the emerging world.

Cooperation in Latin America

Latin American countries have a great deal to offer each other in terms of human resources and infrastructure development. Even their financial resources are generally greater than those of the struggling countries of Asia and Africa. To take the measure most pertinent to this discussion—human resources—only Haiti, of all the American countries, falls in the lowest, the "underdeveloped" level of the Harbison-Myers composite index; nine Latin American countries—Guatemala, Dominican Republic, Bolivia, Brazil, Colombia, Paraguay, Ecuador, Jamaica and Peru—are ranked as "partially developed"; six—Mexico, Cuba, Costa Rica, Venezuela, Chile and Uruguay—as "semiadvanced"; and one, Argentina, as "advanced." [1]

[1] Frederick Harbison and Charles A. Myers have constructed a composite index of human resource development in which they rank 75 countries and group them

Argentina

Even though Argentina's human resources are considerable, relatively few are shared with other countries of the hemisphere. Assistance has been limited to some technical services provided to Bolivia, Paraguay, Uruguay and Chile and to the cosponsorship of a few specialized training facilities, such as the Latin American Center of Mathematics, and of courses offered by the UN's Latin American Institute for Economic and Social Planning.

Argentina's major contribution to hemispheric development of human resources has been the traditional open-door policy of its universities, where study is tuition-free for all students, including foreign students. According to the estimate of an OECD expert working in Argentina, there were between 4,000 and 5,000 foreign students in Argentine universities in 1965, or almost 3 per cent of the total student body.[2] This probably represents a decline from 1958, when new qualifying (*equivalencia*) examinations were introduced for all entering students.

More than half the foreign students at Argentine universities in 1965, according to the OECD survey, are from Peru, followed by Bolivia and Paraguay. Although most of them apparently receive no government assistance, the Argentine Government subsidizes their studies indirectly through its support of the universities. Assuming that there were 4,500 foreign students in Argentine public universities in 1965, the Argentine Government's subsidy amounted to about $1.5 million.[3]

Argentina has for several years discussed a plan to make large numbers of public school teachers available to other countries. The

into four ascending levels of human resource development: underdeveloped, partially developed, semiadvanced and advanced. (*Education, Manpower and Economic Growth: Strategies of Human Resource Development,* McGraw-Hill, New York, 1964, p. 33.)

[2] Estimate of the number of students from M. Hecquet, OECD expert temporarily assigned to Argentina's National Development Council (CONADE) in 1965; the percentage estimate is based on published 1960 attendance data.

[3] Estimate based on data quoted by Morris A. Horowitz in *Manpower and Education* (Harbison and Myers, editors), McGraw-Hill, New York, 1965, pp. 23, 31.

elaboration of an ambitious plan known as "Maestros para America" (Teachers for America) indicates Argentina's awareness of its potential role, but this plan has not yet been executed.

Chile

Argentina's neighbor, Chile, also ranks relatively high in human resources,[4] but its sharing with other countries has been limited to accepting a small number of foreign trainees and university students and to occasional technical assistance missions to other countries, such as recent ones of railroad and electrification experts to Ecuador.

The largely state-supported University of Chile, which accounts for about half the total higher education student population of the country, had about 350 foreign students in 1965, roughly 1 per cent of the student body. About 50 per cent of these came from Bolivia, Venezuela and Ecuador.[5]

Mexico

Mexico, less well-endowed than either Argentina or Chile,[6] is apparently sharing its human resources and educational facilities with other countries of Latin America more generously than either of those countries. Mexico's national university has an enrollment of about 1,500 foreign students, or about 2 per cent of the student body of about 74,000 (1964). Roughly two thirds of the foreign students are from countries south of Mexico, principally Central America.[7] Because of increasingly crowded conditions at the university, the percentage of foreign students admitted has been declining over the past few years. However, Mexico also provides facilities for foreign trainees at many specialized institutes, and has taken a leading role in establishing in Mexico various inter-American institutes and organizations. A

[4] It stands about midway in a group of 21 "semiadvanced" (third level) countries on the Harbison and Myers composite index. (*Op. cit.*, p. 33.)

[5] University Relations Office, University of Chile, Santiago.

[6] Harbison and Myers rank it at the bottom of the "semiadvanced" countries. (*Op. cit.*)

[7] Estimates from the National Autonomous University of Mexico, Mexico City.

catalog of Mexican training facilities published in 1965 by U. S. AID lists more than 60 institutions or Government departments which accept foreign trainees.[8] A few examples illustrate Mexico's potentialities and accomplishments in mutual cooperation.

With the support of the United Nations Educational, Scientific and Cultural Organization (UNESCO) and the OAS, the Mexican Government has established the Latin American Regional Center for School Construction. Its function is to assist school construction programs throughout the hemisphere through technical assistance missions, research and training courses conducted at the Center. The first training course, with participants from Mexico, Chile and Ecuador, was conducted in 1963, with some support from U. S. AID. Since then several courses have been given, and the Center has sent technical experts to a number of countries, including Guatemala, El Salvador, Costa Rica, Nicaragua, Ecuador, Peru, Chile and Brazil; in some cases, actual model schools made of prefabricated material were sent, while in others the experts taught local people the proper use of such material.

Mexican Government departments and institutions have accepted many trainees from abroad, and in some cases have sent their own technical assistance missions to other countries of the hemisphere. Nacional Financiera, the Government's highly successful development corporation, has sent experts on missions lasting three or four months to its counterparts in Bolivia, Peru and Ecuador; the Bank of Mexico has assisted the Central Bank of Guatemala; and Mexico has sent an agricultural survey mission to British Honduras.

A new chapter in Mexico's cooperation activities was opened in January 1966, with the visit of Mexican President Gustavo Díaz Ordaz to Central America. In connection with this visit, Mexico confirmed an economic development loan of $10 million to El Salvador, and a loan of $10 million to the Central American Bank for Economic Integration at Tegucigalpa, Honduras.[9] Technical assistance agreements are in effect with Honduras, El Salvador and Nicaragua.

Mexican officials report that they get more requests for assistance

[8] *Training Facilities in Mexico,* Agency for International Development, Mexico City (no date, mimeo.).

[9] *Survey of International Development,* January 15, 1966, p. 3.

than they can handle. Difficulties in meeting these requests are due partly to funding problems and partly to the reluctance of Mexicans to undertake foreign assignments.[10]

Despite its considerable sharing activities, Mexico seems content to respond to *ad hoc* requests with *ad hoc* activities and arrangements. It thus far has no coordinated framework of policy or administration for the varied programs in which it participates.

Cooperation in Africa

It has been said that the poor can share only their poverty. But some of the countries of Africa, the poorest of the world's inhabited continents, have already proved otherwise by showing both the desire and the ability to aid their neighbors. Especially in the sphere of training and higher education they are, on a small scale, sharing their resources. A few significant examples are described below.

Ghana

Ghana, the first new country in Africa, is better endowed with trained manpower than are other African countries.[11] In line with Kwame Nkrumah's avowed policy of African unity, Ghana inaugurated a program of scholarships for other African countries, and soon after achieving independence even extended financial assistance to them.[12] However, some of the training offered, especially courses at the so-called "Kwame Nkrumah Ideological Institute," was clearly designed to indoctrinate foreign students in the philosophy of "Nkrumahism"; regular academic scholarships, on the other hand, provided instruction in a variety of useful professions at Ghanaian institutions.

[10] This phenomenon is in contrast to the situation in most other developing countries, which seem to be the unwilling victims of a "brain drain."

[11] Ghana falls in the second level of the Harbison-Myers index, and ranks forty-sixth in this index. Of the African countries included in the index only the United Arab Republic and South Africa, both of which fall in the third level, rank higher. (*Op. cit.*, pp. 33 and 44–48.)

[12] Ghana has made loans of G£10 million ($28 million) to Guinea; G£4 million ($11.2 million) to Mali; and G£5 million ($14 million) to Upper Volta.

During 1964–65 Ghana reportedly provided 250 academic scholarships, which included tuition, maintenance, clothing, transportation and pocket money—at an average annual cost of G£500 ($1,400) per student. Foreign students in Ghana studied veterinary medicine, education, community development, mining, nursing and general secondary school subjects, but partly because of the political reputation of the program during the Nkrumah regime, few African countries took advantage of Ghana's facilities. Prior to Nkrumah's overthrow in 1966 the largest student contingents were from Somalia, Congo (Brazzaville) and Zanzibar, with only a scattering of students from other countries. Ghana has also sent a small number of experts abroad on technical missions.

Nigeria

Nigeria, not nearly so well endowed with skilled manpower as Ghana,[13] has had a small assistance program since 1964–65, when it allotted N£20,000 ($56,000) for technical assistance to other countries out of the central government's budget. Additional costs are absorbed by participating Nigerian institutions. Activities have included secretarial courses for trainees from Bechuanaland, Liberia, Kenya, Gambia, Tanzania and Malawi; technical training for a few Dahomeyans at the College of Technology; secondary school education for a few students from the Congo (Kinshasa); sending magistrates to Tanzania and Malawi and medical officers to Sierra Leone; and assistance on the revision of civil service procedures in Kenya and Uganda. Nigeria also worked out a small exchange arrangement under which Guineans have studied English at Nigeria's Federal Advanced Teachers' College and Nigerians have gone to Guinea to study French.[14] Under U. S. AID's Third-Country Training Program students have gone to Nigeria from the Cameroon for training in home economics and from Ethiopia for training in port authority management and medicine.

Nigeria has been careful to keep its assistance program clear of

[13] Nigeria is thirteenth from the bottom in the Harbison-Myers composite index. (*Ibid.*)

[14] Information for this section was supplied by officials of the Nigerian Government.

political overtones. Its policy in this respect was laid down in a statement to Parliament by the late Prime Minister Sir Alhaji Abubakar Tafawa Balewa shortly before Nigeria became independent in 1960:[15]

> It will be our aim to assist any African country to find a solution to its problems and to foster the growth of a common understanding among all the nations, and especially among the new nations of this continent. We are not going to ask to give advice, we are not going to ask to give assistance. People must make requests to us.

Nigeria has apparently adhered to this policy and has not advertised or otherwise publicized its assistance.

Ethiopia

Ethiopia is by almost any measure one of the world's poorest countries.[16] Yet it has a dynamic, growing university, which has received strong support from the Imperial Government and foreign sponsors. The language of instruction at Haile Selassie I University is English, thus reducing the language problem for foreign students.

Evidently as part of an effort to project Ethiopia as an important African political and intellectual center, the Ethiopian Government initiated a program of Haile Selassie I scholarships for students from other African countries, and encouraged foreign donors, notably U. S. AID, to do likewise. As a result, foreign students, sponsored mostly by AID and the Ethiopian Government, became an important element at Haile Selassie I University in the academic year 1963–64, accounting for 10 to 15 per cent of the student body.[17] The following year, however, foreign student enrollment declined by almost 25 per cent (Table 14-1), reportedly reflecting problems with housing, health, food and social facilities for the foreign students. While these problems may be only temporary, they emphasize the need for adequate preparation and planning before facilities are opened to students from abroad.

[15] Statement to Parliament, August 20, 1960, by courtesy of Ministry of External Affairs, Lagos, Nigeria.

[16] Its per capita GNP is estimated at $55 and it is next to the lowest country in the Harbison-Myers composite index. (Harbison and Myers, *op. cit.*, p. 45.)

[17] Registrar's Office, Haile Selassie I University, Addis Ababa.

TABLE 14-1 *Students From Developing Countries at Haile Selassie I University, First Semesters, Academic Years 1963–64 and 1964–65, by Country of Origin*

Country of Origin	1963–64				1964–65			
		Sponsorship				Sponsorship		
	Total	HSI [a]	AID [b]	Private [c]	Total	HSI [a]	AID [b]	Private [c]
Total	130	32	78	19	99	14	55	28
Aden					1			1
Cameroon	8	2	6		6	2	4	
Colombia	2			2				
Gambia	2	1	1					
Ghana	1		1					
India	12			12	15			15
Israel	3			3	2			2
Jordan					1			1
Kenya	29	15	14		17	6	11	
Lebanon	1			1	3			3
Liberia	7		7		1		1	
Malawi	11	7	4		9 [d]	3	5	
Mexico					3			3
Mozambique	1		1					
Nigeria	17	1	16		14	1	14	1
Philippines	1			1	1			1
Sierra Leone					1			1
Southern Rhodesia	3		3					
Sudan	4	1	3		2		2	
Tanganyika	7	2	5		6	1	5	
Uganda	13 [e]	3	9		10 [e]	1	8	
Zambia	2		2		1		1	
Zanzibar	6		6		4		4	

SOURCE: Registrar's Office, Haile Selassie I University, Addis Ababa.
[a] Haile Selassie I scholarship.
[b] U. S. AID scholarship.
[c] Private student.
[d] Includes one Malawi Government scholarship.
[e] Includes one separate university scholarship.

Ivory Coast

The Ivory Coast, which also shares its limited facilities[18] on a modest scale, is one of the first countries in Africa to have sought,

[18] Ivory Coast ranks in the bottom eight countries in the Harbison-Myers composite index. (*Op. cit.*)

through a small student exchange program, to bridge some of the language barriers dividing Africa. An agreement with English-speaking Liberia, financed by the two governments, provides for 20 students to be exchanged annually between the two countries. In addition, the Ivory Coast sponsors a Higher School of Statistics which trains some 50 statisticians yearly for most of the French-speaking countries of Africa. The Center is maintained by the Ivory Coast Government, but the students are usually supported by international organizations or foreign governments.

Middle Eastern Programs

In the Middle East, the United Arab Republic (UAR), Turkey and Kuwait, in addition to Israel, are sharing some of their resources with other developing countries. A few examples of the types of cooperative activities being carried out are presented below.

The United Arab Republic

With encouragement from the Government of the UAR, some 3,500 Egyptian teachers are working in neighboring Arab countries; at the same time, some 5,000 foreign students are studying in Egypt.[19] Students from 82 countries, including about 1,000 from African countries, are studying at Cairo's famous Al Azhar University.[20] Some of these students are on Egyptian Government scholarships. In addition, Egypt makes available short-term training scholarships, notably in irrigation and land use. Lately it has also offered scientific training and in 1965–66, for example, offered 50 fellowships to the Organization of African Unity for courses in medical, agricultural and geological research, chemical technology, radioisotopes and radiation biology, dissemination and documentation of information.[21]

Perhaps partly in response to Israeli activity in Africa, the UAR

[19] Angus Maddison, *Foreign Skills and Technical Assistance in Economic Development,* Development Centre, OECD, Paris, 1965, p. 59.

[20] *Jerusalem Post,* February 11, 1966.

[21] *Daily Nation* (Lagos), January 27, 1965.

has sent teachers and some technical experts to a number of African countries. In 1964 about 270 Egyptian technical experts were reportedly serving in neighboring Arab states or in Africa under technical assistance agreements with the UAR. UAR assistance has been particularly notable in Somalia, where the UAR Government has established Arab-language teaching and is maintaining several schools.[22]

Kuwait

Kuwait is an anomaly among developing countries, with an estimated per capita GNP in 1965 of $3,196, almost as high as that of the United States. In contrast, the population of 500,000 is 70 per cent illiterate,[23] and per capita imports are among the highest in the world. Since its independence in 1961 Kuwait has used some of its revenues derived from oil to extend capital assistance to its Arab neighbors—partly through loans from its state reserves and partly through the government-supported Fund for Arab Economic Development (KFAED).

Kuwait's assistance programs began in the late 1950's with grants to educational and social welfare projects in the neighboring countries along the Persian Gulf. Since 1961 Kuwait has carried on this activity through the Gulf Permanent Assistance Committee (GUPAC). In 1964–65 GUPAC spent $2.8 million for construction and maintenance of schools and hospitals in the area, and reportedly has expanded its activities recently to Yemen with a grant of $3.9 million for similar purposes.[24] Kuwait has given Egypt $7.4 million toward the salvaging of the Abu Simbel Temples, jeopardized by the Aswan Dam project.

Loans by Kuwait to other Arab states fall into two broad categories: budget support loans from state reserves and economic development loans from KFAED. By 1966, state reserve loans totaling some $294

[22] *Al Ahram,* Cairo, September 14, 1964.

[23] Statistics and Reports Division, Office of Program Coordination, U. S. Agency for International Development, Washington; and Population Reference Bureau, Washington.

[24] For a more detailed description of GUPAC activities and other aspects of Kuwait's assistance activities, see Ragaei el Mallakh, "Kuwait's Foreign Aid," *International Development Review,* December 1965, pp. 24–26.

TABLE 14-2 *Kuwait Loan Assistance to Other Arab Countries, by Country and Type of Loan, 1962–1965*

	State Reserve Loan			Fund for Arab Economic Development (KFAED) Loan			
Country	Amount (Millions)[a]	Year	Terms	Amount (Millions)[a]	Year	Purpose	Terms
Total	$294.0			$110.6[b]			
UAR	70.0	1964	4% over 15 years; payments starting after 5 years	27.4	1964	improvement of Suez Canal	4% over 15 years; payments starting after 5 years
Iraq	84.0	1963	interest free				
Algeria	28.0	1963	interest free	21.0	1964	oil pipeline construction	c
Lebanon[d]	14.0	c	c				
Sudan				19.6	1962	improvement and expansion of railway system	c
				4.8	1965	sugar factory construction	4% over 15 years
Jordan	14.0	1964	c	1.4	1962–63	Industrial Development Fund (hotel in Amman; electricity and hotel in Jerusalem)	c
				11.2	1962–63	Yarmouk River Dam	c
				8.4	1962–63	phosphate development	c
Tunisia	28.0	c	c	11.2	1963–64	electric power development	c
				5.6	1963–64	agricultural development and irrigation	c
Morocco	28.0	c	c				
Syria	28.0	c	c				
Yemen				c	c	Wadi Surdud agricultural development and settlement scheme	c

SOURCES: *Third Annual Report, 1964–65,* Kuwait Fund for Arab Economic Development (KFAED); *Economist,* April 24, 1964; Ragaei el Mallakh, "Kuwait's Foreign Aid," *International Development Review,* December 1965, pp. 24–26.

[a] Converted from Kuwait dinars (KD) at the rate of $2.80 to 1 KD.
[b] Excludes amount of loan to Yemen (unknown).
[c] Not available.
[d] Loan to Beirut municipality.

million had been extended to most of the Arab countries, reportedly on liberal terms, sometimes even interest-free. KFAED loans, on the other hand, are tied to specific projects, usually bear 3 to 4 per cent interest over 10 to 25 years and, according to the Fund's criteria, must be "technically and economically sound, financially viable, and [of] high priority . . . in the development plans of the borrowing countries." [25] Established by the Kuwait Government in 1962 with an authorized capital of $280 million, the Fund had assets of $160.4 million in 1965, of which $110.6 million had been committed on 11 loans.

Kuwait's loan assistance to other Arab countries from 1962 to 1965, exceeding $400 million, is summarized in Table 14-2. While more than two thirds of this amount was committed without regard to strict developmental objectives, the Government's present policy seems to be to eliminate lending from state reserves and to emphasize KFAED. The Fund, in turn, is moving in the direction of concerting its loans with the programs of international lending institutions, such as the World Bank and the UN Development Programme.

Through its assistance programs, Kuwait has in a few years earned itself an important place among its Arab neighbors. As it places increasing reliance on KFAED, with its economic development orientation, to channel its assistance, its international stature will grow correspondingly. But already, "Kuwait has demonstrated that developing economies which may vary in stages of economic development and specialties of skilled labor, surplus capital or physical resources, can advantageously participate in intra-help programs." [26]

Turkey

Turkey's sharing activities, involving primarily training facilities within Turkey, are more like those of other developing countries than are Kuwait's. As an active member of three regional groupings—the Central Treaty Organization (CENTO), the Organization for Economic Cooperation and Development (OECD) and the three-nation

[25] *Third Annual Report 1964–65,* Kuwait Fund for Arab Economic Development, pp. 9–10; and "Kuwait Spreads Its Riches," *The Economist,* April 25, 1964.

[26] Ragaei el Mallakh, *op. cit.,* p. 26.

Regional Cooperation for Development (RCD)—Turkey's activities inevitably bear a strong regional character.

The outstanding Turkish training effort is probably the Middle East Technical University (METU) located in Ankara. Financed by the Turkish Government but with additional support from the UN, OECD, CENTO, U. S. AID and the Ford Foundation, METU began with a faculty of 3 and 49 students in 1956. By 1965 it had about 3,000 students, including 235 from abroad.[27]

In part because the university was conceived as a regional institution, English is the prevailing language of instruction. Although this has proved to be an advantage in attracting foreign students, it has also caused difficulties for many Turkish applicants, and has necessitated the addition of a preliminary year of English language study for all students whose English is found to be inadequate at time of admission. Almost half the students at METU are studying engineering. This department also has the greatest concentration of foreign students. As Table 14-3 shows, the number of students from Iran and Pakistan, Turkey's partners in CENTO and RCD, has risen faster than the number from other Middle Eastern countries, so that by 1965 Pakistani and Iranian students outnumbered those from the Arab states.

METU's foreign student population continues to hover around 8 per cent, despite special efforts to attract students from abroad. A U. S. AID-sponsored Kennedy Memorial Scholarship Fund may boost foreign attendance by providing 350 scholarships over a 4-year period for students from Middle Eastern countries, in addition to providing 350 scholarships for Turkey itself. As this program gets under way and METU gains in academic reputation, its attraction for foreign students will undoubtedly grow, provided it maintains its international character and does not bow to internal pressures to shift some of its courses to Turkish-language instruction.

Turkey's other higher educational institutions usually have small quotas set aside for foreign students, often supported by CENTO scholarships. At Ankara University's Hacettepe Medical Center, for example, perhaps a dozen physicians from Pakistan, Iran, Afghanistan

[27] *Middle East Technical University—General Catalog 1964–65;* and "Middle East Technical University" (brochure); and statistics from METU Registrar's Office.

TABLE 14-3 *Foreign Students at Middle East Technical University*

Country of Origin	1961–62	1962–63	1963–64	1964–65
All countries	86	98	169	235
Per cent of student body	9	8	8	8
China	1	—	—	—
Cyprus	21	27	49	37
Germany	—	—	1	1
Holland	1	1	—	—
Iran	3	12	24	53
Iraq	4	2	3	2
Jordan	33	29	33	45
Lebanon	9	8	11	17
Pakistan	6	10	28	52
South Africa	1	1	1	1
Syria	3	5	6	14
U.S.A.	3	1	8	6
Israel	1	1	—	—
Egypt	—	1	—	—
Greece	—	—	1	2
India	—	—	—	1
Korea	—	—	1	1
Sudan	—	—	—	1
Bahreyn	—	—	1	1
Saudi Arabia	—	—	1	1
Canada	—	—	1	—

SOURCE: Registrar's Office, Middle East Technical University, Ankara.

and Iraq are pursuing postgraduate studies, and at the nursing school there are students from Cyprus and Iran. Instruction is in Turkish and foreign students are expected to learn the language.

Short-term training for foreigners is given at the State Highway Department, which took over some of the training activities carried out in 1955 to 1958 by the then existing UN Middle East Highway Training Center. Most other training activities and the work of Turkish experts abroad—both still on a relatively small scale—are carried out under the auspices of CENTO's Multilateral Technical Cooperation Fund (MTCF) and the RCD. (See Chapter 13.)

Turkey is one of the few developing countries that has developed a positive policy of sharing its human resources and development experience with other emerging countries and has also taken practical steps to implement this policy. The results are somewhat evident in the mutually profitable bilateral relationships with Israel, described in Chapter 12, and will become even clearer within the framework of the RCD, which is apparently Turkey's principal focus at present.

The Government in 1965 canvassed over 100 institutions to determine their capacity for training students from other developing countries and for supplying experts to work abroad. It also initiated a modest new program of cooperation with Iran and Pakistan, Turkey's RCD partners in that year. The 63-page catalog resulting from the canvass lists facilities and services ranging from training facilities for the study of tobacco diseases to courses in banking, and from expert services in regional planning to the operation of alcoholic beverage monopolies.[28] It illustrates not only the diversity achieved by the Turkish economy but also indicates the active role Turkey intends to play in promoting mutual aid between developing countries.

The Yugoslav Program

Yugoslavia, like many other countries, was initially impelled by political considerations to seek contacts and build friendships with the developing world. Considered an outsider both by the Communist bloc and by the so-called "Western" bloc, it wanted to escape political isolation and find a channel for asserting its views on world affairs. In 1960 President Tito took the initiative at the UN General Assembly in formulating proposals for a "third force," and a year later he was instrumental in convening the "Conference of Nonaligned States" in Belgrade.

Simultaneously, Yugoslavia began to develop its program of cooperation with developing countries. As a result, more than 1,000 Africans and Asians were trained in Yugoslavia between 1959 and 1965, and more than 2,000 Yugoslav experts worked abroad during the same

28 *Tentative Inventory of the Government of Turkey in Fields of Training Experts/Advisory Services Available for RCD Countries,* Ankara, 1965.

period.[29] Official estimates of expenditures for technical assistance during this period are some 1.5 billion dinars (about $2 million).

Like Israel, Yugoslavia has experimented with joint commercial ventures in developing countries. (See Chapter 9.) Its heavy industry has installed or equipped more than 200 plants in developing countries. Many of these projects were made possible through the extension of more than $360 million in long-term credits.

As of 1966, Yugoslavia had 23 long-term agreements on economic cooperation and 35 technical and scientific cooperation agreements with Asian and African countries. It seems clear that its assistance program has become an important element in Yugoslavia's political and trade relations with the developing world.

Taiwan's Program

Taiwan's political interest in promoting technical cooperation with African countries has apparently been no less keen than Yugoslavia's. "All nations need friends in the present-day world, and for this reason we are anxious to expand this program," said a Nationalist Chinese Government official in reviewing Taiwan's activities.[30]

Taiwan (Nationalist China) has long shared the considerable experience in training it gained through the U. S.–financed Third Country Training Program, discussed in Chapter 13. In 1960 it began a bilateral program of its own with an agricultural mission which visited Togo, Liberia, Senegal, Cameroon and the Malagasy Republic. By 1966 technical cooperation agreements, largely in agriculture, had been signed with at least 16 African countries, and Taiwan was also giving assistance in agriculture to non-African countries, including Saudi Arabia, the Philippines, Brazil and the Dominican Republic.[31]

So-called "farming demonstration missions" are the heart of Taiwan's program. The first of these missions, which went to Liberia in 1961,

[29] This and subsequent data in this section were supplied by the Yugoslav Embassy, Washington.

[30] *New York Times,* April 13, 1964.

[31] "Sino-African Technical Cooperation," Republic of China Information Service, Taiwan, September, 1965 (pamphlet); and "The Open Hand," *New York Times,* June 19, 1966.

reportedly raised Liberia's rice production substantially, and introduced the cultivation of many vegetable and field crops. Similar missions have been sent to Libya, Dahomey, Gabon, Rwanda, Senegal, Sierra Leone, Niger, Cameroon, Upper Volta, Togo, Chad and Ivory Coast. Unlike Israeli missions, which are usually small (see Chapters 6 and 7), Taiwan's agricultural missions normally comprise about a dozen experts, and sometimes many more. The mission sent to the Ivory Coast, for example, began with 14 experts in 1963, and by 1966 had expanded to 160.

Part of the success of Taiwan's missions, according to a Nationalist Chinese official, can be credited to the fact that mission members adapt well to the lower living standards of host countries. This seems plausible, for they reportedly earn only $200 a month [32]—less than half as much as the lowest paid Israeli experts and far less than U. S. and international experts. (See Chapter 3.) Probably another reason some countries welcome Taiwan's assistance is that sometimes the Nationalist Chinese Government has been willing and able to back its technical assistance with capital grants. In 1965, for instance, it announced a $3 million grant to Chad, one third of which is being used for construction projects in Fort Lamy, the capital, and the rest for the improvement of agriculture, forestry, public health and handicrafts.[33]

In addition to farming demonstration missions, Taiwan sends out experts in nursing, medicine, handicrafts, fisheries, engineering and other specialties, and conducts 5-month agricultural training courses for African technicians in Taiwan. By mid-1966 some 300 trainees from at least 26 African countries had attended these courses.[34] Training includes all phases of rice cultivation and vegetable and sugarcane production.

Some indication of the political effects of Taiwan's program can be seen in the vote at the UN General Assembly in 1966, when Albania introduced a resolution to expel Nationalist China (Taiwan) from the United Nations. Of the 39 African nations represented, 22 voted against the resolution or abstained; of these, 16 had cooperative pro-

[32] *New York Times,* April 13, 1964.

[33] *Survey of International Development,* July 15, 1965.

[34] "The Open Hand."

grams with Taiwan. Among the countries voting for expulsion, only two had received assistance from Taiwan. Taiwan's program of sharing, it seems, has been favorably received by countries that otherwise might have been at best indifferent to its fate.

The programs described in this brief survey, though by no means all-inclusive, are a fair indication of the scope of individual assistance programs by developing countries other than Israel. The limitations on what can be offered are no doubt considerable, but the broad range of training and experience that these countries can and do already share with each other is impressive.

Part III

New Perspectives

Chapter 15

Outlook for Mutual Assistance

AT THE MEETING of American Presidents at Punta del Este in April 1967, Mexican President Gustavo Díaz Ordaz declared: "We must pool our own efforts, our imagination, our resources . . . We all have much to learn and all have something to teach . . . the Mexican people . . . accepts that the more advanced countries have a responsibility toward those that are less developed . . ."[1] These propositions reflect to some extent both the thinking and the actions of many emerging countries, as this study has shown.

The sharing of human and institutional resources and development experience cannot, of course, solve the problems of capital shortages, trade imbalances and political conflicts, nor can it serve as a substitute for broader forms of economic cooperation. It is clearly only one element in the total process of social and economic transformation of developing countries. As this study has also shown, however, mutual assistance is a practical step that can be taken long before more complex forms of international cooperation—such as multinational development of resources and broad economic integration—are undertaken.

[1] *El Día,* Mexico City, April 13, 1967.

Some Problems of Mutual Assistance

The number of developing countries actually engaged in serious programs of mutual assistance is nonetheless still quite limited. This can be attributed only partly to the scarcity of financial resources and the lack of administrative tools, discussed earlier in this study. It is also due partly to the absence for many countries of a political stimulus—as exists for Israel, Yugoslavia, Taiwan, the United Arab Republic and Kuwait, for example. In addition, psychological and political barriers have greatly inhibited the spread of cooperation between developing countries.

The psychological barriers were particularly apparent in field interviews in connection with the present study. Many leaders of developing countries professed agreement with the desirability of mutual assistance programs but at the same time expressed doubt as to the potential of their countries to contribute meaningfully. Lack of funds was by no means the major reason for their skeptical attitudes.

A typical reaction was the disbelief expressed by officers of an African country when an Israeli expert suggested that Israel's police could learn something from them about communications in rugged, sparsely settled areas. A similar reaction greeted Israel's invitation to an alumnus of an Israeli training course to return to Israel as a staff member. Not only was the ex-trainee surprised and unbelieving, but it was difficult to convince his suspicious superiors that their man could indeed make a contribution by sharing his practical experience with others.

The skepticism of the people of developing countries about their own capacities, it was found, is accompanied by distrust of the capacities of people from other developing countries. "What could he teach us?" was the reaction of faculty members of an English-speaking African academic institution when it was suggested that a distinguished French-speaking African professor be added to the staff of the institution. Similarly, a Near Eastern country that needed a rural sociologist employed one from Great Britain rather than from nearby Pakistan, where a man with excellent qualifications was available.

Many a Latin American professional, while secretly cursing the North American "gringo" expert, may still prefer him to one from a sister Latin American country. These attitudes are the heritage of an earlier era of domination.

As countries progress economically and become not only politically but culturally and intellectually independent of the metropolitan powers, attitudes change. Latin Americans, for example, are apparently more prepared to agree that their countries have something to offer to others than are Africans, and are becoming increasingly agreeable to accepting the experience and expertise of nationals of other Latin American countries. Even in Africa there are stirrings in this direction. In drafting new company legislation Nigeria was at first inclined simply to take over the British Company Act of 1948, but upon reflection decided to base its legislation on Ghanaian and Indian models. In a similar move, the Tanzanian Government has been seeking to replace British expatriates, in positions for which no qualified Tanzanians are available, with nationals from other African countries, especially Nigeria. Tanzania's highly respected former Minister of State for Development, A. H. Jamal, gave the background for his country's views on the problem at a seminar on public policy at the University of East Africa in Dar es Salaam in 1964: [2]

> . . . we, the developing countries . . . may have become altogether too preoccupied with relationships between the developed and the developing countries. . . . Within our own family of developing countries . . . we may have a great deal to give and take from one another. . . . I see great advantages in increased economic cooperation between ourselves and those other countries which have only recently accumulated know-how and experience in planning and executing economic development. If we really mean to be self-reliant, we cannot afford to ignore the vast fund of information and experience which is available from those countries in the wake of political revolution.

Political considerations are probably even more important than psychological ones, however, in explaining the lag between mutual assistance in practice and the intellectual commitment or public declarations favoring it. India will not share with Pakistan, nor the Arab states with Israel, nor Congo (Kinshasa) with Congo (Brazzaville), nor South Korea with North Korea, and so on.

[2] "Problems of Foreign Aid," September 22, 1964.

Furthermore, extension of the policy of sharing has been impeded by the taint that rightly or wrongly attaches to bilateral aid. Because of sometimes crude and often shortsighted policies by countries extending aid, the stigma of charity or political exploitation tends to adhere to many forms of international assistance, including assistance by developing countries.

In Africa some of the stigma is the result of the policies of Kwame Nkrumah, who was perhaps the first of the African leaders to grasp the possibilities of cooperation between African countries, but who corrupted the concept through blatant political exploitation. The hundreds of students from other African countries invited to study at Ghana's fairly well-developed universities and training institutes were treated to heavy doses of Nkrumah's propaganda. Besides, along with offers of legitimate training scholarships, Ghana sought to attract dissidents to be trained in political agitation and apparently even military subversion at secret training camps and the Kwame Nkrumah Ideological Institute. When this became known, Ghana's reputation as a source of technical assistance and training became tarnished, and the concept of mutual aid between African countries was seriously damaged. Nigeria's decision to assist only when specifically requested to do so has no doubt been influenced by the Ghanaian experience.

Mutual assistance does not constitute national policy in most Latin American countries, despite clear commitments to the concept in the Alliance for Progress and persistent efforts of the Organization of American States to assure recognition of its importance. Though the capacity for sharing is larger and the intracontinental political conflicts are more subdued in Latin America than in Africa or Asia, the Latin American mutual assistance efforts are not commensurate with resources or opportunities. Perhaps the ambivalence that continues to haunt relationships between Latin America and the "Colossus of the North" saps the will and distorts awareness of the need for mutual aid between developing countries in the hemisphere. In any event, nowhere is there greater evidence of the gap between promise and achievement.

This analysis is not meant to imply that every developing country should necessarily launch a broad program of sharing scarce resources. As this study has shown, hastily conceived or inadequately supported activities often do not justify the heavy financial and human investment such programs require. The analysis does suggest, however, that every developing country should survey its own needs and resources and determine what resources it might be able to share with other developing countries and which of its needs, in turn, other developing countries might be able to satisfy. Each country would then be able to decide whether cooperative programs with other developing countries would be in its best interest, and if so, what the scope and character of the programs should be.

Obviously the success of sharing will be determined largely by the quality of assistance given. A program of mutual assistance could affect a country adversely if the quality of aid given were poor or if the program were badly organized and inadequately funded. This does not mean that lack of funds or inadequate organizational machinery need deter developing countries from sharing their resources with each other. These inadequacies might, however, suggest the need for tripartite or multilateral rather than strictly bilateral arrangements—a new "mix" for a new dimension in international cooperation.

Short-Run and Long-Run Effects

The experiences of Israel and other developing countries indicate that mutual aid can bring both partners rich rewards. In the political sphere it can promote friendly relations and increase a country's international stature; in the material sphere it can lead to expanded trade and enriching professional exchanges; and in the sociopsychological sphere it can enhance the morale of other countries, as it has enhanced Israel's. There are other concrete advantages that are immediately apparent.

The costs of technical assistance from one developing country to another, particularly within the same region, are often considerably lower than those from an economically advanced country. Travel costs for a Turkish expert going to Iran, for example, are a small fraction of those for a European or a U. S. expert going to Iran. Also, salaries of experts from developing countries, except those sent under UN sponsorship, are as a rule considerably lower than those of U. S. and European experts. Salaries and maintenance costs of Israeli experts—who are by no means the lowest paid in the profession—are only about half those of their colleagues sent by the United States and the United Nations. Training expenses, too, are often lower in developing countries. U. S. officials have estimated that the cost of their "third-country" training in Mexico ran about half that of comparable activities in the United States.

When these cost advantages are combined with linguistic and cultural affinity—as in Mexico for trainees from Spanish-speaking countries of Latin America—the benefits of mutual assistance between developing countries are obviously even greater.

Providing opportunities for technicians and leaders from developing countries to observe each other's developmental achievements is another simple and effective way of passing on experience and quickly initiating the process of mutual assistance. Thus, experts from other struggling African countries can profit from observing Tanzania's accomplishment in organizing 7,000 local village development commissions to spearhead numerous self-help projects; Venezuela's "Dividendo Voluntario para la Comunidad" (Voluntary Dividend for the Community), which has mobilized extensive local resources for community development, can provide incentive and precedent for similar efforts in other developing countries. And the frequent visits of foreign leaders and others to observe Israel's achievements have, as has been shown, inspired new ventures in other parts of the emerging world. While many observation programs, usually sponsored by economically advanced countries, have taken place in developing countries, this rich experience could be better utilized if more of the developing countries themselves would take the initiative.

The long-run effects of mutual assistance between developing countries are likely to be even more profound. As sharing grows in volume, it can be expected to generate a new spirit of mutuality to replace the prevailing donor-recipient relationship. This, as indicated earlier, can profoundly benefit relations between developing countries and between developing and developed countries.

Steps to Promote Mutual Assistance

On the basis of the findings of this study, some new policies and institutional arrangements seem advisable. As a start in this direction, the following steps for stimulating cooperation and improving related aspects of technical assistance should be considered.

Financial Measures

Lack of capital should not prevent the launching of otherwise viable and sensible programs of cooperation between developing countries or limit the effectiveness of these programs once they are undertaken. International agencies and developed countries could alleviate the problem of financial shortages by assigning higher priority to the support of such activities. The financing patterns developed by Israel and the UN Special Fund in Upper Volta and by Israel and the OAS in Latin America might serve as examples.

Another approach might be for developed countries and international organizations with established programs of technical assistance to earmark a certain amount or percentage of their technical assistance funds for the support of programs of cooperation between developing countries.

In a companion move the United States might make some of its local currency holdings in developing countries available for mutual assistance activities.[3] These funds could be used, for example, to help finance or develop additional training establishments in India, Taiwan, Israel, and elsewhere for trainees from developing countries or to support local costs of other cooperative programs initiated by developing countries. Consideration should also be given to allowing use of United States–owned local currencies to finance international

[3] In a 1965 OECD study, *Foreign Skills and Technical Assistance in Economic Development* (Paris, p. 70), Angus Maddison made a related suggestion: "It would be very useful if bilateral donors gave financial support and cooperation to the technical assistance efforts of those developing countries which may be able to export skills or provide training. This form of self-help within the developing world is often more valuable than technical assistance from the developed world and deserves every encouragement."

travel costs of trainees and experts participating in programs of cooperation between developing countries.

Since the cost of air travel is a major deterrent to increased contacts between developing countries (particularly foreign short-term training and observation visits), reduced fare arrangements should be considered for those who participate in programs of cooperation sponsored by developing countries. There is precedent and operational experience for such arrangements in the special youth and student fare plans available in some countries.

Training Programs

Cooperation arrangements should be introduced into both national and international training programs for developing countries, when this is at all feasible. Judging from Israel's experience, one easy and effective way of accomplishing this is to invite personnel from developing countries to participate as staff members in training programs. Preferably such personnel should be alumni of programs similar to those in which they would be participating as staff members. Another technique successfully developed by Israel is joint planning and staffing with host countries of on-the-spot training courses.

Other countries might also adopt Israel's use of the trainees' own languages in courses expressly prepared for particular national groups; the employment of leader-guides (*madrichim*); and the principle of team training, which makes it possible for trainees to reinforce each other after they return home and thus better retain the effects of their training. While Israel, like most other countries engaged in training programs, has no organized system of follow-up for the graduates of its courses, the alumni magazine, *Shalom,* does provide a limited, but apparently welcome, link between alumni and training staffs. An expanded version of such a magazine, internationally sponsored, would provide a forum for the exchange of experience at the nontechnical level.

Developing countries should examine the capacities of their training and educational institutions and, if feasible, open these institutions to other countries. The developed countries can aid in this process by expanding or initiating new third-country training programs. In this connection the United States might utilize local currencies to extend its own Third Country Training Program to countries not included at the present time.

When new training agreements, particularly for middle-level personnel, are concluded, beneficiary countries should be asked to pledge the services of at least one alumnus of a particular program as a staff member for a later course or for short-term assignments to another developing country at a later date. This could help to establish the practice of reciprocity in technical assistance and would stimulate the chain reaction effect.

Volunteer Programs

The use of volunteers or "associate experts" in technical cooperation can and should be expanded. The UN Associate Expert system offers valuable experience, but its relatively high cost suggests that other approaches should be explored. Countries with successful domestic volunteer programs should be encouraged to make some of their volunteers available for service abroad. This is the concept underlying Argentina's proposed Maestros para America Latina and the U. S. Volunteers to America pilot program. Properly conceived, such use of volunteers would be a way of initiating or strengthening programs of cooperation at relatively low cost.

Capital Funds

Developing countries that have capital surpluses or large reserves of hard currency should share these surpluses with other countries to a greater extent than they are now doing, either through bilateral loan arrangements, as Kuwait does, or through active participation in consortia and international financial institutions. The capacity of some countries to contribute capital resources and of other countries to share human and institutional resources might form the basis of fruitful bilateral cooperation programs.

Expert Services

In some specialties where the need for experts is most critical (such as medicine), developing and developed countries should adopt the concept of service abroad as part of the total educational process. Thus part of the period of internship or practical training of physicians and specialists would be spent working in institutions of another country, preferably a developing country. The reciprocity ingredient of such a program is very high, since both student and host institution benefit from the arrangement. A successful prototype of this plan has been developed in the Ophthalmology Department of the Hebrew University–Hadassah Medical School in Jerusalem, and could serve as a model. Israel could take the lead in regularizing this kind of arrangement as part of its program of cooperation by establishing it as an integral part of the training in all departments of the medical school and in other institutions of higher learning.

Similarly, the concept of service abroad for a limited period could be introduced in other disciplines and professions as part of regular career development programs and as a public service responsibility. Israel's collective settlements furnish something of a precedent for this principle, since they allot about 8 per cent of their manpower regularly to temporary duty in public or national institutions.

Experts should be encouraged to act as "relays," transmitting successful development experience of one developing country to another. Because of their professional contacts and opportunities to travel, experts, particularly those who have extensive international experience, are favorably situated to initiate or stimulate chain reaction effects.

The attitudes and behavior of foreign experts are important elements in the success or failure of international cooperation efforts. While it is not necessary that experts have the zeal and motivation of missionaries, they should be sensitive to the needs and aspirations of the host countries and fully understand their role as representatives of their countries or of international agencies. Israeli experts for the most part have such an understanding of their work, which accounts in part for their excellent reputation abroad. Considering the high investment each foreign expert represents for the sending country or international agency and the prestige at stake, orientation programs for experts should be re-examined and improved. Also, additional efforts are needed, through education and perhaps through administrative measures, to bring the foreign experts closer to the people with whom they work. Whenever feasible, experts should live on or near the sites of their projects, and they should be encouraged to maintain a modest mode of living.

An Association for Mutual Assistance

Mutual assistance offers new opportunities and presents specialized problems in international relations that need specialized organizational attention. The heart of the international mutual assistance effort should be an "Association for Mutual Assistance," with membership open to all countries. Its functions would be:

1. *To provide up-to-date information on the capacities of member countries to share human and institutional resources.* Since few developing countries and international agencies have seriously addressed themselves to the implications of active participation in programs of mutual aid, the information gap in regard to national capacities is a critical obstacle to the spread of cooperative programs. As a result of surveys by various individual governments and international and regional assistance agencies, data are available on training facilities in some countries (Mexico, Turkey, the Colombo Plan member countries, for example), but for most developing countries information is inadequate. As a first step an inventory should be taken so that the association could find out what training facilities, expert services and capital resources, if any, countries are able and willing to provide. A pilot study might be conducted to determine whether some form of rating system of facilities is feasible or advisable. The initial inventory, in addition to providing much-needed basic information, would help generate interest in and awareness of the association's purposes among governments and the professional elite in the developing countries. Once the basic data are available, the association should keep the inventory up-to-date through periodic reports from member countries.

2. *To facilitate contacts and negotiations between cooperating countries and assist in matching needs to resources.* Cooperation on a

bilateral basis engages the prestige and interest of the cooperating countries directly, and therefore each country can be expected to put forth maximum efforts for success. Because the developing countries lack funds, information and operational experience in mutual assistance, however, essential and perhaps key functions of the association would be to bring interested parties together, match requests for assistance to offers and find sources of financing.

3. *To encourage new concepts and forms of joint ventures.* Joint technical assistance efforts by two or more developing countries, perhaps through some type of pooling arrangement, should be facilitated by the association. Similarly, it should explore prototypes for joint capital ventures that, for a reasonable return on investment, would provide a strong local training program and allow an orderly, gradual withdrawal of the foreign partner.

4. *To centralize, store and disseminate useful experience in development for the benefit of member countries.* The thousands of people in responsible positions in the international development effort are gaining valuable experience and insight into problems of developing countries. Much of this experience is not recorded, or if it is, may gather dust in seldom-used files. Little of it is exchanged between countries or between different agencies engaged in development activities. The association would develop a standardized reporting system on development experiences and centralized, computerized storage facilities for the reports, thus making them readily accessible to member countries and research organizations. Selected material of broad interest to development specialists could be disseminated periodically to member countries and other interested agencies.

5. *To provide administrative assistance.* Many countries participating in programs of cooperation do not have the desire, the ability or the experience to establish special administrative machinery for the programs. When necessary the association would share administrative responsibility with the country in which activities are being conducted. Since the association would be basically nonoperating, it would, with the consent of the parties concerned, have the option to contract for administrative services with existing national or international agencies.

6. *To stimulate research in mutual assistance.* The association would not itself conduct or sponsor research. However, as the leading cen-

ter of information on programs of mutual assistance, it would be in a favorable position to facilitate and encourage research into various aspects of cooperation between developing countries. Research on such questions as the effect of mutual assistance on the drain of professional manpower or the effectiveness of different types of chain reactions in technical cooperation—difficult if not impossible to study at present—could be materially facilitated by the association.

The association would be primarily a service agency, and its staff would consequently be small. Eventually, most of its operating expenses would be defrayed from charges and other fees for services performed. The initial investment and operating costs for the first few years, however, would be financed by foundation grants, major contributions from developed countries and minor contributions from developing countries. Service charges would be nominal until the association could prove its value to its members and users.

The association would have a close relationship to the UN family, which is striving for similar goals, but would function independently of it. It would need much flexibility and imagination to be effective, and therefore should not be tied to established, sometimes cumbersome, procedures and structures. Much of its success, particularly during the early period, would also depend on the attitude of the developed countries. They could show their faith in the association by contributions to the initial fund required to establish it; by their willingness to assist in financing programs of cooperation of other members of the association; and by using the services of the association to promote new mutual relationships between themselves and developing countries. All these steps would be essential to the success of the association. The last step, particularly, would have great psychological impact.

If the developed nations were to demonstrate, through the association, that they too have a real need for cooperation with other countries, then the concept of mutual aid and the association as the instrument to carry it forward would be established. With an association for mutual assistance, and the two-way flow of experience between countries growing in volume, the potentially dangerous status gap would rapidly disappear.

APPENDIX TABLE 1 *Participation of Developing Countries in UN Expanded Program of Technical Assistance (EPTA), by Country, 1962–1965*

Area and Country	Experts [a]				EPTA Fellows [a]			
	1962	1963	1964	1965	1962	1963	1964	1965
Total, EPTA	2,381	2,817	3,292	3,130	3,831	3,099	5,109	3,657
Africa	71	81	90	115	307	417	705	515
Algeria	—	—	—	2	—	—	8	12
Basutoland	—	—	—	—	1	—	—	—
Cameroon	—	—	1	2	1	16	15	84
Central African Republic	—	—	—	—	—	24	25	—
Congo (Brazzaville)	—	—	1	1	—	—	—	—
Congo (Léopoldville)	—	—	—	3	—	9	5	40
Dahomey	3	1	—	1	—	—	—	—
Ethiopia	—	1	1	4	3	16	118	15
French Somaliland	—	—	—	—	—	3	—	—
Ghana	2	2	1	12	13	19	24	36
Ivory Coast	—	—	—	1	11	21	19	9
Kenya	1	1	—	2	12	67	43	25
Libya	4	—	—	—	8	—	1	—
Malagasy	1	—	—	—	—	—	—	—
Malawi	—	—	—	—	—	—	25	—
Mali	—	—	—	1	15	—	1	1
Morocco	—	—	1	2	10	8	55	43
Niger	—	—	—	—	—	4	8	4
Nigeria	1	1	1	8	12	10	19	26
Senegal	—	—	2	3	72	26	35	79
Sierra Leone	—	1	—	—	—	—	—	—

APPENDIX TABLE 1 (*continued*)

Area and Country	Experts [a]				EPTA Fellows [a]			
	1962	1963	1964	1965	1962	1963	1964	1965
Africa (cont'd)								
Sudan	4	5	5	6	14	36	6	6
Tanzania	—	—	—	1	2	—	—	19
Tunisia	2	6	6	4	25	28	39	23
Uganda	—	1	1	1	37	42	61	19
United Arab Republic	53	62	68	61	71	88	188	64
Upper Volta	—	—	—	—	—	—	10	10
Zambia	—	—	2	—	—	—	—	—
Latin America	204	267	298	425	273	256	455	319
Argentina	35	42	53	63	24	27	55	44
Bolivia	4	6	7	13	1	—	—	—
Brazil	25	23	29	45	21	26	56	20
Chile	40	56	57	61	78	77	97	86
Colombia	6	9	15	20	5	6	8	11
Costa Rica	8	11	10	11	1	—	66	13
Cuba	8	10	7	6	—	—	—	—
Dominican Republic	5	4	3	3	1	—	—	—
Ecuador	15	15	19	50	14	22	23	20
El Salvador	1	1	1	—	1	—	—	—
Guatemala	2	3	3	3	1	2	1	1
Haiti	11	21	29	33	—	—	—	—
Honduras	—	2	1	2	—	—	—	—
Jamaica	1	2	6	5	2	1	5	1
Mexico	13	17	18	20	108	60	110	78
Netherlands Antilles	1	1	—	—	—	—	—	—
Nicaragua	3	1	1	—	1	—	—	—

Panama	—	3	2	2	7	1	—	1
Paraguay	2	2	4	29	—	—	—	—
Peru	14	14	14	32	7	13	9	—
Surinam	—	—	—	—	—	1	—	—
The West Indies	1	—	—	—	—	—	—	—
Trinidad and Tobago	1	2	3	3	1	3	10	2
Uruguay	6	17	12	21	—	—	1	2
Venezuela	2	5	4	3	—	17	14	40
Asia and the Far East	215	232	254	287	323	290	552	244
Afghanistan	2	—	1	—	—	—	26	—
Burma	2	4	3	5	24	1	7	8
Cambodia	—	—	1	—	1	—	—	—
Ceylon	9	11	12	18	37	7	21	16
China (Taiwan)	16	28	13	22	32	2	1	4
Fiji	—	—	—	—	—	—	—	2
India	130	136	166	170	78	136	118	41
Indonesia	1	1	1	3	3	—	—	—
Iran	5	6	5	8	2	12	87	23
Malaysia [b]	1	—	1	3	21	4	26	1
Nepal	1	—	—	—	—	—	—	—
New Caledonia	—	—	—	—	1	—	1	2
Pakistan	25	22	20	16	9	2	6	6
Philippines	14	14	21	26	34	47	140	93
Republic of Korea	1	—	1	3	—	1	—	—
Republic of Vietnam	3	3	5	7	—	—	—	—
Thailand	5	7	4	6	81	78	115	48
Western Samoa	—	—	—	—	—	—	4	—
Middle East	66	86	101	83	154	78	156	157
Iraq	3	4	4	6	—	1	27	6
Israel	17	33	42	31	87	31	60	63

(*Continued on following page*)

APPENDIX TABLE 1 (*continued*)

Area and Country	Experts [a] 1962	1963	1964	1965	EPTA Fellows [a] 1962	1963	1964	1965
Middle East (cont'd)								
Jordan	16	14	18	9	1	—	2	—
Lebanon	14	18	15	11	31	35	64	78
Saudi Arabia	—	—	—	—	1	—	—	—
Syria	8	8	13	13	4	—	3	3
Turkey	8	9	9	12	30	11	—	6
Yemen	—	—	—	1	—	—	—	1
Other developing countries	30	45	59	54	77	11	44	56
Cyprus	2	2	3	1	11	—	—	—
Malta	—	1	0	1	3	—	1	—
Yugoslavia	28	42	56	52	63	11	43	56
Developed countries	1,795	2,106	2,490	2,166	2,697	2,047	3,197	2,366

SOURCES: 1962, *Annual Report of the Technical Assistance Board for 1962, Final Report on the Implementation of the 1961–1962 Programme,* Technical Assistance Committee, Economic and Social Council, UN, New York, 1963, Annex VIII, pp. 129 ff., and Annex XI, pp. 149 ff.; 1963 and 1964, *Programmes of Technical Cooperation, Expanded Programme of Technical Assistance: Annual Report of the Technical Assistance Board to the Technical Assistance Committee for 1964, Final Report on the Implementation of the 1963–1964 Programme,* Economic and Social Council, UN, New York, May 1965, Annex VIII, pp. 1 ff., and Annex XI, pp. 1 ff.; and 1965, *Report on the Activities of the United Nations Special Fund and the Expanded Programme of Technical Assistance in 1965, Report by the Administrator,* Development Programme, UN, New York, April 1966, Annex I, pp. 3 ff., and pp. 15 ff.

[a] The countries indicate the origin of the experts, the destination of the fellows. Placements exceed number of fellowships granted because some fellows studied in more than one country.

[b] Includes Singapore.

APPENDIX TABLE 2 *Training Scholarships Provided by Colombo Plan Developing Countries, Fiscal Years, 1950–1965*

Receiving Country	Supplying Country: Burma			Ceylon			India			Indonesia			Malaysia			Pakistan			Philippines			Thailand		
	1950–58	1958–64	1964–65	1950–58	1958–64	1964–65	1950–58	1958–64	1964–65	1950–58	1958–64	1964–65	1950–58	1958–64	1964–65	1950–58	1958–64	1964–65	1950–58	1958–64	1964–65	1950–58	1958–64	1964–65
Total	10	15	7	46	31	—	718	1,722	280	12	6	—	62	233	46	78	86	54	—	29	1	10	—	—
Afghanistan	—	—	—	—	—	—	—	—	4	—	—	—	—	—	—	—	—	—	—	—	—	—	—	—
Australia	—	—	—	—	—	—	1	2	4	—	—	—	—	—	—	—	—	—	—	—	—	—	—	—
Brunei	—	—	—	—	—	—	—	—	—	—	—	—	—	11	—	—	—	—	—	—	—	—	—	—
Burma	—	—	—	15	4	—	36	35	3	10	—	—	28	10	—	21	12	—	—	2	—	2	—	—
Cambodia	—	—	—	—	—	—	—	2	—	—	—	—	—	—	4	—	4	—	—	—	—	—	—	—
Ceylon	—	—	—	—	—	—	116	141	45	2	1	—	2	12	4	10	2	—	—	5	—	—	—	—
India	—	—	—	—	—	—	—	—	—	—	—	—	1	—	1	—	—	—	—	3	—	—	—	—
Indonesia	—	—	—	7	—	—	11	45	—	—	—	—	1	11	—	19	19	—	—	2	—	—	—	—
Japan	—	—	—	—	—	—	5	5	—	—	—	—	—	—	—	3	—	—	—	—	—	—	—	—
Korea	—	—	1	—	—	—	—	8	20	—	—	—	—	2	4	—	6	1	—	—	—	—	—	—
Laos	—	—	—	—	—	—	—	12	—	—	—	—	—	4	2	—	1	—	—	—	—	—	—	—
Malaysia	8	4	—	12	7	—	17	92	38	—	4	—	15	123	—	18	21	3	—	12	—	8	—	—
Maldives	—	—	—	—	—	—	—	17	—	—	—	—	—	—	—	—	—	—	—	—	—	—	—	—
Nepal	—	3	—	8	5	—	439	1,100	89	—	—	—	—	9	1	—	2	49	—	—	—	—	—	—
New Zealand	—	—	—	—	—	—	—	1	—	—	—	—	—	—	—	—	—	—	—	—	—	—	—	—
Pakistan	—	1	—	2	6	—	39	—	—	—	1	—	15	14	8	—	—	—	—	5	—	—	—	—
Philippines	—	3	—	1	5	—	40	103	23	—	—	—	—	8	—	3	9	—	—	—	—	—	—	—
Thailand	2	3	6	1	3	—	14	138	54	—	—	—	—	29	21	—	7	—	—	—	1	—	—	—
Vietnam	—	1	—	—	1	—	—	21	—	—	—	—	—	—	1	4	3	1	—	—	—	—	—	—

SOURCES: Colombo Plan Bureau, Colombo, Ceylon: *Technical Co-operation Under The Colombo Plan: Report by the Colombo Plan Council for Technical Co-operation in South and South-East Asia for the Year 1 July 1963 to 30 June 1964*, pp. 56–57; and *Report for the Year 1 July 1964 to 30 June 1965*, pp. 86–87.

APPENDIX TABLE 3 *Experts Provided by Colombo Plan Developing Countries, Fiscal Years, 1950–1965*

Receiving Country	Supplying Country																	
	Ceylon			India			Indonesia			Malaysia			Pakistan			Vietnam		
	1950–58	1958–64	1964–65	1950–58	1958–64	1964–65	1950–58	1958–64	1964–65	1950–58	1958–64	1964–65	1950–58	1958–64	1964–65	1950–58	1958–64	1964–65
Total	2	1	—	26	637	238	—	1	—	—	1	—	1	1	—	—	1	—
Afghanistan	—	—	—	—	—	5	—	—	—	—	—	—	—	—	—	—	—	—
Australia	—	—	—	—	—	—	—	1	—	—	—	—	—	—	—	—	—	—
Bhutan	—	—	—	—	—	—	—	—	—	—	—	—	—	—	—	—	—	—
Brunei	—	—	—	—	—	—	—	—	—	—	—	—	—	—	—	—	—	—
Burma	—	—	—	2	—	—	—	—	—	—	—	—	—	—	—	—	—	—
Cambodia	—	—	—	—	1	—	—	—	—	—	—	—	—	—	—	—	—	—
Ceylon	—	—	—	15	24	2	—	—	—	—	—	—	1	—	—	—	—	—
India	1	—	—	—	—	—	—	—	—	—	—	—	—	—	—	—	—	—
Indonesia	—	—	—	4	1	—	—	—	—	—	—	—	—	—	—	—	—	—
Korea	—	—	—	—	—	—	—	—	—	—	—	—	—	—	—	—	—	—
Laos	—	—	—	—	—	1	—	—	—	—	—	—	—	—	—	—	1	—
Malaysia	1	—	—	4	5	—	—	—	—	—	—	—	—	1	—	—	—	—
Maldives	—	—	—	—	1	3	—	—	—	—	—	—	—	—	—	—	—	—
Nepal	—	—	—	—	598	226	—	—	—	—	—	—	—	—	—	—	—	—
Pakistan	—	1	—	—	—	—	—	—	—	—	—	—	—	—	—	—	—	—
Philippines	—	—	—	—	—	—	—	—	—	—	—	—	—	—	—	—	—	—
Thailand	—	—	—	—	—	—	—	—	—	—	—	—	—	—	—	—	—	—
United States	—	—	—	—	—	—	—	—	—	—	1	—	—	—	—	—	—	—
Vietnam	—	—	—	1	—	1	—	—	—	—	—	—	—	—	—	—	—	—
Mekong River	—	—	—	—	7	—	—	—	—	—	—	—	—	—	—	—	—	—
Regional	—	—	—	—	—	—	—	—	—	—	—	—	—	—	—	—	—	—

SOURCES: Colombo Plan Bureau, Colombo, Ceylon: *Technical Co-operation Under The Colombo Plan: Report by the Colombo Plan Council for Technical Co-operation in South and South-East Asia for the Year 1 July 1963 to 30 June 1964*, p. 64; and *Report for the Year 1 July 1964 to 30 June 1965*, p. 94.

Index of Sources

Subject Index

A

B

C

D

G

H

I

L

M

N

R

S

T

U